D0876165

Business Interruption Insurance

AND EXTRA EXPENSE INSURANCE
AS WRITTEN BY FIRE INSURANCE COMPANIES
in the
UNITED STATES AND CANADA

By

HENRY C. KLEIN

Secretary, New York Underwriters Insurance Co.

(Retired January 1956)

A Publication of

Rough Notes

Devoted to

INSURANCE AGENCY SALESMANSHIP AND MANAGEMENT

Business Interruption Insurance

COPYRIGHT 1950

By THE ROUGH NOTES CO., INC.

Indianapolis, Indiana

PRINTED IN THE UNITED STATES OF AMERICA

Third Edition, May, 1957

To

FREDERIC C. WHITE

CONTENTS

CHAPTER   PAGE

1 FUNCTION—ORIGIN—NAME 1

2 INSURABLE INTEREST—TIME ELEMENT............................... 14

3 THE PER DIEM POLICY FORM.. 30

4 THE WEEKLY AND MONTHLY POLICY FORMS...................... 36

5 THE TWO ITEM CONTRIBUTION POLICY FORM.................... 52

6 THE GROSS EARNINGS POLICY FORM................................. 72

7 THE EARNINGS INSURANCE POLICY FORM........................ 104

8 AGREED AMOUNT CONTRIBUTION AND ADJUSTABLE
   PREMIUM POLICIES 111

9 MULTI-LOCATION DIRECT AND CONTINGENT COVERAGES...... 133

10 STOCK COVERAGES 152

11 CANADIAN METHODS: SPECIFIED TIME POLICIES.................. 166

12 WARTIME METHODS 195

13 RATING METHODS 205

14 UNDERWRITING BUSINESS INTERRUPTION INSURANCE........ 224

15 EXTRA EXPENSE INSURANCE.. 236

16 MISCELLANEOUS 259

    APPENDIXES 1-8—LOSS ADJUSTMENTS.............................. 297

    APPENDIX 9—TESTIMONIAL LETTERS................................ 307

    APPENDIX 10—LEGAL DECISIONS..................................... 311

    INDEX 323

Business Interruption Insurance

CHAPTER 1

FUNCTION — ORIGIN — NAME

The Problem—Scarcely a day passes that a newspaper somewhere does not contain an item similar to the following:

"Early this morning the business premises of the John Doe Company were destroyed by fire of unknown origin. It is reported that full insurance was carried and rebuilding operations will begin as soon as possible."

The average reader assumes that the reference to "full insurance" means that the buildings, machinery, equipment, and stock—which comprised the destroyed premises—were insured to their full physical value and that therefore all's well with the Doe Company.

But what are the thoughts of the stockholders, the local bank, the creditors, the employees; of the local merchants, landlords and physicians who serve the employees, the local church and Community Chest treasurers, and the competitors of the Doe Company?

The stockholders are fearful dividends will cease; the bank and other creditors are worried about the firm's ability to repay loans and meet interest payments, in addition to financing rebuilding costs.

The employees, faced with the probability of prolonged unemployment, are worried (as are the merchants and others who serve them) about their ability to pay necessary marketing, clothing, rent, medical bills and church and community chest pledges. Even the tax collector speculates about the effect of the fire on his collections and tax sales.

Probably the only persons viewing the future with complacency are the competitors of the Doe Company. They see the possibility of benefiting while the business is shut down, and anticipate that when and if it is resumed, it will probably be on a substantially reduced scale, because of financial difficulties resulting from the fire loss.

If only Property Damage Insurance had been carried on the physical value of the Doe Company's buildings and contents, all of these people would be justified in their fears. But the management of the Doe Company—realizing that the dollars of its earnings are as valuable as the dollars invested in the buildings and their contents, and that Property Damage Insurance indemnifies for only part of the loss when fire strikes—had followed the advice of their insurand advisor and had also bought Business Interruption Insurance.

Coverage Under Business Interruption—As a result, the net profit that would have been realized, and the business expenses that necessarily continued while the business was shut down during reconstruction, were paid by the Business Interruption Insurance. In consequence, the stockholders received dividend checks as usual, the bank and other creditors had no grounds for apprehension, the essential skilled employees were retained on the payroll, and others were assisted while they found employment elsewhere, merchants, landlords and others dependent upon the pay envelopes of the employees breathed a sigh of relief, and competitors could only anticipate competition as usual after reconstruction.

In short, Business Interruption Insurance did for the John Doe Company what the company would have done for itself in the production of earnings—through its ability to use and occupy the premises—had there been no interruption of business. It paid for their loss of net profits, plus fixed charges and expenses that necessarily continued, while business operations were suspended.

The day following the Doe Company fire, Mr. White—an agent for insurance companies—while attending a Chamber of Commerce luncheon, found himself seated at a table with Messrs. Smith and Jones, respectively the managers of

Plants Nos. 1 and 2 of the Brown Manufacturing Company; Davis of the Ray Foundry—which was supplying special castings to the Brown Company; Gray, the Selling Agent for products of the Brown Company; Williams and Green, operators respectively of a local drug store and theatre; Clay, a credit man; and Jackson, operator of a laundry.

Conversation turning to the Doe Company fire and its consequences, White—who was the insurance advisor of the Doe Company—explained the function of Business Interruption Insurance. He started his explanation dramatically by producing two $1 bills, saying: "One of these bills represents the dollars invested in the purchase and maintenance of the buildings, equipment, and materials of a business for the purpose of producing the earnings for which the business is conducted—and which are represented by the other $1 bill.

"The first dollar was spent to produce the second dollar. Both dollars have the same value. Therefore, if the property value represented by the first dollar is worthy of protection by Property Damage Insurance, the earnings value represented by the second dollar is obviously also worthy of protection by Business Interruption Insurance. Fortunately for the Doe Company, its earnings were protected by Business Interruption Insurance."

At this point Smith and Jones inquired how the earnings of their factories could be protected. Mr. White explained that since their operations are interdependent, one Business Interruption Insurance policy could be purchased, blanketing both factories which would reimburse for the loss of net profit and continuing business expenses if production at either factory were interrupted by property destruction. Another policy, known as Contingent Business Interruption Insurance, he said, could be bought to protect the earnings of the Brown Company factories against loss if the Ray Foundry were prevented by property destruction from manufacturing the castings required by the

Brown Company. Both policies could be extended to protect against loss of earnings to the Brown Company—resulting from stoppage of electric power resulting from damage to the municipal power plant producing, or the transmission lines carrying, electricity for and to the Brown and Ray plants.

Similarly, Mr. White said, the management of the Ray Foundry could purchase direct Business Interruption Insurance against loss of earnings—should property destruction at the foundry prevent production; and Contingent Business Interruption Insurance against loss of earnings—should either of the Brown factories be prevented by property destruction from receiving the castings made by the foundry. Moreover, Mr. Gray—as the Selling Agent for the products of the Brown factories—could also secure a form of Business Interruption Insurance, known as Selling Agents Commissions Insurance, to protect his commission earnings against loss in case the factories were prevented by property destruction from manufacturing the products sold and to be sold by Mr. Gray.

Williams and Green could also protect the earnings of their drug store and theatre against loss in the event business was interrupted due to property destruction, Mr. White continued, pointing out that the theatre particularly should extend its Business Interruption Insurance to cover against loss of earnings if the local electric light and power plant or the power lines were so damaged as to prevent them from supplying the electric current essential to the showing of motion pictures.

"But," remarked Jackson, "what about my situation? If my laundry is shut down by property destruction, my sales will not stop, because I can continue to serve my customers with the help of Mr. Black's laundry—under an agreement I have with him to help each other if either of our laundries is shut down by property destruction.

"We believe that our customers will hardly know the difference, our sales will not be reduced, and the only loss we can sustain will be the extra expense of continuing business. Is there not some form of insurance that each of us can secure to reimburse us only for the extra expense we will incur until property destruction has been repaired, costing less than full coverage Business Interruption Insurance?"

"Yes," Agent White replied. "There is a limited form of Business Interruption Insurance called 'Extra Expense Insurance,' which you can carry as an alternative—provided you are certain that Mr. Black will process for you all of the laundry of your customers without loss of sales and profits to you. Many service-rendering businesses—such as yours—dairies, bottling and printing plants, banks, offices, schools, etc., carry Extra Expense Insurance—provided they are so situated as to be able to continue in business by paying for outside assistance until the damage to their business premises is repaired—and therefore do not require insurance against loss of earnings. I carry Extra Expense Insurance on my own office," Mr. White added, "because I can continue my business in temporary quarters—although at considerable extra expense."

Credit Man's Viewpoint—Mr. Clay, a credit man, had been listening with deep interest.

"Gentlemen," he said, "everything that Mr. White has told you about Business Interruption Insurance and the experience of the John Doe Company is true. I should know because at the time of their recent fire, the Doe Company, which is an old and highly valued customer of ours, was heavily indebted to us.

"But we did not worry. We knew that the Doe Company carried Business Interruption Insurance. In fact, we strongly supported Mr. White at the time he convinced the Doe Company that, for complete protection, Business Interruption Insurance should be carried in addition to Property Damage Insurance.

"Our object was to keep the Doe Company as a good credit

risk, and therefore a valued customer. We knew that unless Business Interruption Insurance was carried, serious financial embarrassment, even bankruptcy, for the Doe Company—and a bad debt loss for us—could result.

"Our experience in extending credit has taught us that, frequently, Business Interruption Insurance is the factor which determines whether or not a business will resume operations. A certain frequently cited survey of the credit histories of 100 businesses that had experienced fire losses (conducted by the Safe Manufacturers National Association) developed data which demonstrates the value of Business Interruption Insurance. The survey disclosed that fire losses involving destruction of records caused 14% to suffer a reduction of from 30% to 66-2/3% in their credit rating, and 43% to permanently discontinue business.

"Although some of the 57% that did resume business may not have carried Business Interruption Insurance, we are convinced that it was not carried by any of the 43% that did not resume business.

"Credit men and loan offices have two objectives—to secure their loans against loss, and to keep good customers. Both are achieved when customers are adequately covered by Business Interruption Insurance, because it is both indirect collateral security and business preservation insurance."

War Time Experience—"Mr. Clay's testimony," said Mr. White, "to the value of Business Interruption Insurance has been demonstrated during every cycle of our nation's economy, in times of peace, war, postwar period, prosperity, and depression.

"How effectively Business Interruption Insurance protects business earnings in wartime was amply demonstrated during World Wars I and II, particularly during the latter, when tremendous amounts of this form of insurance were bought, ranging from the small policies carried by drug stores, markets and other small mercantile businesses, to the policies like the $300,000,000 policy bought by a large steel corporation to cover its various plants.

"Time being of the essence of our nation's war program as well as of the essence of Business Interruption Insurance, it was only natural for American businesses to turn to Business Interruption Insurance for protection against loss of the money value of time—resulting from the effects of shortages of materials and manpower in the rehabilitation and replacement of damaged and destroyed business premises.

"As a result, many more business managements became aware of the value of Business Interruption Insurance than in any previous period in our history, and it is not surprising—considering the uncertainties that darkened the path of business in the post-war period—that the purchase of Business Interruption continued to increase.

"Faced by the prospects of rationing of raw materials, as our Government set out to increase our nation's stockpile of the many critical and strategic materials in short supply for civilian as well as military needs—with the continuing shortage of steel, and while Marshall Plan shipments abroad were reducing domestic supplies—business managements realized that Business Interruption Insurance was as necessary during post-war as during war years.

"Should business conditions develop into a recession (or a full scale depression such as followed World War I Business Interruption Insurance will again be the indispensable form of insurance coverage, both for the business operating with normal earnings, or the business operating 'in the red.' Business Interruption Insurance will protect such policyholders from the greater losses that otherwise, in their weakened financial condition, would have wrecked them."

(Note to Reader. The foregoing, plus the testimonial letters presented in Appendix 9, briefly explain the function and value of Business Interruption Insurance, and

7

serve as an introduction to the detailed exposition which follows in this and subsequent chapters.)

ORIGIN

How old is Business Interruption Insurance? Unfortunately, a definite answer to this question is not available, since historians do not agree on details. However, here is a summary of the events which contributed to the development of this form of Earnings insurance in the United States.

First Record—In 1834, Charles Wright, Keeper of the Ship Inn at Dover, England, attempted to recover from the Sun Insurance Office under a policy covering his interest in the Inn "for the loss he has sustained in his business by not being able to occupy the said Ship Inn and Offices during the time that elapsed between the fire and rebuilding of the said premises."

In 1842, a similar attempt was made in the United States by Michaela Leonardo to recover, from the Phoenix Assurance Company loss of rents sustained because of fire damage to buildings situated in the State of Louisiana.

In 1847, Robert Menzies, proprietor of a corn grinding mill in Scotland, filed claim against the North British Insurance Company, not only for loss of profits and rent sustained because the premises were damaged by fire, but also for the wages which he was obliged to pay the servants, and for which he could receive no recompense—since he had no building for them to work in.

In each of these cases, which occurred under ordinary Fire Insurance policies, the English, American and Scottish Courts all held that profits and rents were insurable, but were not recoverable under a policy of insurance that does not specifically insure them as such.

The inference is that insurance specifically covering profits and rents, although possibly obtainable at that time in England and the United States, was practically unknown.

Chomage Insurance—In 1860, "Chomage Insurance" was developed in France to cover loss of profits to the extent of an agreed percentage of the property loss—"chomage" being the French word for enforced idleness. Manifestly "Chomage Insurance," which continues to be written in France and Scandinavian countries, is based on the inaccurate assumption that loss of profits is directly proportionate to the degree of property loss. It is therefore not surprising that attempts to introduce it in the United States were unsuccessful.

Use and Occupancy—The next development was recorded in C. C. Hines' Book of Forms for 1879, which contained a policy form covering the Newton Mills of Newton, Massachusetts, against "damage or destruction of their buildings or machinery by fire, either or both, which damage or destruction may prevent manufacturing of goods" and providing that if, in consequence of fire, the non-delivery of goods causes the purchaser to void his contract, the insurers are to pay the difference between the contract price and the price for which they actually sell to the amount of $400 per day. The amount of insurance was $36,000, reducing at the rate of $400 each day during the three months the insurance was in force.

Some historians credit Henry R. Dalton, a Boston insurance agent, collaborating with A. W. Damon—then secretary of the Washington Insurance Company and later President of the Springfield Fire and Marine Insurance Company —with devising the first Profits or Use and Occupancy form of insurance policy written in the United States and with actually writing such insurance on the Newton Mills.

Mr. Dalton, spurred by the necessity of protecting his substantial commission income against mutual competition for insurance required by New England textile mills which had been equipped with the newly invented automatic sprinkler system, conceived the plan of offering textile mills a valued form of policy, agreeing to pay the insured the stated sum

9

of 1/300ths of the face amount of the policy for each day a mill was entirely prevented by fire from producing goods until the mill be rebuilt or repaired, and for that proportion of the Per Diem sum which the product prevented from being manufactured bore to the average daily production previous to the fire.

Other historians give credit to Edward Atkinson, a textile mill operator, as the father of Use and Occupancy Insurance. However, they admit that it was not until 1895 that he, then president of the Boston Manufacturers Mutual Fire Insurance Company, succeeded in getting the approval of the directors of that company to issue Use and Occupancy policies.

Profits Insurance—Meanwhile, in England, a form of Profits Insurance was developed on the basis that the reduction in "turnover" following a fire bears to the "turnover" previous to the fire, the insured's recovery continuing until the "turnover" is restored to normal. This type of Profits Insurance, which was perfected in 1899 or 1900, is presently written under a standardized form in Canada—where it competes with Business Interruption Insurance which is written there under forms practically identical with forms which are standard in the United States.

Since Business Interruption, or Use and Occupancy, Insurance has therefore been written in the United States for more than 75 years, the previous insurance advisers who had failed to recommend its purchase to the John Doe Company probably did so, not because they were unaware of its existence, but because they were under the influence of the too widely held belief that Business Interruption Insurance is a mysterious form of coverage which is understood only by specialists. The purpose of this discussion is to present to salesmen, buyers and underwriters as much of the background, functions and procedures of Business Interruption Insurance as are necessary for a working knowledge.

THE NAME

A brief history of the name, or names, by which this form of insurance is known, may be interesting.

Origin of Terms—Assuming that the early editions of Hines' Book of Forms recorded all the special forms in current use, it appears that the words "Use and Occupancy," as applied to insurance, were first used between 1879, when the second edition of the Hines' Book of Forms was published—and 1882, when the third edition was published. The policy form by which the plant of the Newton Mills was covered and which was published in the edition of 1879, did not employ the words "Use and Occupancy." In the edition of 1882, however, there appeared a form captioned "Product Policy—Consequential Damage," which opened with the words "Do Insure $5,000 on the Use and Occupancy of their mill buildings"—the recovery being valued at $16.66 per day for entire prevention of production of goods and such proportion of $16.66 as the product prevented from being made bears to the average yield previous to the fire.

Legal Decisions—Evidently this set the pattern for many years, since in the famous case of Michael vs. Prussian National Insurance Company (171 NY 25), decided by the Court of Appeals, April 18, 1902, the policies covered "on the Use and Occupancy" of the property and elevator building of the Buffalo Elevating Company in a fixed, i.e., valued, amount per day, against prevention of the handling and elevating of grain, but without a definition of "Use and Occupancy."

In its decision, the Court said: "Insurance on 'Use and Occupancy' evidently relates to the business use which the property is capable of in its existing condition. If it is destroyed by fire, and its use becomes impossible, then, during the period required for its reinstatement as property capable of use and occupation, the owner is to be compensated according to the terms of the policy.

11

"The peculiar feature of the contract is that it contemplates, as its subject matter, not the mere material loss of the plant, or any part of it, but the loss to the owner of the ability to use it. Use and Occupancy, as terms of insurance, may assume within their general scope the expectation of profits and earnings derivable from property, but the terms appear to have a broader significance as to the subject of insurance, and to apply to the status of the property and to its continued availability to the owner for any purpose he may be able to devote it."

Since the court held that the insurance was valid and, therefore, "Use and Occupancy" was not insurance of earnings or income, the insurance companies were compelled to pay more than $60,000 for 259 days suspension of ability to use and occupy the elevator by an insured who, because of lack of unconditional and sole ownership of the elevator, had not actually lost it.

This decision and similar subsequent decisions in the cases of Tanenbaum vs. Freundlich (81 NY Supp. 292), and Tanenbaum vs. Simon (81 NY Supp. 655), resulted in the revision of later policy forms which, although covering the "Use and Occupancy" of described property, stated that the subject of insurance is net profit and continuing expenses.

Business Interruption Indemnity—In an address by Frederic C. White, then an executive of the New York Underwriters Agency, delivered at a meeting of the Wisconsin Association of Insurance Agents on July 10, 1918, Mr. White said:

"About 10 or 11 years ago, we decided in our office that a clearly descriptive title for this form of indemnity would be helpful to agents and insured and also would give a little individuality to our forms; so we got together and, from a long list of titles suggested by men in our office, we selected 'Business Interruption Indemnity' as being the most clearly descriptive. We printed it in our forms and we alone used it for several years thereafter. Then, one by one, other companies adopted the title, which was quite in order—since it was not copyrighted."

Although other titles such as "Prospective Earnings Insurance" have also been used, the name "Business Interruption Insurance" has been accorded virtually universal acceptance and official recognition in Manuals of Rules and Standard forms. Nevertheless, the name "Use and Occupancy Insurance" continues to be extensively used as an alternate title, and even those who frequently refer to "Business Interruption Insurance" just as frequently speak of "U & O" —thereby avoiding the confusion resulting from the use of "B.I.I." which also refers to Bodily Injury Insurance in the field of Automobile Insurance.

CHAPTER 2

INSURABLE INTEREST—TIME ELEMENT

Every properly written Business Interruption Insurance policy is based upon two essential ingredients: Insurable Interest, and the Time Element. Without Insurable Interest a policy purporting to provide Business Interruption Insurance is a wager, not insurance, and without the Time Element it lacks the one constituent distinctive of Business Interruption Insurance.

INSURABLE INTEREST

Who May Be Insured?—In the realm of direct Property Damage Insurance, Insurable Interest is not confined to the owner of the property covered but is created on behalf of whoever might suffer a pecuniary loss in the event the object is damaged or destroyed. Similarly, in the realm of Business Interruption Insurance, Insurable Interest exists when there is an interest in earnings derived from business occupancy or use of or dependency upon the object of coverage, irrespective of its ownership.

For instance, the lessee of a building occupied for his business or the lessee of machinery or equipment used for his business purposes has a Business Interruption Insurable Interest in them as complete as though he owned them. The user of electric power generated by a Public Utility Corporation, of castings purchased from a certain foundry, or of cloth purchased from a certain mill, has a Business Interruption Insurable Interest in the Power Plant, Foundry or Mill, even though he does not own or even occupy or operate it. His Insurable Interest is created by his dependence upon it for the supply of services or materials essential to his business operations, for the lack of which, due to property damage or destruction at the Power Plant, Foundry or Mill, he will suffer a pecuniary loss.

14

Earnings Must Be In Prospect—Occupancy, use of, or dependence upon the object of coverage alone does not create Business Interruption Insurable Interest in it. There must also be the prospect of business earnings, consisting of net profits or fixed charges and operating expenses that would have been earned but for property damage to or destruction of the object.

Since a business enterprise earns a net profit only after all costs, expenses and fixed charges have been earned the management manifestly has a Business Interruption insurable interest in the business premises if a net profit is being earned. However, the earning of a net profit is not the only prerequisite of Business Interruption Insurable Interest. To the extent that a business earns its expenses and fixed charges, to that extent does its management have a Business Interruption Insurable Interest in the premises.

But expenses and fixed charges not being earned, or to be earned by the operation of a business, do not create Insurable Interest, since they are normally a loss and suspension of business due to property damage will not increase the normal loss. On the contrary, the loss normally sustained while a business is in operation will decrease to the extent that expenses are discontinued during the time of business suspension. When a business is idle for an indefinite period of time, obviously the complete absence of present or prospective earnings means a complete absence of Business Interruption Insurable Interest.

However, since Business Interruption Insurance covers against loss of prospective earnings, if an idle factory is definitely scheduled to resume operations, the operator has a potential Business Interruption Insurable Interest therein, and any loss of earnings would be payable as of the date operations would have begun had not property damage prevented.

Similarly, the operator of a business, the premises of which are in course of construction, also has a Business Interruption Insurable Interest in the premises. Any loss thereto is payable as of the prospective date of occupancy when business earnings would have begun had not property damage or destruction postponed the date of completion of construction.

Limited to Earned Charges—All standard Business Interruption policy forms not only specify that indemnity is for "actual loss sustained" by the insured, but also state that coverage for continuing charges and expenses is limited to the extent that they would have been earned had no fire occurred. Even under a policy written to cover Actual Loss sustained, but without limiting coverage of charges and expenses to such as would have been earned, courts have held that there can be no claim for loss of charges and expenses that would have been a loss anyway had no fire occurred.

A case in point was that of Goetz vs. Hartford Fire Insurance Company (Wisconsin Supreme Court 1927; 215 NW 40; 70 Insurance Law Journal 108). In that case the Peterson Manufacturing Company of Milwaukee held policies providing for recovery "for the actual loss sustained consisting of net profits of the business which is thereby prevented and such fixed charges and expenses pertaining thereto as must necessarily continue during a total or partial suspension of business."

After finding that the Insured would have operated without net profit had no fire occurred, and at a loss of $4062.64 during the 49 days the plant was shut down by fire, and that the necessarily continuing fixed charges and expenses during the period of suspension were $3,820.30, for which the Insured claimed reimbursement, the Court held that, since the Insured could not have earned sufficient during the 49 days to meet the sum claimed, they could not properly be said to have sustained an actual loss due to the fire. The Court said that the insurance was not to indemnify against liabilities incurred during the suspension period; that it was necessary to show that, but for the fire, the Insured could have made the wherewithal to meet the expenses, and that the Insured had sustained no actual loss since, with respect to the expenses, its position would be the same, fire or no fire.

VALUED FORM POLICIES

The foregoing discussion of Insurable Interest relates particularly to Business Interruption policies written to indemnify for "Actual Loss Sustained," generally termed "Non-Valued Policies."

Valued Policies—Very infrequently, and only in the few territories where they are permitted (at a substantially increased rate) or where Lloyds, or a domestic insurance company has received approval of a filed deviation from standard non-valued forms, Business Interruption Insurance policies, which are termed "Valued Policies," are written to hold the Insurer liable for a fixed sum per day, week or month without limiting recovery to actual loss sustained. Necessarily, Valued Form policies lack the flexibility of standard non-valued policies particularly where the Insured's earnings fluctuate.

The great majority of Valued Form Business Interruption Insurance policies are written where the Insured, although having an Insurable Interest in the object of coverage, feels unable to predict the amount of future earnings or anticipates great difficulty in proving the actual amount of loss sustained. He therefore desires a policy which will pay a fixed sum per day, per week or per month of business suspension, without proof of actual loss sustained.

While it is possible that Valued Form policies have been or may be secured by parties without any Insurable Interest whatever in the object of coverage, or with an Insurable Interest considerably less than the fixed amount of insurance secured, such cases are believed to be exceedingly rare.

The applicant for a Valued Form policy ordinarily either discloses the existence of his Insurable Interest at the time of purchase, or if he conceals his lack of it, becomes guilty of fraud and risks voidance of the policy. Courts may be expected to support the insurer's refusal to pay fixed sums under Valued Business Interruption Insurance policies where either complete lack of Insurable Interest or excessive amounts of insurance is proven.

That Boiler and Machinery Use & Occupancy policies are writable under a Valued Form is sometimes cited as precedent for similarly writing Fire Business Interruption policies. The fact, however, is that in the majority of cases, Boiler and Machinery policies cover specific objects—such as a boiler or a particular machine which, when damaged or destroyed by explosion, will not shut down the entire plant. Therefore, to avoid compliance with a Coinsurance clause based on the annual earnings of the entire plant and being unable to determine the Use & Occupancy value of the specific object on which coverage is desired, it is covered for an arbitrary amount under a Valued Form policy. Fire Business Interruption policies invariably, and necessarily— because fire is a spreading peril, cover the entire plant and contents which are subject to a catastrophic loss.

Valued Form policies, in their relation to an insured's liability for Income and Profits Taxes payable on recoveries from Business Interruption policies, are discussed under Subdivision 9 of Chapter 16.

THE TIME ELEMENT

The other ingredient of every Business Interruption policy is the Time Element—the yardstick which determines the required amount of insurance and the amount of recoverable loss.

Determine Time Element Factor—Because the element of time is peculiar to Business Interruption, Tuition Fees, Rent and Rental Value, Leasehold Interest, Extra Expense and Selling Agent's Commission Insurance, they are known as forms of "Time Element Insurance." Of these, Business Interruption is of chief interest because of its tremendously important function of protecting the vast earnings of business enterprise against loss resulting from interruption of business operations during the time required to repair or replace property damaged or destroyed.

Since time is required to produce business earnings, much of the haze that has obscured Business Interruption Insurance is dissipated when buyers, salesmen, inspectors, adjusters and underwriters thoroughly understand the part that the Time Element plays in determining the extent of the need for Business Interruption Insurance, the amount of it required, the price paid, and the extent of the purchaser's indemnification for loss of earnings resulting from damage to or destruction of property used for business purposes.

This chapter presents illustrations selected with the purpose of impressing upon the mind of the reader the importance of the time element, so that henceforth every building, machine, device, fixture and stock of materials used for business purposes, will be appraised not alone for its appearance, quality and physical value, but also in terms of time required to repair or replace it in the event of damage and consequent loss of earnings while its user is deprived of its services.

BOTTLENECKS

No term is quite so descriptive of situations to be found in practically every business which threaten to impede business operations, as the expressive term "bottleneck." Among the many types of business bottlenecks, Business Interruption Insurance is concerned only with physical situations where damage or destruction of property will throttle business operations. Indeed, a good name for Business Interruption Insurance would be "Bottleneck Insurance."

Bottlenecks and vulnerable situations requiring time-consuming repairs and replacements can exist in building construction, machinery, power supply, raw materials and other physical attributes of business premises.

BUILDING CONSTRUCTION

● When fire destroyed the Arcade Building, which provided the only entrance to the lobby of Loew's Lincoln Square Theatre in New York City, the theater, although not damaged, was forced to shut down. The Arcade Building was one of the theater's bottlenecks.

● The walls of a Greenwich Village restaurant in New York City were decorated with South Sea Island scenes by a well known artist. Since this artist could not be hurried in the reproduction of the damaged paintings, the claim for Business Interruption Insurance was settled on a six month's basis. The underwriter, unconscious of this possible bottleneck, had figured on a maximum loss of three months to rehabilitate the restaurant.

● Unsprinklered open communications over the crosswalls between the joist channels under the grade floor of a Birmingham department store permitted fire to spread beyond control of the sprinkler system in the upper floors. The total destruction of the building resulted in a Business Interruption loss exceeding $200,-000.

● Fire spreading through the unsprinklered under-floor air space of an otherwise sprinkler equipped Michigan refrigerator factory caused the floor to collapse, seriously damaging essential machinery. The property loss was $73,000 but the Business Interruption loss was $221,000.

● Lack of waterproof floors was responsible for a heavy Business Interruption loss in an art metal factory when water, discharged by the automatic sprinkler system to extinguish a paint spraying booth fire on an upper floor, seriously damaged raw materials and stock in process on lower floors.

● Because the naphtha soap compounding building of a Pennsylvania factory was of frame instead of fire resistive construction and was the bottleneck of the Insured's operations, its destruction by explosion and fire resulted in total suspension for 3-3/5 weeks, 2/3 suspension for 1-3/5 weeks and 1/3 suspension for one week.

● Unanchored roofs, vulnerable to windstorm damage, have

caused large Business Interruption losses. When a large portion of the unanchored roof of a Georgia Cotton Mill was torn off by a tornado and heavy rain wet down machinery, production equivalent to three weeks' full time was lost.

PROCESSES: MACHINERY

In a manufacturing plant, the arrangement, hazards and protection of processes and machinery furnish the greatest number and the most important and threatening bottlenecks.

● At an East Peoria, Illinois, factory, fire in an oven—used to bake enamel on metal—spread to concealed places in oven walls and ceilings. Result—a Property Damage Insurance loss of $9,000, but a Business Interruption Insurance loss of $22,000.

Elsewhere, fire in an enameling furnace caused a property loss of $40,000 to furnace and stock but, since the furnace handled half of the production of the factory, the equivalent of 35 days of production was lost and Business Interruption Insurance paid the loss of $70,000.

● At a Grand Rapids, Michigan, electroplating plant, an explosion and ensuing fire in an electric oven, (through which a conveyor passed over plating tanks using a flammable solvent), resulted in a two hour suspension of production and a Business Interruption Insurance loss of $1,256.

In another plant, an inadequately ventilated oven operating seven days a week was wrecked by an explosion and could not be replaced for six weeks.

A japan-oven explosion in another factory caused a Business Interruption Insurance loss of $15,000 for 12 days interruption of oven production and extra expense to have materials finished elsewhere.

A large gas heated lithographing oven in another factory was damaged by an explosion resulting in a property loss of $15,000 but a Business Interruption loss of $60,000.

● Water from the opening of low test automatic sprinkler heads, due to high temperature from steam in a hosiery drying enclosure in Boston following an employee's failure to close the steam valve at the close of a workday, deluged the premises of various tenants on lower floors resulting in the recovery of amounts ranging from $389 to $4,113 by some of the tenants carrying Sprinkler Leakage Business Interruption Insurance.

● Fire originating from an explosion of wood flour in the dry kiln of a Massachusetts toy factory, although extinguished by

21

26 automatic sprinklers, caused a Business Interruption loss of $37,000, compared with a property loss of $8,500, because operation of the factory was dependent upon a special type of dried lumber.

● Fire caused by a hot bearing on the improperly oiled main shaft of a Massachusetts paper mill operating 24 hours a day destroyed a large pulley, a 32″ by 111″ leather belt and two 20″ belts, shutting the mill down for one week.

● In a Michigan refrigerator factory, two unusual woodworking machines were wrecked by fire. Eight weeks would have been required to reproduce the machines, causing a Business Interruption loss in excess of $100,000 per week. Fortunately duplicate machines were located (one in North Carolina, the other in Ohio), costing less than $7,500 each. They were shipped by truck and were ready to operate when building repairs were completed. Instead of a loss of approximately $1,000,000, the Business Interruption Insurance actually paid $200,000.

SPECIAL MACHINES

● The destruction by fire of two large specially built machines in the total destruction of a New Jersey floor covering factory was chiefly responsible for a Business Interruption loss of $508,-000, or 70% to insurance, whereas the underwriter had not anticipated a loss in excess of 40%.

● When the harness on three looms in a Philadelphia lace works was damaged by fire and water and expert reharness men refused, under the rules of their union, to work double time, the $14,000 Business Interruption loss payment was nearly seven times the property loss, because lost time was more expensive than loss values. In this case, the bottleneck could be said to be the union rules.

● Fire in the breaker-picker of a thread mill caused property loss of $7,500 but, in addition, nearly 1,000,000 spindle hours of production were lost for which Business Interruption Insurance paid $6,000.

● When a Springfield, Massachusetts, plant burned while partially inundated by water, the intense heat damaged 32 drop forge hammers, weighing from 500 to 3,000 lbs. each, by stresses set up in the upper portions while the lower portions were under water. A Business Interruption loss of approximately $250,000 was paid for loss of earnings during the 25 days required for demolition and 105 days to replace the damaged hammers and tune up the new hammers before production could be resumed.

Who could have predicted that a Business Interruption loss of this magnitude would result from fire damage to heavy forge hammers?

● Foreign built machinery is likely to be a bottleneck, as was demonstrated when the German-made soy-bean oil extracting machinery of a Chicago manufacturer was damaged in 1935 and replacement required 9½ months suspension of the insured's production. The loss amounted to 80% of the amount of Business Interruption insurance.

Nearly a seven months Business Interruption loss was paid when the German-made machinery of an Illinois liquid oxygen plant was damaged by explosion in 1941.

● That even animals can be a bottleneck was demonstrated when nearly 1,000 rats, used to test the potency of vitamin tablets, were destroyed by fire and smoke in the biological laboratory of a drug manufacturer. Since the rats were of a special breed exceptionally suitable for biological tests, their speedy replacement was impossible and a $20,000 Business Interruption loss resulted.

ELECTRIC POWER SUPPLY

● When the cable tower at the power house of a New Hampshire paper mill was struck by lightning which damaged the insulation of two generators, the greater cost of electric power generated in a reserve steam station caused a Business Interruption Insurance loss of approximately $100,000, which was double the property loss.

● A Tennessee rayon manufacturing plant was shut down for 24 hours, and an Ohio chemical plant four hours, by cable box fires—demonstrating that unless cables are wrapped with fire resistive insulation, cable boxes and ducts are vulnerable production bottlenecks.

● Power plant stacks, both brick and metal, are bottlenecks responsible for substantial Business Interruption Insurance losses when damaged by wind, lightning or explosion.

When the brick stack of a Minnesota paper mill collapsed as the result of the explosion of unconsumed fuel gases, it damaged the turbine house so that four paper machines were shut down until the power load could be transferred to another turbine house and additional power secured through a temporary connection.

When the brick chimney of a textile mill was toppled by a windstorm, it wrecked the power house, caused a loss of production equivalent to seven working days, for which the Business Interruption policies paid $65,000.

Chimneys without lightning rod protection are vulnerable production bottlenecks. This was demonstrated when the 115 foot brick stack of a Rhode Island textile mill was struck, felling the upper half and blasting a large hole in its side. The damage to boiler, engine house and equipment, plus the shortening of the stack, prevented operation of the engine for generating electric power, resulting in the total suspension of the mill's production for several weeks.

Too numerous to mention individually are the windstorm damages to bottleneck metal smoke stacks, upon which power and heat, and therefore production, is dependent.

● A fire box explosion in a natural gas fired boiler completely shut down a large wall board mill which recovered a loss of $33,000 from Business Interruption Insurance, compared with a property loss of $11,000.

● At a cotton mill, an insulation breakdown resulted in a fire in a large electric generator which so damaged the windings that a complete rewinding of the generator was required; the mill meanwhile was forced to get along with 25% less power.

● Oil filled electric transformers are bottlenecks when they are damaged by fire, as happened at a Michigan factory when production was stopped for two days until borrowed transformers were installed.

For instances of Business Interruption losses sustained when damage to Public Utility or other off-the-Insured premises property damage interrupts supplies of power, heat, gas and water, the reader is referred to the discussion of Contingent Business Interruption Insurance in Chapter 9.

WINDSTORM LOSSES

Outside conveying and handling equipment, such as traveling cranes and bridges, are particularly susceptible to damage by windstorm, resulting in prolonged suspension of manufacturing operations dependent upon such equipment.

For instance, a sudden violent storm rolled an ore-loading

bridge out of control along 500 feet of its curved track, crashing it into another bridge at a steel company's lakeside plant in Ohio. Although the bridge was equipped with safety brakes, it could not be checked, and both bridges were totally destroyed, with a property loss of nearly $400,000. The Business Interruption Insurance loss was held to less than $100,000 by renting large shovels and diverting many boatloads of ore to other storage yards. The Business Interruption loss was thus largely composed of expediting expense.

● Similarly, a 50-mile wind drove an unanchored 10-ton overhead crane with a 90-foot span along 200 feet of wet rails. At the end of the track it collapsed, causing a heavy Business Interruption loss to a Pennsylvania manufacturer's plant, the production of which was dependent upon the materials handled by the crane.

RAW MATERIALS AND STOCK IN PROCESS

Since Business Interruption Insurance written for manufacturers covers raw materials and stock in process, the following actual losses illustrate how damage to such materials contributes to Business Interruption losses.

● At a Michigan pulp and paper mill, a pile of pulpwood 425 feet long, 200 feet wide and 80 feet high, containing more than 15,-000 cords, was totally destroyed by fire, shutting down the mill for one week.

● More than $350,000 worth of No. 1 grade ash sticks 12 feet long, but for the fire which destroyed them, would have been manufactured into the famous "Louisville Slugger" baseball bats. Since the ash was being air-dried in the yard of the factory, it was "stock in process" as defined in the Business Interruption policy. Since the reconditioning of similar stock, which normally requires up to 24 months, was covered for only 30 days, the bat manufacturer recovered only $28,000 from Business Interruption Insurance totaling $500,000.

● When most of the hides in the vats of a Virginia tannery were damaged by fire and all plank covers of the vats were destroyed, a 92% loss to Business Interruption Insurance was paid, including a "stock in process" loss of 120 days, whereas the loss to property damage insurance was 67%.

● Fire in the large lumber yard of a manufacturer of fine cabinets destroyed specially selected and graded oak, walnut and

BUSINESS INTERRUPTION INSURANCE

mahogany which required a minimum of two and one-half years seasoning. Had Business Interruption Insurance been carried, the loss paid would have depended upon the number of days *stock in process* coverage purchased by the Insured.

● When the warehouse of a Wisconsin felt pad manufacturer was destroyed by fire, together with the total supply of a raw material required to manufacture a certain type of cushion, the plant was forced to shut down for two eight-hour shifts until substitute raw material could be obtained and machinery adjusted. Loss paid was $10,612, including $3,625 for expediting expense incurred to reduce the U & O loss that would have been sustained.

MISCELLANEOUS

Not the least of the various types of bottleneck situations that can cause or increase Business Interruption losses are the following, in each of which the time element is responsible for the extent of the resulting loss.

Climate—can greatly affect the time required to repair or rebuild. To illustrate, a certain loss adjuster relates how in his experience three similar factories were destroyed by fire: One in the early Spring, one in the late Summer, and one at the start of Winter. The Business Interruption losses were adjusted respectively on the basis of 170, 190 and 270 days because the weather conditions encountered controlled the speed of rebuilding operations.

Municipal Fire Limits—In some municipalities, a building of combustible construction located within the fire limits must be rebuilt of fire resistive construction if damaged in excess of 50% of its value. Since the undamaged portion must therefore be demolished, and the time required for that operation plus the time required to rebuild of fire resistive construction will invariably exceed the time required merely to repair the damage or to completely rebuild of the original type of construction, the Business Interruption loss will manifestly be greater than normal—provided

26

the insurance has been extended by special endorsement to assume liability for the additional loss.

Building Ownership—Where the Insured is the lessee and not the owner of the building he occupies, and the lease does not give him control over repairs and rebuilding, disagreements with and delays by the lessor prolong the time required to rehabilitate, and may result in an increased claim for loss.

Plans and Specifications of Buildings, Patterns and Dies for Machinery and Products—When destroyed and duplicates are not available, these delay rehabilitation and resumption of business.

Lack of Adequate Fire Protection results in more extensive and frequently total property losses, increasing the time required for rebuilding and, consequently, the Business Interruption Insurance loss.

Processes not duplicated in separate buildings or fire divisions are bottlenecks, since destruction of their machinery and equipment results in complete interruption of production.

Special and Obsolete Machines are bottlenecks requiring increased time for repairs and replacements.

Seasonal and Imported Materials are bottlenecks unless replacements are in reserve supply, or obtainable in the open domestic market.

Housing for Employees (whether or not provided by manufacturers in "mill villages"), when the dwellings are included in the coverage of Business Interruption Insurance on the factory, can become a bottleneck when a conflagration or tornado renders the homes of employees untentantable and suspends factory production while the families of employees are re-housed.

Offices and Office Records are bottlenecks when destroyed, handicapping executive direction of continued business operations and rehabilitation measures.

Motor Vehicles Used for transportation of raw materials or finished products, and **Garages** required to house and service them, are bottlenecks when covered by Business Interruption Insurance, since their destruction eliminates a vital link in the chain of operations, whether the business be manufacturing or mercantile.

Sprinkler System Tanks cause heavy business interruption as well as property losses when they collapse because of weak supports or wind pressure, and crash through buildings.

Bridges connecting buildings become production bottlenecks when closed by property damage. For example, the two mills of a Virginia cotton manufacturer located on opposite sides of a river, connected by a steel truss bridge, experienced production difficulties resulting from the disruption of gas and telephone service when the bridge was destroyed by fire and utility cables severed. Due to this destruction of electric power cables, one of the mills was shut down for a day and production was further reduced because of the destruction of a 14-inch pipe supported by the bridge and used for blowing cotton from one mill to the other.

Government Directives such as Priority Regulations. Unless a Business Interruption Policy denies liability for increased loss resulting from the enforcement of a Government regulation, or if the policy specifically assumes liability for such increased loss, as was done under the Priorities Assumption clause during World War II, or if the Demolition coverage or Contingent Liability from Operation of Building Laws Endorsement is attached to a policy, Business Interruption Insurance losses are increased because of the increased time required to rehabilitate the damaged or destroyed property. For a discussion of the effect of wartime government regulation supon Business Interruption Insurance, the reader is referred to Chapter 12.

CHAPTER 3

THE PER DIEM POLICY FORM

The reader may feel that an undue amount of space is devoted, in this and the following chapter, to the Per Diem, Weekly and Monthly Business Interruption forms, since these forms are either obsolete, or nearly so. If so, he should realize that:

(1) The Per Diem form was the first under which Use & Occupancy Insurance was written in the United States;

(2) It was the medium through which the principle of coinsurance was first applied to Use & Occupancy Insurance;

(3) The modern Two Item Contribution and the Gross Earnings forms were the result of a direct line of development through the Per Diem, Weekly and Monthly forms; an understanding of the weaknesses and bad features of the older forms will help in understanding and appreciating the advantages of the modern forms.

(4) In the past, many businessmen refused to buy Business Interruption Insurance because of the inflexibility and the seeming complexity of the old forms. An understanding of the basis of their objections will help in the sale of the modern forms, in which these objections are completely eliminated.

Indemnity Per Day—The Per Diem Policy form indemnifies the Insured at the rate of a specified sum per day for the loss of net profit and necessarily continuing business expenses during the time the Insured's business is totally or partially prevented from operating because of damage to or destruction of business property by fire or other perils insured against.

In the latest editions of this policy form, the indemnity per day in the event of total suspension of business is expressed as a fraction of the total amount of insurance—

1/365th if the Insured's business normally operates seven days per week, 1/300th if it normally operates six days per week and 1/250th if it normally operates five days per week. In the event of partial suspension of business, the Insured's daily recovery is proportionate to the recovery provided for total suspension.

If the earnings of the Insured's business fluctuate seasonally so that an amount of daily insurance which is uniform throughout the year will provide overinsurance per day during some seasons and insufficient insurance per day during other seasons, the Per Diem fractions of 1/365th, 1/300th, or 1/250th are replaced by a table listing the varying dollars of the Insured's recoveries per day of total suspension of business between specified dates. The aggregate of the totals for each season equals the amount of insurance for which the policy is written.

The earliest Per Diem Policy forms were "valued," in that the Insured's recovery in the event of loss was a fixed sum per day or on the basis of an agreed daily value of goods produced. This plan disregarded the actual loss per day or the actual value of goods produced. The latest standard editions of the Per Diem form are "non-valued" by stating that the Insured's recovery is limited to the "actual loss sustained not exceeding 1/ . . . .th of the amount of this policy for each business day."

Historical Development—The Per Diem Policy form is of historical importance because it was the first form of contract to apply the principle of Coinsurance or Contribution in the writing of Business Interruption Insurance. In the policy form covering the Newton Mills (described in Chapter 1) no provision was made for the measurement of the amount of loss resulting from less than a total prevention of production.

In the later forms, this omission was corrected by providing that in the event of a partial suspension of production, settlement was to be for that proportion of the Per

Diem amount of insurance which the product prevented from being manufactured bore to the average daily yield previous to the fire. The average daily yield, for the purpose of the insurance, was agreed to be a stated sum per day. Thus came into existence the "Partial Suspension Clause," which was the equivalent of a 100% Coinsurance Clause.

Partial Suspension Clause—Because of the many variations of the Partial Suspension Clause which were devised, some based upon past net profits, some on past sales, others on past production, a standardized clause emerged in which the Insurer's liability for partial suspension was "not to exceed that proportion of the Per Diem liability which would have been incurred by a total suspension which the decrease in production (or business) bears to the full daily production (or business) at the time of the fire." This clause was supplemented by a clause basing the daily production (or business) at the time of the fire upon the average daily production (or business) of all properties described in the policy for a period of not less than 30 days of full operation next preceding the fire.

Without this supplemental provision, the rate was at least 10% higher than the rate which would otherwise apply. Moreover, if the policy covered more than one plant, either a pro-rata distribution clause or a coinsurance clause was required.

The latter provided that liability be for no greater portion of any loss than the amount of the policy bears to the amount of loss incurred by a total suspension of operations of all described properties during an entire year beginning with the date of the fire. This coinsurance clause was so severely criticized that it was withdrawn.

Meanwhile, controversy raged over the propriety of continuing to base the Partial Suspension Clause upon past production or business, thereby setting up a fraction to measure recovery, the numerator of which represented the decrease in production resulting from the fire, the denominator representing the daily production for a stated period immediately preceding the fire. It was pointed out that only in a business operating with absolute uniformity would there be any uniformity between a numerator reflecting future probabilities and a denominator reflecting past experience. Moreover, attention was called to the hardship to the insured where a slight decrease in production resulted in a disproportionate loss of profits; yet recovery was based solely on the decrease in production.

As a result, the following revised Partial Suspension Clause became standard, thus establishing a coinsurance fraction of related members, both numerator and denominator reflecting the future probabilities of the insured's business:

"Partial Suspension: The per diem liability under this policy during the time of a partial suspension of business shall be limited to the actual loss sustained, not exceeding that proportion of the per diem liability that would have been incurred by a total suspension of business which the actual loss sustained during the time of such partial suspension bears to the loss which would have been sustained by a total suspension of business, for the same time, of all properties described herein, due consideration being given to the experience of the business before the fire and the probable experience thereafter."

Since the new Partial Suspension Clause provided an iron-clad full coinsurance condition, the pro-rata distribution clause which had been required when two or more plants were blanketed became superfluous.

Per Diem Form—Subsequently the Partial Suspension Clause was again revised, but only to make clear the intention that where there is a reference to actual loss sustained it is to the loss sustained "by the Insured" and not by the Insurance Company. For the sake of their historical value, following are the essential portions of the Per Diem Form as it was constituted at the time it was discontinued.

"The conditions of this contract are that if the building(s) situate .... and occupied as....................and/or machinery and/or equipment and/or Raw Stock contained therein (Strike out "and/or Raw Stock" if rate does not contemplate raw stock coverage), be destroyed or damaged by fire occurring during the term of this policy so as to necessitate a total or partial suspension of business, this Company shall be liable under this policy for the ACTUAL LOSS SUSTAINED, for not exceeding such length of time as would be required with the exercise of due diligence and dispatch, to rebuild, repair or replace such part of the property described as covered by this policy as has been destroyed or damaged, commencing with the date of the fire and not limited by the date of expiration of this policy, to wit:—

    I. Net profits on the business which is thereby prevented;

    II. Such charges and other expenses as must necessarily continue during a total or partial suspension of business, to the extent only that such charges and expenses would have been earned had no fire occurred;

    III. Such expenses as are necessarily incurred for the purpose of reducing the loss under this policy; for not exceeding, however, the amount by which the loss covered is thereby reduced.

Total Suspension Clause: The per diem liability under items I and II of this policy during the time of total suspension of business of all the properties described herein shall be limited to the "Actual Loss Sustained," not exceeding:

    (a) 1/*........(insert 250)........the of the amount of this policy for each business day, if during the period of total suspension, the business would have operated not more than five days per week, and the period for which this Company is liable in any week shall not exceed five days, due consideration being given to the experience of the business before the fire and the probable experience thereafter.

    (b) 1/*........(Insert 300)........th of the amount of this policy for each business day, if during the period of total suspension the business would have operated not more than six days per week, and the period for which this Company is liable in any week shall not exceed six days, due consiberation being given to the experience of the business before the fire and the probable experience thereafter.

(c) 1/*........(Insert 365)........th of the amount of this policy for each business day, if during the period of total suspension, the business would have operated more than six days per week, due consideration being given to the experience of the business before the fire and and the probably experience thereafter.

*Insert the amount designated in parentheses *under one item only;* the other two items remaining blank shall be of no force and effect.

Note:

Partial Suspension Clause: The per diem liability of this Company under Items I and II of this policy during the time of a partial suspension of business shall be limited to the "Actual Loss Sustained" by the Insured, not exceeding that proportion of the per diem liability under said Items that would have been incurred by this Company by a total suspension of business, which the actual per diem loss sustained under said Items during the time of such partial suspension bears to the per diem loss which would have been sustained by the Insured under said Items by a total suspension of business, for the same time, of all properties described herein, due consideration being given to the experience of the business before the fire and the probable experience thereafter.

The good and bad features of the Per Diem Form, which are practically identical with the good and bad features of the Weekly Form, are analyzed in the next chapter.

A typical loss adjustment under the Per Diem Policy Form is reproduced in Appendix No. 1.

CHAPTER 4

The Weekly and Monthly Policy Forms

The Weekly Form indemnifies the Insured at the rate of a specified sum per week for the loss of net profit and necessarily continuing business expenses during the time the Insured's business is totally or partially suspended by fire or other perils insured against.

Weekly Indemnity Fraction—The indemnity per week is expressed as a fraction—1/50th of the total amount of insurance in the event of total suspension of business, and as a proportion of 1/50th per week in the event of partial suspension of business. As in the case of the Per Diem Form, if the Insured's earnings fluctuate seasonally, the uniform Weekly Indemnity fraction of 1/50th is replaced by a Table listing varying dollar amounts which the Insured recovers for each week of total suspension between specified dates, the aggregate of the totals for each season equalling the amount of insurance for which the policy is written.

The creation of the Weekly Form resulted from objections to the Per Diem Form from lines of business the earnings of which fluctuate during the week; for example, coal mining properties, which seldom operate every day, and department stores, which experience days of both low and high earnings in the same week.

Assume, for example, earnings on the peak day of a six day week are $1,000, and on each other day to be $800, or aggregating $5,000 per week. The operator of a department store with this pattern of earnings was compelled under the Per Diem Form to carry $300,000 (300 times $1000) insurance in order to recover $1000 if shut down on the peak day. Under the Weekly Form, insurance of only $250,000 (50 times $5,000) is sufficient for the recovery of $1000 for the peak day, plus $800 for each of the other five days.

Since the Weekly Form will probably have become obsolete

in all states by the time this discussion is published, the following analysis and comments are recorded for whatever historic value they may have, and because students of the later forms discussed in subsequent chapters should understand the process by which they were developed.

Composition of Form—Following are the portions of the Weekly Form essential to an understanding of its operation. Of greatest importance are the "Total Suspension Clause" and the "Partial Suspension Clause."

"If the building(s) and /or structures and/or machinery and equipment contained therein (for stock see Sections 7, 8 and 9 of this form) be destroyed or damaged by the perils insured against occurring during the term of this policy so as to necessitate a total or partial suspension of business, this Company shall be liable under this policy for the ACTUAL LOSS SUSTAINED, for not exceeding such length of time as would be required with the exercise of due diligence and dispatch, to rebuild, repair or replace such part of the property described as covered by this policy as has been destroyed or damaged, commencing with the date of such damage or destruction and not limited by the date of expiration of this policy, to wit:—

I. Net profit which is thereby prevented from being earned;
II. Such charges and other expenses, including salaries of officers, executives, department managers, employees under contract and other important employees, as must necessarily continue during a total or partial suspension of business, to the extent only that such charges and expenses would have been earned had no loss occurred.

Expense to Reduce Loss: This policy also covers such expenses as are necessarily incurred for the purpose of reducing any loss under this policy (except expense incurred to extinguish a fire), not exceeding, however, the amount by which the loss under this policy is thereby reduced.

Total Suspension Clause: The liability per week under Items I and II of this policy during the time of total suspension of business of all the properties described herein shall be limited to the "Actual Loss Sustained," not exceeding 1/50 of the amount of this policy for each business week of such suspension.

Partial Suspension Clause: The liability per week of this Company under Items I and II of this policy during the time of a partial suspension of business shall be limited to the "Actual Loss

Sustained" by the Insured, not exceeding that proportion of the liability per week under said Items that would have been incurred by this Company by a total suspension of business, which the actual loss per week sustained by the Insured under said Items during the time of such partial suspension, bears to the loss per week which would have been sustained by the Insured under said Items by a total suspension of business, for the same time, of all properties described herein.

Experience of the Business: In determining the actual loss sustained, covered under this policy, or the loss per week which would have been sustained by the Insured by the total suspension of business, due consideration shall be given to the experience of the business before the loss and the probable experience thereafter had no such loss occurred.

Definition of "Suspension"—Upon first consideration of the Total and Partial Suspension Clauses, it would seem that there should be no disagreement as to their operation or the definition of a total and of a partial suspension of business.

Nevertheless, there are adjusters and underwriters who contend that a "total suspension" is a complete cessation of business for any period of time even if less than one week, and a "partial suspension" is a suspension of business which is less than complete for any period of time less than one week; whereas others contend that a "total suspension" is a complete cessation of business for not less than the Insured's full work week, and a "partial suspension" is any suspension of business, total or partial, which continues for a period of time less than the Insured's full work week.

Moreover, some claim that the words "for the same time" near the end of the "Partial Suspension Clause" are intended to mean that the denominator of the fraction which measures the Insured's recovery is the loss that the Insured would have sustained had his business been totally suspended **during the same time** it was partially suspended, whereas others claim that these words mean that the denominator is the loss that the Insured would sustain if his business were totally suspended **during the full week** in which it was partially suspended.

To illustrate the effect of these conflicting interpretations, a few examples are presented in which the operation of the Partial Suspension Clause is expressed as follows:

$$\frac{\text{Insured's actual loss per week}}{\text{Insured's loss per week if totally suspended "for the same time."}} \times \frac{\text{The insurer's maximum liability per week in the event of total suspension for a week.}}{} = \frac{\text{Loss paid per week}}{}$$

Assume Weekly Insurance of $500, and that the Insured's loss is $300 if business is totally suspended for one day and is $1500 if totally suspended for one full week of five days.

Example No. 1—Assume that business is totally suspended for two full days, loss sustained $600.

(a) If loss is construed to fall under the *"Total* Suspension Clause" the Insured recovers not exceeding the Weekly Insurance of $500.

(b) If loss is construed to fall under the *"Partial* Suspension Clause" and the words "for the same time" refer to the same two days, the Insured recovers $500 as follows:

$$\frac{\$600}{\$600} \times \$500 = \$500$$

(c) Same as (b) but words "for the same time" are contrued to refer to the full week.

$$\frac{\$\ 600}{\$1500} \times \$500 = \$200 \text{ recovery}$$

In Examples Nos. 1 (a), (b) and (c), if the Weekly Insurance had been $1500, the Insured in each case would have recovered the full actual loss of $600.

Example No. 2—Assume business is 50% suspended on each of four days and the Insured sustains loss of $150 x 4 or $600.

(a) If the words "for the same time" are construed to refer to the same four days, the Insured recovers $250, as follows:

$$\frac{\$\ 600}{\$1200} \times \$500 = \$250$$

(b) If the words "for the same time" are construed to refer to the full week:

$$\frac{\$\ 600}{\$1500} \times \$500 = \$200 \text{ recovery}$$

In Examples Nos 2 (a) and (b), if the Weekly Insurance had been $1500, the Insured's recoveries would have been as follows:

Example No. 2 (a)

$$\frac{\$\ 600}{\$1200} \times \$1500 = \$750, \text{ but not exceeding } \$600, \text{ the "actual loss sustained," is paid.}$$

Example No. 2 (b)

$$\frac{\$\ 600}{\$1500} \times \$1500 = \$600 \text{ recovery}$$

The interpretation of the Weekly Form which adopts the insurable value of the unit of time which is the yardstick of the contract (the Insured's work week) as the denominator of the fraction which measures the Insured's recovery, and views every suspension of business which is shorter than that unit of time as a "partial suspension" is the interpretation which would appear to be in line with the intent of all Contribution and Coinsurance Clauses. Under that interpretation, the Insured's recoveries as developed in the foregoing examples Nos. 1 (c) and 2 (b) are the maximum recoveries to which he is entitled because of inadequate insurance to value.

The foregoing examples assume business is suspended for less than one week and all expenses necessarily continue during the period of suspension.

Longer Partial Suspension—The following examples assume that the Insured's business is partially suspended for a prolonged period of time. Since all expenses that necessarily continue during a suspension of one week or less do not necessarily continue during a prolonged suspension, the loss per week in the following example is assumed to be $1000 in case of total suspension (instead of $1500 as in Example 1), and the actual loss per week is again assumed to be $600.

Example No. 3—Assume Weekly Insurance of $500 and the interpretation followed in Examples No. 1 (c) and No. 2 (b) applies:

$$\frac{\$\,600}{\$1000} \text{ x } \$500 \,=\, \$300 \text{ per week recovery}$$

The foregoing examples illustrate a feature of the Weekly Form which is both an attraction and a danger for the Insured—that Coinsurance applies for the duration of the loss. In examples Nos. 1(c) and 2(b), because the suspension of business is for only one week or less, all expenses necessarily continue and, therefore, the denominator of the coinsurance fraction is $1500. In Example No. 3, because the suspension is for a prolonged period during which all expenses do not necessarily continue, the denominator is $1000. In all three examples, the Weekly Insurance is $500 and the Loss is $600. Nevertheless, since the lower its denominator the greater the value of a fraction, the recoveries differ, being $200 when the denominator is $1500 and $300 when the denominator is $1000.

Moreover, in the event of total suspension of business for only one week, with $1500 Weekly Insurance carried, the recovery under the total suspension clause would be $1500, whereas in the event of total suspension for the prolonged period, with $1500 Weekly Insurance carried, the recovery would be only $1000 per week, i.e., the "actual loss sustained," and the same recovery that would be received had Weekly Insurance of only $1000 been carried.

Two Alternatives—Therefore the buyer of Weekly Form, when determining the amount of insurance to purchase, must choose between the following alternatives, bearing in mind that many expenses which must necessarily continue during a short suspension of business may be discontinued during a prolonged suspension of business:

Over-insurance in case of prolonged suspension of business but full recovery in case of short partial suspension of business;

or;

Insurance sufficient only in case of prolonged suspension of business, resulting in under-insurance and the Insured suffering the coinsurance penalty in case of short partial suspension of business.

Disadvantages of Weekly Form—The Weekly Form is therefore attractive to the Insured who is willing to purchase only the minimum amount of insurance necessary for full recovery in the event of a catastrophe, and is prepared not to recover the full amount of loss sustained in the event of a short partial suspension of business. It will be dangerous and disappointing to the Insured who, buying an amount of insurance designed to cover the average loss, discovers that he is over-insured for a prolonged suspension and under-insured for a short suspension of business.

Moreover, the Weekly Form can be dangerous and disappointing to the Insured operating a business the earnings of which are seasonal or fluctuate throughout the year, unless the amount of weekly indemnity is adjusted from a uniform 1/50th of the total amount of insurance to the amount required for full recovery of loss occurring at those times when the Insured's earnings increase or decrease according to business conditions.

Seasonal Earnings Weekly Form—For such lines of business, a seasonal or fluctuating earnings Weekly Form has been available in which, in place of the straight weekly indemnity of 1/50th of the total amount of insurance, a table of varying weekly indemnities is substituted, establishing the dates between which each specific amount of weekly insurance applies. However, even in the case of a business with one or more regular operating seasons, the opening and closing dates of each season cannot be accurately predicted.

Canneries, for example, must accommodate their operations to weather conditions. If unseasonable weather delays or speeds the maturity of crops to be canned, the cannery must delay or advance the start of its operating season as the case may be. Therefore, to adjust the weekly seasonal operations forms to the needs of canneries, the form is endorsed to provide that the table of weekly amounts of insurance begins on the day the cannery began operations or would have begun operations if fire had not prevented.

Department stores are representative of other lines of business with seasonal fluctuations of earnings. However, although the dates upon which Christmas Day and Easter Sunday fall are fixed by the calendar, the actual opening dates of the shopping seasons that precede them cannot be determined. In addition, there are other times during the year when sales increase or decrease due to weather conditions, special events, etc. Therefore the department store buyer of the Weekly Fluctuating Earnings Form must do the best he can in predicting the opening and closing dates of each period of time during which earnings increase or decrease, so that the listing of such dates and the varying amounts of weekly insurance for each period in the table inserted in this form, will be as accurate as possible under the circumstances.

If the Insured has not accurately predicted the dates during the term of his policy and for one year thereafter, as of which his earnings will change because of seasonal or other business conditions, as well as the amount of each change, or both, he will either have uncollectible over-insurance or be penalized for insufficient insurance when a loss occurs.

The accompanying chart, which is based on the actual weekly earnings of a department store, illustrates the sea-

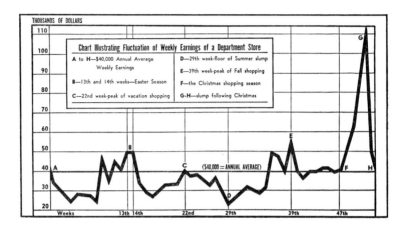

Chart Illustrating Fluctuation of Weekly Earnings of a Department Store

A to H—$40,000 Annual Average Weekly Earnings

B—13th and 14th weeks—Easter Season

C—22nd week-peak of vacation shopping

D—29th week-floor of Summer slump

E—39th week-peak of Fall shopping

F—the Christmas shopping season

G-H—slump following Christmas

sonal fluctuations which normally occur, and is the basis for the following comparison of several methods of using the Weekly Form where earnings are not uniform.

The chart discloses that earnings range from the low figure of $23,000 in the 29th week in mid-summer, to $110,-000 in the peak 51st week in December, with a high of $50,000 per week during the 13th and 14th weeks in the Easter Season, and another high of $54,000 in the 39th week in September.

Examples of Use—Following are several of the ways of using the Weekly Form under such circumstances. In these examples an 80% coinsurance building rate of $1 is assumed, and premium costs are shown computed at the rate of $0.65 (65% of the building rate) formerly charged in all states except Texas and Canada.

Method I.—Uniform weekly insurance of $110,000 can be carried to assure recovery for the actual loss in the 51st week. $110,000 times 50 weeks equals $5,500,000, premium $35,750. Manifestly this is the most expensive method, since Weekly Insurance of $110,000 is needed for the 51st week only.

Method 2.—The next most expensive method is to divide the year into periods, the amount of weekly insurance for each period being the peak weekly amount in that period. The division might be as follows:

Period	Peak Week		Weeks	Total Insurance
1st through 8th week	35,000	x	8	$ 280,000
9th-12th week	46,000	x	4	$ 184,000
13th-24th week	50,000	x	12	$ 600,000
25th-35th week	36,000	x	11	$ 396,000
36th-48th week	54,000	x	13	$ 702,000
49th-52nd week	110,000	x	4	$ 440,000

Total Insurance $2,602,000

Premium $16,913.

Under this method, the amount of Weekly Insurance is needed for only the few peak weeks of the year—six in the foregoing example—so that the amount of insurance maintained for the remaining 46 weeks is excessive.

Method 3.—Next in order of premium cost is to maintain the average amount of Weekly Insurance uniformly for all weeks, $40,000 being the average obtained by dividing the sum of all weekly amounts by 52. $40,000 x 52 weeks = $2,028,000, premium $13,182. While the total amount of insurance is the lowest produced by any method, the amount of Weekly Insurance is less than required for each of 15 weeks and is more than required for each of 33 weeks. Weekly Insurance of $40,000 is exactly the amount required for each of only 4 weeks.

Method 4.—By this method, a specific amount of Weekly Insurance is assigned to each week in the table of Weekly

45

Insurances in the Fluctuating Earnings Weekly Form. The first few lines of such table would be as follows:

January 1 to the following January 7 inclusive—$35,000
January 8 to the following January 14 inclusive— 31,000
January 15 to the following January 21 inclusive— 27,000
January 22 to the following January 28 inclusive— 25,000
January 29 to the following February 4 inclusive— 28,000
     and so on throughout the 52 weeks.

The sum of the weekly amounts would be the total insurance of $2,028,000 produced by Method No. 3, and the premium cost would also be the same, i. e., $13,182.

But where is the Insured who can predict accurately the amounts of Weekly Insurance that will be required under any of the foregoing methods? This conclusion is inevitable —the Weekly Form can be depended upon to furnish protection for actual loss sustained at a premium cost based on the proper amount of insurance, only when the Insured's Weekly Earnings are uniform throughout the year. Moreover, the Insured must choose between the purchase of insurance sufficient only for a prolonged suspension when necessarily continuing expenses are at a minimum, and be resigned to being a coinsurer if loss results from a short suspension when all expenses continue, or purchase an amount sufficient for full recovery in case of a short suspension and be over-insured in case of a prolonged suspension.

How to Determine Amount of Weekly Form Insurance— In the light of the foregoing how is the amount of insurance purchased under the Weekly Form determined? It is computed by means of a Work Sheet such as the specimen shown at the end of this chapter.

A typical loss adjustment under the Weekly Form is reproduced in Appendix No. 2.

THE MONTHLY FORM

It is not surprising that dissatisfaction with the Weekly Form spurred efforts to devise a form possessing greater flexibility in the coverage of lines of business with seasonal and fluctuating earnings.

Since the Per Diem Form used the day as the yardstick, thereby blanketing the hours of the day under one unit of measurement, and the Weekly Form used the week as the yardstick, thereby blanketing the days of the week, the next development was logically the Monthly Form, which used the month as the yardstick, thereby blanketing the weeks of the month.

Under the monthly Form, the amount of monthly insurance was 1/12th of the total amount of insurance except when the Fluctuating or Seasonal Earnings type of the Form was used and then, as in the case of that type of Weekly Form, a Table of Monthly Insurance was inserted in the Form.

Very little study of the preceding Chart is necessary to reach the conclusion that the Monthly Form possessed the same weakness that is inherent in the Weekly Form, i.e., inflexibility, which was soon experienced in the comparatively few territories in which it was adopted.

Efforts to achieve needed flexibility therefore continued, and logically produced a form of coverage using the year as the yardstick, thereby blanketing the months of the year. This form is discussed in the next chapter.

WORK SHEET FOR WEEKLY FORM

COLUMN A
Estimated Amounts for
the year beginning

1. Annual Net Sales of Mercantile or Non - Manufacturing Establishment or Net Sales Value of finished goods produced during year by a Manufacturing Plant... $.................
(See Formula X)

47

2. Cost of Merchandise sold by Mercantile or Non-Manufacturing Establishment or Raw Stock and Supplies consumed during the year in production of finished goods of a Manufacturing Plant plus in either case cost of services purchased from outsiders which do not continue under contract. .... $.................
   (See Formula Y)

3. Sales Taxes if included in No. 1......... $.................

4. Bad Accounts if included in No. 1.... $.................

5. Sum of No. 2, 3, and 4....................... $................. $.................

6. Subtract No. 5 from No. 1................... $.................

7. Add other receipts of business
   (a) Cash discounts unless deducted under No. 2........................... $.................
   (b) Income from departments leased to others........................ $.................

8. Gross Earnings (total of No. 6 and No. 7 .... $.................

9. Total of all expenses listed in Column B .... $.................

10. Net Profit (Subtract No. 9 from No. 8) .... $.................

11. Total of all continuing Expenses listed in Column C................................... $.................

12. Amount of Insurance (*)
    No. 10 plus No. 11................................. $.................

(*) The amount entered here is the amount of Business Interruption Insurance to be carried if this Work Sheet has been made up on an Annual Basis. If the business is subject to seasonal fluctuations and a separate sheet has been made up for each period of level business less than a year, the amount of insurance to be carried for the year will be the sum of the period amounts entered at No. 12

EXPENSES AND FIXED CHARGES	COLUMN B Estimated full amounts for year ending as in Column A	COLUMN C Estimated portion that will continue during total suspension of business during year ending as in Column A (Note 1)
Advertising Expense		
Automobile and Truck Expense		
Branch Office Expense		
Depreciation of property not destroyed		
Heat, unless included in Rent		
Insurance Premiums		
Interest on Indebtedness		
Legal Expenses		
Light, unless included in Rent		
Office Expenses		
Power, unless included in Rent		
Rent (see Note 2)		
Repairs		
Royalties		
Salaries and Wages		
Taxes (except Income and Profits)		
Traveling Expenses		
Watch Service		
Other Expenses—Dues, Fees, etc.		
Total		

Note 1. Enter in Column C the amounts, on an *annual* basis, for which the Insured desires full recovery, taking into consideration the selected duration of the suspension of business for which full recovery is desired.

Note 2. If the Insured does not own the building, insert entire annual rental in Column B and in Column C only the amount for which Insured is legally liable during untenantability.

FORMULA X

Annual Net Sales (Gross less outgoing transportation, expense and returns, discounts and allowances to customers) including income from services rendered to others during the year.... $.......................

If a Manufacturing Plant *Deduct* Inventory (*) of finished goods at beginning of year............................... $.......................

and *Add* Inventory (*) of finished goods at close of year........................... $.......................

Total—if a Manufacturing plant—Net Sales Value of goods produced during the year (See Note 2)................... $.......................

(*) "Compute inventories at selling price at time of inventory."

FORMULA Y

Inventory of Merchandise (plus Raw Stock if a Manufacturer) and Supplies on hand at beginning of year (See Note 1).. $.......................

Add Merchandise (plus Raw Stock if a Manufacturer) and Supplies purchased during the year (less discounts and returns but including incoming transportation expense)...... $.......................

Add cost of services rendered by outside sources during the year which do not continue under contract........ $.......................

Total

Deduct Inventory of Merchandise (or Raw Stock if a Manufacturer) and Supplies at close of the year.............. $.......................

Cost entered at Item 2 of Work Sheet $.......................

Note 1. If the Insured operates a service type business such as a Hotel, Restaurant, Theater, where income is not wholly, or not at all, derived from the sale of merchandise, refer to discussion in Chapter 6.

Note 2. If the Insured is a manufacturer selling finished goods shortly following their production, the term "Annual Net Sales" and "Net Sales Value of finished goods produced during the year" are identical. But if the Insured has accumulated finished goods in storage to be held for future sale along with goods currently produced, then the amounts described by these two terms differ and the basis of the Work Sheet should be the "Net Sales Value of finished goods produced during the year," because it is a fundamental principle of Business Interruption Insurance that since a manufacturer's earnings are produced at the time his product is manufactured they should be insured as of that time and not as of the time the goods are sold and delivered.

CHAPTER 5

THE TWO ITEM CONTRIBUTION
POLICY FORM

A Double Contract—The Two Item Contribution Policy Form is a contract divided into two items, one indemnifying for loss of net profit and necessarily countinuing expenses except ordinary payroll, the other indemnifying, at the option of the Insured, for necessarily continuing ordinary payroll for a specified number of days not less than ninety.

Unlike the Per Diem and Weekly Forms, the Two Item Contribution Form does not limit the Insured's recovery to a specified sum per day or per week but, as its name implies, includes a Contribution (Coinsurance) Clause which limits the Insured's recovery, in the event of a partial loss, to the proportion of the amount of loss that the amount of insurance bears to a specified percentage of the Insured's annual Business Interruption value as heinafter described. Wherever the Two Item form is used, it is known as Form 2 (formerly "A") when applied to manufacturing properties, and as Form 1 (formerly "D") when applied to non-manufacturing and mercantile properties.

Since the Per Diem, Weekly and Monthly Forms successively enlarged the unit of time by which the Insured's recovery for loss was limited and measured, and since the principle of applying contribution (Coinsurance) had become established in the partial suspension clauses in those forms, the Two Item Contribution Form was the next logical step in development of Business Interruption Insurance.

Historical Development—That step was taken in the six years that followed 1923, the year in which the Sheppard Company Department Store in Providence, Rhode Island, was forced by fire damage to partially suspend business for five months, and suffered a coinsurance penalty in excess of 40% under the Partial Suspension Clause in the Per Diem Form,

52

whereas the shortage of recovery would not have exceeded 17% had the suspension of business been total. It was also in 1923 that the National Retail Dry Goods Association, acting through its Controllers Congress, began a study of Business Interruption Insurance because of the dissatisfaction of its members with policy forms available.

It was the inelasticity of the Per Diem Form in the face of the needs of retail merchants operating with fluctuating earnings, and the failure of the Weekly and, subsequently, the Monthly Form, to provide the complete elasticity required, that led the National Retail Dry Goods Association to request insurance carriers to furnish a contract without a daily, weekly or monthly limit upon recovery, and with a definite coinsurance requirement based upon annual earnings.

Chief among the early forms of contracts devised to satisfy these requirements was one offered by the New York Reciprocal Underwriters, covering Net Profits and such fixed charges and expenses as would necessarily continue, and containing a Coinsurance requirement of 75% of full annual gross earnings in place of the Partial Suspension Clause with its 100% Coinsurance requirement. The Controllers Congress of the Dry Goods Association proposed a similar contract, but with a 90% Coinsurance requirement and provision for limited coverage of Ordinary Payroll.

In many, but not all states, the capital stock companies offered a standard Single Item Coinsurance Clause form; and in New York State the Rating Organization filed with the State Insurance Department a 100% Coinsurance form, whereby an elective percentage of certain enumerated expenses could be insured for an elective number of working days. Such expenses, however, were not to exceed, on an annual basis, 25% of all fixed charges and expenses, and no elective period of time to be less than three months.

So many, diverse, and strong were the opinions expressed as to the relative merits of the various available and proposed forms, and their prices compared with the rates charged for the Per Diem and Weekly Forms, and so numerous were the conferences held by Eastern and Western Committees, separately and jointly, that a sizable book could be written detailing only the six year history of the controversy which absorbed the attention of the fire insurance world.

The Two Item Form—It is sufficient to report that in 1929 the capital stock companies agreed upon a form of contract which became standard in all states including New York and was practically the Two Item Contribution Form, as we know it today.

The form was divided into an Item insuring Net Profits and all necessarily continuing expenses except Ordinary Payroll, and a second Item separately insuring Ordinary Payroll for a minimum of 90 days, both Items subject to the 100% Coinsurance requirement.

A few years later coverage of payroll for a period exceeding 90 days, also 80% Coinsurance, was offered as optional, the former at a reduced, and the latter at an increased rate.

Meanwhile, the Reciprocal Exchanges had improved their form of contract by adopting a Two Item coverage, with provision for separate insurance on Ordinary Payroll for the number of weeks elected by the Insured, and with the maintenance of 80% insurance to value, controlled by an annual audited report of the Insured's earnings and a limit of liability of the Insurer in the event of loss.

Thus it was that merchants secured a type of Business Interruption Insurance which is adjusted to their need for a contract which follows their daily, weekly and seasonal fluctuations in earnings without possibility of coinsurance penalty so long as the total amount of insurance complies with the coinsurance requirement applied on an annual basis. Merchants also secured the privilege of insuring, or not insuring, the wages of the employees classed as "Ordinary Payroll," i.e., employees other than officers, executives, department managers, employees under contract and other important employees.

Present Two Item Form—In its present day edition, the Two Item Contribution Form provides that if the property described as covered by the policy is destroyed or damaged by the perils insured against so as to necessitate a total or partial suspension of business, the Insurer shall be liable for the actual loss sustained by the Insured during such length of time as would be required, with the exercise of due diligence and dispatch, to rebuild, repair or replace such property as has been destroyed or damaged, the recoverable loss to consist of:

Item I. $............On the net profit which is thereby prevented from being earned and such charges and other expenses, including payroll expense of Group I employees but excluding payroll expense of Group II employees, as must necessarily continue during the interruption of business, to the extent only that such charges and expenses would have been earned had no loss occurred.

This item covers expense of necessary heat, light and power, the cost of which is prevented from being earned during the interruption of business.

Definition of Group I employees: Officers, executives, department managers, employees under contract and other important employees.

Item II. $............On the Insured's payroll expense for Group II employees which continues during the interruption of business, for a period of time not in excess of 90*............ consecutive calendar days immediately following the date of damage or destruction but covering only to the extent necessary to resume the normal business of the Insured with the same quality of service which existed immediately preceding the date of damage or destruction and only to the extent that such payroll expense would have been earned had no loss occurred.

Definition of Group II employees: All other employees of the Insured not covered under Group I.

The total payroll expense for Group I or Group II employees shall include the entire payroll expense for each employee in each respective group.

No insurance attaches under Item I or Item II unless an amount is inserted in the dollar blank provided therefor.

BUSINESS INTERRUPTION INSURANCE

(Resumption of Operations clause in form for manufacturing properties.)

3. *Resumption of Operations:* It is a condition of this Insurance that if the Insured,

(a) by resumption of complete or partial operation of the property herein described, whether damaged or not, or

(b) by making use of stock (raw, in process or finished) or other property, at the location described herein or elsewhere, could reduce the loss resulting from the interruption of business such reduction shall be taken into account in arriving at the amount of loss hereunder and, with respect to such use of finished stock, this policy covers any necessary extra expense that would be required to replace the finished stock used by the Insured to reduce the loss resulting from the interruption of business.

(Resumption of Operations clause in form for mercantile and non-manufacurting properties.)

3. *Resumption of Operations:* It is a condition of this Insurance that if the Insured,

(a) by resumption of complete or partial operation of the property herein described, whether damaged or not, or

(b) by making use of merchandise or other property, at the location described herein or elsewhere, could reduce the loss resulting from the interruption of business, such reduction shall be taken into account in arriving at the amount of loss hereunder.

4. *Contribution Clause:* In consideration of the rate and form under which Items I and II are written, this Company shall be liable, in the event of loss, for no greater proportion of the loss under Item I or Item II than the amount hereby covered under each respective item, bears to

(a) Under Item I, insert 80, 90, or 100% of the sum of the annual net profits and the annual amount of all charges and expenses of any nature whether continuing or not, except the Insured's payroll expense for Group II employees and except the expense of heat, light and power to the extent that such expense does not continue under contract, that would have been earned (had no loss occurred) during the 12 months immediately following the date of damage to or destruction of the described property.

(b) Under Item II, insert 80, 90, or 100% of the Insured's payroll expense for Group II employees that would have been earned (had no loss occurred) during the 90*.................... consecutive calendar days immediately following the date of damage to or destruction of the described property.

5. *Experience of the Business:* In determining the amount of net profit, charges and expenses covered under Item I or Item II, whether for the purpose of ascertaining the amount of loss sustained or for the application of the Contribution Clause, due consideration shall be given to the experience of the business before the date of damage or destruction and the probable experience thereafter had no loss occurred.

6. *Expense to Reduce Loss:* This policy also covers such expenses as are necessarily incurred for the purpose of reducing any loss under this policy (except expense incurred to extinguish a fire), not exceeding, however, the amount by which the loss under this policy is thereby reduced. Such expenses shall not be subject to the application of the Contribution Clause.

If there is insurance covering loss described under both Items I and II, the said expenses shall be apportioned to these Items in the proportion that the reduction in amount of loss under each Item bears to the reduction under both Items.

7. *Interruption by Civil Authority:* This policy is extended to include the actual loss as covered hereunder during the period of time, not exceeding 2 consecutive weeks, when, as a direct result of the peril(s) insured against, access to the premises described is prohibited by order of civil authority.

8. *Special Exclusions:* This Company shall not be liable for any increase of loss which may be occasioned by any local or state ordinance or law regulating construction or repair of buildings or structures, nor by the suspension, lapse or cancellation of any lease or license, contract or order, nor for any increase of loss due to interference at the described premises by strikers or other persons with rebuilding, repairing or replacing the property or with the resumption or continuation of business; nor shall this Company be liable for any other consequential loss or remote loss.

9. *Limit of Liability:* The liability under this policy shall not exceed a greater proportion of any loss than the insurance hereunder bears to all insurance, whether collectible or not, covering in any manner the loss insured against by the respective Items of this policy. This provision shall apply separately to Item I and Item II.

When written on a manufacturing plant, this form includes coverage of "raw stock" and "stock in process," limited to 30 days unless the period of coverage is extended by endorsement for additional premium; and denies liability for any loss sustained because of damage to or destruction of finished stock. (For analysis of stock coverages see Chapter 10; and for discussion of clauses see Chapter 16.)

Disadvantages of Two Item Form—Although this Two Item Form met the need of the merchants who originally sponsored it, and has been the form of contract purchased by countless thousands of manufacturers and merchants, it has not escaped adverse criticism from buyers as well as underwriters. The latter find it more difficult to underwrite than the Weekly Form, because it does not disclose any information upon which to predicate an estimate of the probable amount of loss to be expected, whereas the underwriter's limit of liability per week in the Weekly Form affords a basis for predicting loss expectancy.

Moreover, the underwriter knows that, under the Weekly Form, he is assured of the full and sincere cooperation of the Insured in case of loss in determining the Use and Occupancy value for the time required to rehabilitate the damaged or destroyed property since, under the Weekly Form, Coinsurance is applied only for the duration of the loss.

Under the Two Item Form, he fears that, in determining the insurable value to ascertain whether the Contribution (Coinsurance) requirement has been satisfied, it will be difficult to disprove the claim of the Insured who may be tempted to magnify his insurable value for the period of the loss, while minimizing his value for the remaining portion of the twelve months which is the basis for the application of the Contribution Clause.

Required Amount of Insurance—The only serious objection buyers have taken to the Two Item Form is directed at the conflict between the provision in the Contribution Clause that the amount of insurance shall equal the required percentage of the sum of annual net profits and the annual amount of all expenses (except ordinary payroll, heat, light and power), whether or not such charges and expenses necessarily continue during business suspension. On the other hand, the Coverage Clause provides that payment in case of loss is limited to prevented net profits and only such charges and expenses as necessarily continue during business suspension.

Buyers unfamiliar with the reasons for this provision criticize it as an attempt by the insurance companies to compel the Insured to maintain a greater amount of insurance than can be collected in case of loss. They point out that many items of expense can be discontinued in the event of a prolonged suspension (the longer the suspension, the greater the amount of discontinuable expenses) and therefore such discontinuable expenses should be eliminated from the denominator of the coinsurance fraction. Such reasoning, however, disregards the fact that the shorter the suspension of business the greater the amount of necessarily continuing expenses for which the Insurer is liable, and therefore such necessarily continuing expenses should be included in the denominator of the coinsurance fraction.

In short, since Business Interruption Insurance undertakes to indemnify for brief as well as prolonged periods of suspension, the insurance companies are entitled to charge premium on all the expenses for which the Insured will claim reimbursement in the event of a short suspension of business. To have equipped the Two Item Form with a Contribution Clause based on the sum of net profits and only such charges and expenses which necessarily continue during the business suspension would have provided a variable basis Contribution Clause, and would have perpetuated the very feature of the Weekly Form which forces upon the Insured the impossible task of predicting accurately the duration of the time his business will be suspended. Moreover, the Two Item Form is obtainable with 80% Co-insurance, resulting in a leeway of 20%, which frequently offsets most, if not all, of the discontinuable expenses in the event of prolonged periods of business suspension.

Furthermore, with a variable basis Contribution Clause,

the Insured could never feel confident that he has the proper amount of insurance for the loss that he may sustain. Nor would he escape conflicting advice from solicitors competing for the privilege of writing his insurance, each trying to discredit the advice of others as to the adequacy of the basis upon which the Insured's Coinsurance requirement is adjusted.

A Coinsurance Clause, whether in Property Damage or Business Interruption policies, is designed to make sure that all who seek like benefits maintain equality of insurance to value, and contribute their correct proportions of the total premium required to pay losses and expenses, and allow Insurers a fair profit.

If the formula for equalizing amounts of insurance and premium contributions were revised to produce less than the total premium required, the formula for determining rate of premium charged would obviously also require revision so that the end result as to premium cost to the Insured would be the same. If the Contribution Clause in the Two Item Form were revised to permit each Insured to carry an amount of insurance based upon his estimate of the amount of expenses which would continue in case of suspension of business, an increase in the rate would be necessary to produce the required premium income.

An illustration of such a result was afforded in the case of the Loveman Joseph and Loeb Department Store in Birmingham, Alabama, which was destroyed by fire in March, 1934. Due to the ambiguous phraseology of the then 100% Contribution Clause attached to the policies, it was misconstrued by judge and jury to require insurance equal to the sum of net profit and only the necessarily continuing expenses. Therefore the Insured was not held to be a coinsurer, although they had paid premium on an amount of insurance which was approximately 50% of the amount which the Contribution Clause was intended to require.

Work Sheet Necessary—The amount of insurance required by the Contribution Clause in the Two Item Form is determined by a Work Sheet by which the amount of each item is separately computed.

Although the Contribution Clause for Item No. 1 requires the maintenance of the specified percentage of the sum of the annual net profit and the annual total of all charges and other expenses (except ordinary payroll, heat, light and power), it is not necessary to itemize net profit and expenses as in the Work Sheet for the Weekly Form. It is only necessary to determine the annual gross earnings, and deduct expense of ordinary payroll, heat, light and power. The result is the amount of insurance required under Item I if written subject to 100% Contribution. If 80% Contribution is required, 80% of such amount is taken.

A Two Item Form Work Sheet is shown on the following pages.

WORK SHEET FOR TWO ITEM CONTRIBUTION FORM

COLUMN A
Estimated Amounts for the year beginning

1. Annual Net Sales of Mercantile or Non Manufacturing Establishment or Net Sales Value of finished goods produced during year by a manufacturing plant. .... $..................
   (See Formula X)

2. Cost of Merchandise sold by Mercantile or Non Manufacturing Establishment or Raw Stock, materials and supplies consumed during the year in production of finished goods of a Manufacturing Plant, plus in either case cost of services rendered by outside sources for resale which do not continue under contract.................................. $..................

3. Sales Taxes if included in No. 1........ $..................

4. Bad Accounts if included in No. 1.... $..................

5. Sum of Nos. 2, 3 and 4......................... $.................. $..................

6. Subtract No. 5 from No. 1..................... $..................

7. Add other receipts of business
   (a) Cash discounts unless deducted
       under No. 2...................................... $...............
   (b) Income from departments
       leased to others.......................... $...............

8. Gross Earnings (total of No. 6 and
   No. 7) .... $...............

(To this point the Work Sheet for the Two Item Form is a duplicate of the Work Sheet for the Weekly Form—see end of chapter 4. Because of the deductions from Gross Earnings authorized by the Two Item Form the two sheets differ from this point on.)

8. Gross Earnings as above (No. 8)........ $...............

9. Deductions
   (a) Cost of Light, Heat and Power*.. $...............
   (b) Payroll of Group II (ordinary)
       Employees, i.e., total annual pay-
       roll, less salaries of officers, ex-
       ecutives, department managers,
       employees under contract and
       other important employees de-
       scribed under Item 1 of policy
       form .... $...............

   (Include ordinary labor cost directly
   chargeable to Light, Heat and Power
   unless included under 9(a). Include
   also Social Security and Unemployment Insurance Taxes, Pensions,
   Workmen's Compensation and other
   employee insurance costs charged to
   "Ordinary Payroll.")

10. Total of No. 9(a) and (b)................... $............... $...............

11. Amount of Insurance under Policy
    Item 1 with 100% Contribution (Co-
    insurance) Clause (Subtract No.
    10 from No. 8)...................................... $...............

12. Take 80% of Item 11 if 80% Con-
    tribution (Coinsurance) Clause ap-
    plies. 80%

    Amount of Insurance Item I—80%
    Contribution ....$...............

    Annual Rate ....$...............

TWO ITEM CONTRIBUTION POLICY

Annual Premium Item No. 1 of Policy form ....$...............

(*) The amounts entered opposite 9(a) should be the total expense of light, heat and power, except that if the Coinsurance Clause in policy form provides for the deduction of expense of light, heat and power only to the extent it does not continue under contract, the amounts entered opposite 9(a) should be limited to the expense of light, heat and power not under contract.

To Determine the Amount and the Cost of Payroll of Group II (ordinary) Employees Insurance Under Item No. II of the Two Item Form, Fill in the Following:

13. Annual Payroll of Group II employees Transfer amount of Item No. 9(b)............ $....................

	COLUMN B If 90 days coverage of Payroll of Group II Employees	COLUMN C If 180 days coverage of Payroll of Group II Employees
14. Insert 25% of No. 13 in Column B	$....................	
15. Insert 50% of No. 13 in Column C		$....................
16. Increase No. 14 to equal 90 consecutive days of season when payroll is greatest	$....................	
17. Increase No. 15 to equal 180 consecutive days of season when payroll is greatest		$....................
18. Enter 80% of Item No. 16 in Column B and 80% of Item 17 in Column C resulting in amounts necessary to meet requirements of 80% Coinsurance (Contribution) Clause for Item II of Policy Form	80% $....................	80% $....................
Annual Rates*	....	....
Policy Item No. II—Annual Premiums..............	$....................	$....................

63

Policy Item No. 1—Annual Premium .... $........................ $........................

TWO ITEM FORM POLICY TOTAL ANNUAL PREMIUMS .... $........................ $........................

(If 90 days Payroll) (If 180 days Payroll)

*The rates charged are 150% of Item I rate for 90 days coverage, and 100% of Item I rate for 180 days coverage.

FORMULA X

Annual Net Sales (Gross less outgoing transportation expense and returns, discounts and allowances to customers) including income from services rendered to others during the year.... $........................

If a Manufacturing Plant: *Deduct* Inventory (*) of finished goods at beginning of year................................. $........................

and *Add* Inventory (*) of finished goods at close of year........................... $........................

Total—If a Manufacturing Plant—Net Sales Value of goods produced during the year (See Note 2)..................... $........................

(*) Compute Inventories at Selling Price at time of the Inventory.

FORMULA Y

Inventory of Mercandise (plus Raw Stock if a Manufacturer) and Supplies on hand at beginning of year (See Note (1)... $........................

Add Merchandise (plus Raw Stock if a Manufacturer) and Supplies purchased during the year (less discounts and returns but including incoming transportation expense)........ $........................

Add cost of services rendered by outside sources for resale during the year which do not continue under contract .... $........................

Total $........................

Deduct Inventory of Merchandise (and
Raw Stock if a Manufacturer) and
Supplies at close of the year................ $..........................

Cost entered at Line 2 of Work
Sheet .... $..........................

NOTE 1. If the Insured operates a service type business such as a Hotel, Restaurant, Theater, where income is not wholly, or not at all, derived from the sale of merchandise, refer to discussion in Chapter 6, captioned "Service Type Businesses."

NOTE 2. If the Insured is a manufacturer selling finished goods shortly following their production, the terms "Annual Net Sales" and "Net Sales Value of finished goods produced during the year" are identical.

But if the Insured has accumulated finished goods in storage to be held for future sale along with goods currently produced, then the amounts described by these two terms differ, and the basis of the Work Sheet should be the "Net Sales Value of finished goods produced during the year," because it is a fundamental principle of Business Interruption Insurance that, since a manufacturer's earnings are produced at the time his product is manufactured, they should be insured as of that time and not as of the time the goods are sold and delivered.

ORDINARY PAYROLL INSURANCE

When choosing coverage under the Two Item Form, the Insured must answer these questions: "Who are my Group II employes?," "Should their wages be insured?," "For what period of time should the wages be insured?," and "What will it cost?"

Definition of Group II Employees, i.e., "Ordinary Payroll"—As described in Item II of this form, the wages of Group II employees, i.e., ordinary payroll, are the wages of employees who are not Officers, Executives, Department Managers, Employees under Contract, and those who are not important for other reasons—but whose wages nevertheless the Insured desires to pay for a limited time in order that normal operations following reconstruction may be resumed with the same quality of service which existed immediately preceding the suspension of business.

The classification "Group II Employees," which has replaced the former reference to "Ordinary Payroll" in all forms, dates from its initial appearance in the 1953 edition of the West Virginia Form No. 7A for Coal Mining Properties—in which a detailed listing of the special categories of mining employees was inserted (by means of a Standard "Report of Values" definitely tied to the contract), to meet the peculiar needs of the mining industry.

Manufacturers usually refer to Group II employees as "direct" or "factory" labor. They are employees worth retaining when business suspension is of comparatively short duration but not of sufficient importance to justify payment of their wages for a prolonged suspension of business. They are also employees who merit payment of wages for a reasonable time to permit them to locate temporary jobs from which they will return when the Insured's business is ready to resume operations. In some cases, they are employees who can assist in expediting the resumption of business.

Wherever such employees exist, the employer should seriously consider specifically insuring their wages for the minimum 90 day period, to cover the payment of wages which the employer would consider desirable, to assure efficient resumption of business following short suspensions.

Moreover, insurance covering wages of Group II employees can be regarded as insurance against increase in the employer's state unemployment compensation tax in states in which employers are taxed on an experience rating basis. If employees, out of work because operations are suspended, receive continued wage payments made possible by the employer's recovery from Business Interruption Insurance, and do not draw wages from the State Unemployment Compensation Fund, obviously the employer's rate of tax is not increased since insofar as the State Fund is concerned, the employees have no claim for unemployment compensation.

Group II Employees Payroll Period—The minimum period of 90 days for which "Ordinary Payroll" may be insured was established by negotiations between the National Retail Dry Goods Association and the insurance companies at the time the Two Item Form was adopted in 1929. Since insuring the wages of unimportant employees was desired—without being compelled to insure them on an annual basis, as required under the Weekly Form—it was agreed that the contract should include provision for specifically insuring such wages for 90 days. A later development was the privilege of extending the 90 day period to 180 days or longer, in consideration of graded reductions in rate.

The rate of premium charged for 90 day coverage being 150% of the rate charged for insurance carried under Item 1, the graded rates are now as follows:

> 90 Days Coverage—150% of the rate for Item 1
> 120 Days Coverage—125% of the rate for Item 1
> 150 Days Coverage—110% of the rate for Item 1
> 180 Days or longer—100% of the rate for Item 1

Resolving these charges to increases in premium costs compared with increases in amount of insurance, discloses the following:

INCREASES OVER 90 DAYS' COVERAGE

In Amount of Insurance	In Premium Cost
33-1/3% (for 120 days)	11.1%
66-2/3% (for 150 days)	22.2%
100% (for 180 days)	33.3%

Prospective purchasers of coverage of Wages of Group II employees should understand that the period of time for which it is purchased is the outside limit of recovery and is not the period of time for which recovery is guaranteed—irrespective of circumstances.

If a minimum of 90 days' coverage is purchased, recovery will be subject to these limitations: Actual loss sustained, coinsurance, and exhaustion of the amount of insurance.

If, for example, recovery under Item 1 of the contract is for a few weeks' suspension of business, it is altogether likely that recovery for loss to Ordinary Payroll will be received for the same period of time.

However, as the period of business suspension lengthens, the necessity for payment of wages to employees classed as Group II usually decreases—so that only in exceptional circumstances will a total loss to insurance under Item II be recovered, even though the amount of insurance, because of the application of 80% Coinsurance to the actual payroll for 90 days, is exhaustible in 72 days (80% of 90 days). Or, because the loss occurs when payroll is at its peak, the amount that would normally have complied with the requirement of 80% Coinsurance is exhaustible in less than 72 days.

Not a Valued Policy—In any consideration of insurance on wages of Group II Employees, this fact should be borne in mind—it is designed to be realistic, and to reimburse the Insured only to the extent that he would continue wages of unimportant employees—did he not carry the insurance. In no sense is it "valued" as to amount nor as to the period of time for which it assumes liability. Like the remainder of the contract, it covers for "actual loss sustained."

In the light of the foregoing, it is not surprising that few merchants who purchase the Two Item Form include coverage of more than 90 days of Payroll of Group II Employees, and that few manufacturers include even the minimum of 90 days' coverage.

Whether or not the purchaser of coverage under Item I is inclined also to purchase coverage under Item II, the Item II portion of the Work Sheet should be completed, so that the facts as to cost as well as to possibilities of recovery in the event of loss will be on hand when a decision is reached.

Coverage of Group II Employees only—Very occasionally, a purchaser of insurance on wages of Group II Employees desires to insure them alone, without any coverage whatever under Item I of the Two Item Form. Since Business Interruption Insurance covers only charges and expenses that would have been earned had no loss occurred, all charges and expenses that would have been earned (and not only Payroll), should be insured to avoid difficulty in the adjustment of a loss occurring when the Insured's business is operating at a net loss and all charges and expenses will not have been earned. Moreover, insurance companies should not be expected to insure Payroll alone, thereby assuming liability subject to a total loss for a rate of premium designed to be received in addition to and not apart from premium for liability assumed under Item I—under which a total loss, though possible, is seldom experienced.

These considerations apply also where, due to the apportionment of an Insured's insurance requirements among several or more insurers, some are committed under Item I alone and others under Item II alone.

COMPARISON OF PREMIUM COSTS OF TWO ITEM AND WEEKLY FORMS

Comparison of Costs—Using the chart showing the actual weekly earnings of a department store, as reproduced in Chapter 4, four methods of adapting the Weekly Form produce the following results:

	Insurance	Premium Cost
Method 1	$5,500,000	$35,750.00
Method 2	2,602,000	16,913.00
Method 3	2,028,000	13,182.00
Method 4	2,028,000	13,182.00

Applying the Two Item Form Work Sheet to the earnings of this department store determines the amount of insurance required under that form, written subject to 80% Contribution Clause, to be as follows, assuming Ordinary Payroll of Group II Employees to be 40% and Heat, Light and Power expense 2% of Gross Earnings:

	MIDWEST STATES			ELSEWHERE*	
	Amount of Insurance	Rate	Premium	Rate	Premium
Item I	$941,000	.77	$7,245.70	.715	$6,728.15
Item II	162,000	1.155	1,871.00	1.07	1,733.40
	(90 days)				
	$1,103,000		$9,116.80		$8,461.55

*Except Texas and Canada.

Bearing in mind that $2,028,000 of insurance is needed under the Weekly Form to indemnify this store for actual loss sustained in the event of a short suspension of business —when all expenses necessarily continue—but is excessive in the event of a prolonged suspension—when all expenses do not necessarily continue—the forgoing comparison is convincing evidence of the superiority of the Two Item Form over the Weekly Form for a business with fluctuating earnings.

Here we see that $1,103,000 insurance under the Two Item Form, at a substantial saving of cost, furnishes the protection that requires nearly double that amount under the Weekly Form. Moreover, it achieves that result without requiring the Insured to predict accurately at what times and in what amounts his earnings will fluctuate. Under the Two Item Form, so long as the requirements of the Contribution Clause are met on an annual basis, the Insured is indemnified for the actual loss sustained during any week of the year business is suspended—whereas under the Weekly Form the actual loss sustained during any such week is recoverable only if the amount of insurance allocated to that week in advance is adequate.

This illustration demonstrates that the merchants of 1929 were wise in desiring a contract blanketing the weeks of the year, with coinsurance functioning on an annual basis, as a substitute for the inflexible Per Diem, Weekly and Monthly Policy forms. Although using the experience of a department store, this illustration is no less applicable to any business—mercantile, service, or manufacturing—the earnings of which fluctuate to any extent whatever, by weeks or seasons.

A variation of the Two-Item Contribution Form is the West Virginia Form 7A, promulgated in 1953 to meet the needs of the coal mining industry. It covers net profit, expenses and payroll of executives in wording copied from the Two Item Form, but does not include Item II—because coal mining companies refuse to insure miners' wages but do need a Premium Adjustment Contract, which is not obtainable in any territory in connection with the Two Item Contribution Form. For discussion of the West Virginia Form for coal mining properties, the reader is referred to Chapter 16, under the heading "Special Conditions Applicable to Mining Risks."

Good as the Two Item Form was, and in fact continues to be, a better form has been devised. It is known as the "Gross Earnings Form," and is discussed in the next chapter.

Typical loss adjustments under the Two Item Contribution Form are reproduced in Appendix No. 3 and No. 4.

CHAPTER 6

THE GROSS EARNINGS POLICY FORM

The Gross Earnings Policy form, also sometimes termed the Single Item Contribution form, derives its name from the way it operates. In one item of coverages, the Insured is indemnified for loss sustained—measured by the reduction in gross earnings directly resulting from interruption of business—less charges and expenses which do not necessarily continue, subject to a Contribution Clause which limits the Insured's recovery in the event of a partial loss to the proportion of the amount of loss that the amount of insurance bears to a specified 50%, 60%, 70% or 80% of the Insured's annual gross earnings. This form is known as No. 3 (formerly "G") when applied to mercantile and non-manufacturing properties, and as No. 4 (formerly "C" in mid-western States and "H" elsewhere) when applied to manufacturing properties.

A Blanket Coverage on Earnings—The Gross Earnings form improves and simplifies Business Interruption Insurance by blanketing coverage of all earnings. It dispenses with the provision for specific insurance on Ordinary Payroll, and the necessity for determining the amount of annual expense of heat, light and power—which characterize the Two Item Contribution Form. The Gross Earnings Form was adopted for mercantile businesses in 1938-1939, and for manufacturing plants in 1945. It was approved for non-manufacturing businesses (other than mercantiles) in 1940, but was withdrawn from them in a few territories in 1948.

Historical Development—Although hailed as a brand new type of Earnings Insurance contract, the idea was not new. In 1923, at the same time the Two Item Form was being developed, a Chicago loss adjuster, Frank L. Erion, proposed a form to cover "on the gross earnings (less any part thereof that is used during operation to pay expenses that will not be incurred or accrue during inoperation) produced by the Use and Occupancy of buildings, machinery and equipment situate —." Mr. Erion's form defined "Gross Earnings" as the difference between cost of merchandise and the sale price thereof, and included a Coinsurance requirement of 100% of Annual Gross Earnings less discontinuable expenses. It was the severity of this requirement which caused merchants to reject it. It is interesting to speculate whether the Two Item Contribution Form would ever have been adopted had Mr. Erion's idea been coupled with a lower Coinsurance requirement. Probably the disinclination of the merchants of 1923-1929 to purchase more than a minimum of Payroll coverage would in any event have resulted in the adoption of the Two Item Form in 1929 with its provision for 90 days' coverage of Payroll.

It required the experience of the following nine years under the Two Item, Weekly and Per Diem Forms, culminating in the conviction that a simpler form of contract was possible. A campaign, led in behalf of his clients by Warren F. Kimball of New York—a foremost mercantile U. and O. producer who had also contributed to the development of the Two Item Form—and cooperation by underwriters and Rating Bureau representatives (too numerous for individual mention) finally brought about the adoption of the simple Single Item Contract that the Gross Earnings Form has proven to be.

The Gross Earnings Form in Relation to Mercantile Businesses—Since the Gross Earnings Form was originally designed for their exclusive use, its application to Retail and Wholesale Businesses will be discussed before analyzing its application to non-manufacturing and manufacturing businesses to which it was offered in 1940 and 1946 respectively. For the purposes of this discussion, the following selected portions of the present day edition for Mercantile Risks are quoted.

Recovery in the event of loss hereunder shall be the ACTUAL

BUSINESS INTERRUPTION INSURANCE

LOSS SUSTAINED by the Insured directly resulting from such interruption of business, but not exceeding the reduction in gross earnings less charges and expenses which do not necessarily continue during the interruption of business, for only such length of time as would be required with the exercise of due diligence and dispatch to rebuild, repair or replace such part of the property herein described as has been damaged or destroyed, commencing with the date of such damage or destruction and not limited by the date of expiration of this policy. Due consideration shall be given to the continuation of normal charges and expenses, including payroll expense, to the extent necessary to resume operations of the Insured with the same quality of service which existed immediately preceding the loss.

Resumption of Operations: It is a condition of this Insurance that if the Insured,

(a) by resumption of complete or partial operation of the property herein described, whether damaged or not, or

(b) by making use of merchandise or other property, at the location described herein, or elsewhere, could reduce the loss resulting from the interruption of business, such reduction shall be taken into account in arriving at the amount of loss hereunder.

Gross Earnings: For the purpose of this insurance "Gross Earnings" are defined as the sum of:

(a) Total net sales, and

(b) Other earnings derived from operation of the business, less the cost of:

(c) Merchandise sold, including packaging materials therefor,

(d) Materials and supplies consumed directly in service(s) sold, and

(e) Service(s) purchased from outsiders (not employees of the Insured) for resale which do not continue under contract.

No other costs shall be deducted in determining "Gross Earnings."

In determining "Gross Earnings" due consideration shall be given to the experience of the business before the date of damage or destruction and the probable experience thereafter had no loss occurred.

Contribution Clause: In consideration of the rate and form under which this policy is written, this Company shall be liable, in the event of loss, for no greater proportion thereof than the amount hereby covered bears to insert 50, 60, 70 or 80% of the gross earnings that would have been earned (had no loss occurred) during the 12 months immediately following the date of damage to or destruction of the described property.

74

Expense to Reduce Loss: This policy also covers such expenses as are necessarily incurred for the purpose of reducing any loss under this policy (except incurred to extinguish a fire), not exceeding, however, the amount by which the loss under this policy is thereby reduced. Such exepnses shall not be subject to the application of the Contribution Clause.

Interruption By Civil Authority: This policy is extended to include the actual loss as covered hereunder, during the period of time, not exceeding 2 consecutive weeks, when as a direct result of the peril(s) insured against, access to the premises described is prohibited by order of civil authority.

Special Exclusions: This Company shall not be liable for any increase of loss which may be occasioned by any local or state ordinance or law regulating construction or repair of buildings or structures, nor by the suspension, lapse or cancellation of any lease or license, contract or order, nor for any increase of loss due to interference at the described premises by strikers or other persons with rebuilding, repairing or replacing the property or with the resumption or continuation of business; nor shall this Company be liable for any other consequential loss or remote loss.

In all territories, the Insured has the choice of four percentages of Contribution —50%, 60%, 70%, or 80%—at graduated rates of premium, and coverage of time to replace stock is unlimited—see Chapter 10 for analysis of Stock Coverages.

Reduction of Gross Earnings—The feature of the Gross Earnings Form that first attracts attention is the provision that the measure of recovery in the event of loss is the reduction in "Gross Earnings" directly resulting from any interruption of business, less charges and expenses which do not necessarily continue during the period of interruption. This is the feature from which the form derives its name. Although the phraseology differs from that of the Two Item, Weekly and Per Diem Forms, which measure the Insured's recovery by his loss in net profits, plus his loss in charges and expenses which necessarily continue during the period of business interruption, the result is the same.

The sum of Net Profits (income less cost of merchandise and all other expenses), plus necessarily continuing expenses, is the same as Gross Earnings (income less cost of merchandise) less discontinuable expenses, just as 10-5-3 plus 2 equals 4 is the same as 10-5-1 equals 4. Obviously, determination of the amount of loss sustained by the latter formula, involving three steps, is easier than by a formula requiring four or more steps.

All standard Business Interruption forms are designed to indemnify for actual loss sustained, regardless of the formula by which that result is reached. Loss adjusters testify that determination of actual loss sustained is easier in terms of reduction in Gross Earnings less discontinuable expenses, than by building up the loss sustained, beginning with the loss of Net Profits, and adding the loss sustained in necessarily continuing expenses.

Moreover, just as there is always one formula that is simpler than all others for computing the answer to a mathematical problem, so in Business Interruption Insurance there is one formula that is simpler than all others for computing the amount of insurance required. That formula is presented in the Contribution Clause in the Gross Earnings Form and simply consists of subtracting the annual cost of merchandise supplies and services purchased from the annual net sales to determine "Gross Earnings," and taking 50%, 60%, 70% or 80% of Gross Earnings, depending upon the percentage of contribution selected by the Insured.

Simple Work Sheet—That the Work Sheet by which this computation is made is the simplest of all Business Interruption Work Sheets is apparent by reference to the Weekly Form and Two Item Form Work Sheets reproduced at the ends of Chapters 4 and 5. Only Items No. 1 to 8 of those Work Sheets need be used to determine "Gross Earnings." The only deduction from sales is the cost of merchandise, materials, supplies and services, whereas, under the Two Item Form, the additional deductions of the expense of Group II Employees Payroll and of Heat, Light and Power are necessary and, under the Weekly and Per Diem Forms, the Insured must analyze each item of expense to determine what part of it should be deducted, taking into consideration the duration of the loss for which full recovery is desired.

If, at this point, the same objection is raised to the Gross Earnings Form as is sometimes raised to the Two Item Form, i.e., that the Contribution Clause does not track with the coverage, since it requires the maintenance of an amount of insurance based upon all expenses, whereas discontinuable expenses are deducted from Gross Earnings when a loss is adjusted, the reader is referred to the discussion of this criticism in Chapter 5 since the analysis found there applies equally to the Gross Earnings Form. In fact, in some circumstances the leeway in the required amount of insurance which offsets discontinuable expenses is greater under the Gross Earnings Form than under the Two Item Form.

Why is 50% the Basic Percentage of Contribution?—To make sure that the minimum amount of insurance and premium cost under the Gross Earnings Form should approximate the amount and cost of coverage under the Two Item form on the average mercantile business, the authors of the Gross Earnings Form secured data on the earnings of a large number of mercantiles. They found that the percentage to gross earnings of Ordinary Payroll (now known as Group II employees payroll) and the expense of heat, light and power average 40% and 2% respectively, and that, therefore, the total amount of insurance under both items of the Two Item Form with 80% Contribution average slightly more than 50% when Ordinary Payroll was covered for 90 days. The minimum percentage of contribution under the Gross Earnings Form was therefore fixed at 50%. So that merchants would have a wide choice of degrees of contribution at graduated rates of premium, provision was also made for 60%, 70% and 80% contribution. The comparison was based upon the Two Item Form including the minimum of 90 days' coverage of Ordinary Payroll, since

77

the Gross Earnings Form includes coverage of Ordinary Payroll at least to the extent necessary for resumption of normal operations.

Comparison of Premium Costs—The minimum amount of insurance having thus been established, a premium cost comparable to the premium cost of the Two Item Form was secured by establishing 80% of the building rate as the rate for 50% Contribution, and the following rates for the higher percentages available:

80% of building rate for 50% Contribution Clause
70% of building rate for 60% Contribution Clause
65% of building rate for 70% Contribution Clause
60% of building rate for 80% Contribution Clause

In Pacific Coast states the 100% Contribution Clause is available at 55% of the building rate.

These rates were the result of comparison with the Two Item form 80% Contribution rates of $71\frac{1}{2}$% of the building rate for Item I and $107\frac{1}{4}$% ($71\frac{1}{2}$% plus 50%) of the building rate for Ordinary Payroll insurance under Item II, as used in the majority of States outside of Midwestern territory. They were adopted for uniform use nation-wide with the intention that nation-wide uniformity in rates for the Two Item Form would also develop.

Unfortunately, however, while rates for the Gross Earnings Form charged in Midwestern States are uniform with those charged in other states, Midwestern rates for the Two Item form with 80% contribution are approximately 4% higher than elsewhere, being 77% of the building rate for Item I and 1.155% for Group II Employees Payroll coverage under Item II. Since the Midwestern rate for the Gross Earnings Form for mercantile properties is less than the rate charged for the Two Item Form without coverage on Group II Employees Payroll, Midwestern merchants are able to purchase the Gross Earnings Form for premiums substantially lower in comparison with the cost of the Two Item Form than can merchants elsewhere.

Comparison of Gross Earnings Cost—This is graphically demonstrated by the following examples which are based upon an 80% Contribution building rate of $1, assuming Group II Employees Payroll 40% and Heat, Light and Power expense 2% of Gross Earnings:

IN MIDWESTERN STATES

TWO ITEM FORM

	ITEM I		**ITEM II**
$100,000	Gross Earnings	$40,000	Payroll of Group II
42,000	(40% of Payroll of		Employees
	Group II Employees)	25%	
	(2% Heat, Light and		
	Power)		
$ 58,000		$10,000	for 90 days
80%	Contribution	80%	Contribution
$ 46,400	Insurance	$ 8,000	
.77	Rate	1.555	Rate
$ 357.28	Premium Item I	$ 92.40	Premium Item II
92.40	Premium Item II		
$ 449.68	Total Premium		

GROSS EARNINGS FORM WITH 50% CONTRIBUTION

$100,000	Gross Earnings
50%	Contribution
$ 50,000	Insurance
.80	Rate
$ 400.00	Premium

79

BUSINESS INTERRUPTION INSURANCE

ELSEWHERE*

TWO ITEM FORM		GROSS EARNINGS FORM with 50% Contribution
ITEM I	**ITEM II**	
$46,400 Insurance as above.	$8,000 Insurance	$50,000 Insurance
.715 Rate	1.073 Rate	.80 Rate
$331.76 Premium Item I	$85.84 Premium Item II	$400.00 Premium
85.84 Premium Item II		
$417.60 Total Premium		

*Except in New York City, Texas and Canada.

In short, Midwestern merchants, with Group II Employees Payroll 40% and Heat, Light and Power 2% of Gross Earnings, save 11% of premium cost by purchasing the Gross Earnings Form with 50% Contribution instead of the Two Item Form with 90 days' Group II Employees Payroll coverage and 80% Contribution, whereas elsewhere, except in New York City, Texas and Canada, merchants save only 4%.

The foregoing comparisons are for merchants whose Group II Employees Payroll is 40% and the expense of Heat, Light and Power is 2%, totaling 42% of Gross Earnings. This percentage of course varies—as between mercantile establishments. The following tables show the percentages to Gross Earnings of the sum of Group II Employees Payroll, Heat, Light and Power at which the premium costs of the Two Item Form with 80% Contribution, and of the Gross Earnings Form, are approximately identical. Consequently, for merchants whose percentages are less than those in the tables, the premium cost of the Gross Earnings Form of the indicated percentage of contribution will be lower than the premium cost of the Two Item Form and vice versa.

TABLE NO. 1—WHEN TWO ITEM FORM COVERS PAYROLL OF GROUP II EMPLOYEES FOR 90 DAYS

% of Group II Employees Payroll, Heat, Light & Power to Gross Earnings					Gross Earnings Form % of Contribution
Midwest	N. Y. City	Texas	Canada*	Else-where	
56%	48%	44%	61%	46%	50%
51%	40%	38%	57%	40%	60%
41%	32%	28%	49%	30%	70%
35%	28%	22%	42%	24%	80%

TABLE NO. 2—WHEN TWO ITEM FORM DOES NOT COVER PAYROLL OF GROUP II EMPLOYEES

% of Group II Employees Payroll, Heat, Light & Power to Gross Earnings					Gross Earnings Form % of Contribution
Midwest	N. Y. City	Texas	Canada*	Else-where	
34%	32%	28%	39%	30%	50%
32%	25%	25%	36%	26%	60%
27%	20%	19%	31%	20%	70%
22%	18%	14%	27%	15%	80%

*Unsprinklered—see Chapter 11.

The foregoing tables are constructed with the use of the following rates, based on an 80% Coinsurance rate of $1.00 for insurance on building, except that in New York City the basis rate is the contents rate.

BUSINESS INTERRUPTION RATES—BASED ON 80% COINSURANCE RATE OF $1.00

	Two Item Form		Gross Earnings Form			
	Item I	Item II	% of Contribution			
			50%	60%	70%	80%
Midwest	.77	1.155	.80	.70	.65	.60
N. Y. City	.55	.825	.60	.55	.50	.45

Texas	.70	1.05	.80	.70	.65	.60
Canada*	.825	1.24	.80	.70	.65	.60
Elsewhere	.715	1.07	.80	.70	.65	.60
Pacific Coast	.71	1.06	.80	.70	.65	.60

*Unsprinklered—see Chapter 11.

Since the percentage to Gross Earnings of Payroll of Group II Employees, Heat, Light and Power of comparatively few merchants exceeds 45%, it is evident from Table No. 1 that the majority of merchants who would insure Payroll of Group II Employees for 90 days under the Two Item Form find the Gross Earnings Form less expensive, particularly in Midwestern states and Canada. The majority of merchants who do not care to insure Payroll of Group II Employees also find the Gross Earnings Form less expensive than the Two Item Form, since the highest percentage in Table No. 2 is 39%, and comparatively few merchants operate with combined Payroll of Group II Employees heat, light and power expense of 39% or more of gross earnings.

Danger of Excluding Payroll of Group II Employees— Incidentally, if any purchaser of the Gross Earnings Form who does not care to insure Payroll of Group II Employees thinks that, because he will not claim for a loss of such payroll, he can exclude the expense of it from the computation of the amount of insurance and thereby reduce his premium cost, let him beware of becoming a coinsurer and suffering a substantial coinsurance penalty in the event of loss.

Cost Comparison—The Gross Earnings Form is not only less expensive than the Two Item Form for most merchants but is also considerably less expensive than the Weekly Form. Borrowing from the Department Store chart in Chapter 4, and the analyses in Chapters 4 and 5, the following table presents a comparison of the premium costs to merchants of all forms—Weekly, Two Item, and Gross Earnings:

Weekly Form

	Insurance	Premium
Method No. 1	$5,500,000	$35,750
(all ter- No. 2	2,602,000	16,913
ritories) No. 3	2,028,000	13,182
No. 4	2,028,000	13,182

Two Item Form 80% Contribution

	Insurance	West	Elsewhere**
Item I	$ 941,000	$7,245.70	$6,728.15
Item II*	162,000	1,871.10	1,733.40
Total	$1,103,000	$9,116.80	$8,461.55

*These figures for the Two Item Form assume Ordinary Payroll is 40% and the expense of Heat, Light and Power is 2% of Gross Earnings.
**Except Texas and Canada. For Canada see Chapter 11.

Gross Earnings Form	All Territories Insurance	Premiums
50% Contribution	$1,014,000	$8,112
60% Contribution	1,217,000	8,519
70% Contribution	1,420,000	9,230
80% Contribution	1,622,000	9,732

It is difficult to identify any other business requirement of merchants that has been reduced in cost as substantially in the same period of time, as the foregoing table discloses, notwithstanding marked improvement in quality.

Comparison of Treatment of Group II Employees (Ordinary) Payroll of Merchants by Gross Earnings and other Forms—In the foregoing, the Gross Earnings Form is compared with the Weekly and the Two Item Forms as to phraseology, work sheet and premium cost. The comparison has dealt mainly with the Two Item Form because the chief competition between forms of Business Interruption Insurance is between the Gross Earnings and the Two Item Forms.

Since the Gross Earnings Form claims superiority on the ground that it covers all Payroll blanket with all other business expenses, whereas under the Two Item Form, Payroll of Group II Employees receives separate consideration, and since the Gross Earnings Form thereby achieves simplicity, a comparison of Payroll treatment is in order.

Item II of the Two Item form is worded as follows:

Item II. $.......................On the Insured's payroll expense for Group II employees which continues during the interruption of business, for a period of time not in excess of 90*............ consecutive calendar days immediately following the date of damage or destruction but covering only to the extent necessary to resume the normal business of the Insured with the same quality of service which existed immediately preceding the date of damage or destruction and only to the extent that such payroll expense would have been earned had no loss occurred.

Definition of Group II employees: All other employees of the Insured not covered under Group I.

The total payroll expense for Group I or Group II employees shall include the entire payroll expense for each employee in each respective group.

The only reference to Payroll in the Gross Earnings Form is contained in the second paragraph, as follows:

Recovery in the event of loss hereunder shall be the ACTUAL LOSS SUSTAINED by the Insured directly resulting from such interruption of business, but not exceeding the reduction in gross earnings less charges and expenses which do not necessarily continue during the interruption of business, for only such length of time as would be required with the exercise of due diligence and dispatch to rebuild, repair or replace such part of the property herein described as has been damaged or destroyed, commencing with the date of such damage or destruction and not limited by the date of expiration of this policy. Due consideration shall be given to the continuation of normal charges and expenses, *including payroll expense*, to the extent necessary to resume operations of the Insured with the same quality of service which existed immediately preceding the loss.

Manifestly, both forms cover executive and important payroll, the Two Item Form doing so under its first item, which covers "salaries of officers, executives, department managers, employees under contract and other important employees." The Gross Earnings Form simply states that "Payroll" (meaning ALL payroll) is included in its coverage.

Comparison of Payroll Coverages—A question frequently asked is—To what extent does the Gross Earnings Form cover wages of Group II Employees, i.e., Ordinary Payroll in comparison with the specific coverage of wages of Group II Employees, i.e., Ordinary Payroll under Item II of the Two Item Form?

Payroll of Group II Employees is covered under Item II of the Two Item Form "to the extent necessary to resume the normal business of the Insured with the same quality of service which existed immediately preceding the loss." The Gross Earnings Form states in similar wording that payroll is covered "to the extent necessary to resume operations of the Insured with the same quality of service which existed immediately preceding the loss."

In one case, the reference is to resumption of the "normal business of the Insured"; in the other, to resumption of "operations of the Insured." Both obviously mean the resumption of normal business operations.

But, assuming business is suspended for 90 or more days, will the recovery for Payroll of Group II Employees under the Gross Earnings Form be for the 90 days which is the minimum under Item II of the Two Item Form? The answer is the recovery up to 90 days should be identical under both forms and under the Gross Earnings Forms can exceed 90 days.

Simply because 90 days coverage has been purchased under Item II of the Two Item Form is not a guarantee that the Insured will recover for 90 days if retention of the employees classifying as Group II for 90 days is not necessary for the resumption of the normal business operations of the Insured "with the same quality of service which existed immediately preceding the loss."

Both forms of contract are non-valued, indemnifying for actual loss sustained. The coverage under both is designed to be realistic. If suspension of business is short, all payroll is necessarily continuing. In proportion as the period of suspension lengthens, the need for retaining certain employees is necessarily reduced.

Each case must be considered upon its merits and necessities, taking all facts and circumstances into consideration. No single rule can be laid down for all cases.

If to pay an Insured's Payroll of Group II Employees for 60 days when his business is suspended for 60 days is agreed to be equitable under either of these forms, it does not follow that the same Insured would recover such Payroll for 60 days should his business be suspended for nine months. In such case, the reasonable and realistic recovery might be for only 30 days.

Blankets Payroll Coverage—At this point it is in order to call attention to the fact that the Gross Earnings Form is not the only Form that blankets the coverage of all payroll with other business expenses. Both the Per Diem and Weekly Forms also provided such blanket coverage, subject to the daily or weekly limit on recovery and to the Partial Suspension Clause, the latter operating (as explained in Chapter 4) on the basis of the amount of loss, including loss chargeable to necessarily continuing payroll, sustained in the event of total suspension considering the duration of the period of suspension.

Under the Two Item Form, the amount of insurance purchased under Item II for Payroll coverage is definitely earmarked for that purpose and cannot be used for any other purpose. Under the Gross Earnings Form, however, the coverage of all expenses is blanket, and no portion of the amount of insurance is earmarked for the coverage of Payroll or any other item of expense.

Therefore, under the Two Item Form, the Insured will

naturally try to recover as much as possible of the amount of insurance earmarked for Group II Employees Payroll coverage. Under the blanket coverage of the Gross Earnings Form, however, every dollar claimed by the Insured on account of such Payroll is one less dollar available for the indemnification of loss of net profits and expenses that necessarily continue for the duration of the loss.

The Insured sustaining loss under the Gross Earnings Form can be expected to weigh carefully the consequences to his own recovery of the size of his claim for Ordinary Payroll of Group II Employees. The smaller the amount of insurance carried in proportion to loss expectancy, the greater the Insured's caution will be with respect to the size of his claim for such Payroll. Policyholders in states with Unemployment Compensation Funds on the experience rating basis will doubtless take into consideration the cost of claiming for such Payroll under Business Interruption Insurance compared with the increased tax paid to the State Fund.

The fact that Insureds under the Gross Earnings Form are faced with a choice respecting their claim for Payroll of Group II Employees which depends upon the capacity of the amount of insurance to support a maximum claim, leads to a discussion of

THE ADEQUACY OF AMOUNT TEST

Wherever an insurance contract contains a Contribution Clause, clearly the amount of insurance must satisfy the requirements of the clause if the Insured is to avoid being a coinsurer. However, to carry Business Interruption Insurance under the Gross Earnings Form in an amount which is only 50% of annual gross earnings may, in certain circumstances, result in only a partial recovery of actual loss if total suspension of business is for a prolonged period of time.

Test Sufficiency of Coverage—The amount of Business

Interruption Insurance to be carried should be checked not only to determine whether it meets the requirement of the Contribution Clause, but also by the Adequacy of Amount Test, to determine whether the amount is also sufficient to indemnify the Insured fully for actual loss sustained under the worst conceivable circumstances.

These two tests are complementary. Both should always be made before any amount of insurance is finally approved as adequate.

The Adequacy of Amount Test is simple, and consists merely of

(1) an estimate of the longest conceivable period of time the Insured's business is likely to be totally suspended.

(2) an estimate of the Insured's loss of net profit and of the amount of business expenses that will necessarily continue during that period of time.

In the latter estimate should be included the amount of Payroll of Group II Employees, the payment of which will be necessary, bearing in mind that every dollar claimed for an item of expense of questionable necessity means a dollar less insurance available for payment of loss of net profit, and loss of expenses, the continued payment of which is mandatory and inescapable.

The greater of the amounts resulting from these two tests is the amount of insurance to be carried.

If the Adequacy of Amount Test produces a figure less than 50% of Gross Earnings, the amount of insurance needed to comply with the requirement of the 50% Contribution Clause should be carried. If the Adequacy of Amount Test produces a figure greater than 50% of Gross Earnings, the amount of insurance should comply with the requirement of the 60%, 70% or 80% Contribution Clause, and be written at the reduced rate of premium applying thereto.

For example, assuming Gross Earnings of $100,000, and the Adequacy of Amount Test produces $65,000, the amount of insurance carried should be $70,000, written with the 70% Contribution Clause.

That substantial increases in amount of insurance are obtainable at comparatively small increase in premium cost is demonstrated by the following table, based upon Gross Earnings of $100,000, and a 50% Contribution rate of .80 per $100 of insurance.

				Compared with 50% Contribution	
Insurance		Rate	Premium	Increase in Insurance	Increase in Prem.
50% — $50,000		.80	$400	....	....
60% — $60,000		.70	$420	20%	5%
70% — $70,000		.65	$455	40%	13¾%
80% — $80,000		.60	$480	60%	20%

IS 50% OF GROSS EARNINGS SUFFICIENT INSURANCE?

Attention is also called to the mistaken idea occasionally encountered that the amount of insurance needed under the 50% Contribution Clause is sufficient for only a six months' suspension of business, or that insurance of 100% of annual gross earnings would be sufficient for only a 12 months' suspension of business. Insurance in the amount of 50% of annual gross earnings has been found in many actual loss adjustments to be sufficient for a total business suspension of substantially more than six months. The excess over six months depends upon the extent to which expenses can be discontinued, thereby releasing insurance to apply to the payment of loss of net profit and necessarily continuing expenses.

However, this should not be construed to advocate 50% insurance to Gross Earnings as sufficient for every business. In the case of a seasonal business, it is quite possible that 50% will be insufficient for payment of the loss sustained during the time required for replacement of building and contents in the event of total destruction. For such situations, insurance greater than 50% of Gross Earnings should be purchased, choosing one of the higher percentages of contribution (60%, 70% and 80%) available, and benefiting by the reduced rate of premium charged therefor.

Period of Indemnity—All that has been said on the Adequacy of Amount Test should be digested in the light of the Period of Indemnity, if any, subject to which the insurance is written. If the Insured is in a territory in which Business Interruption Insurance is written subject to a minimum Period of Indemnity of 12 months, consideration should be given to whether an amount of insurance equal to the requirement of a percentage of contribution higher than 50% can be recovered within 12 months. For an explanation of the 12 month Period of Indemnity, and of the shorter Periods of Indemnity available in Pacific Coast states and in the Dominion of Canada, the reader is referred to chapters 11 and 12.

SUMMARY FOR MERCANTILE BUSINESSES

Summarizing, the Gross Earnings Form is superior to other forms of Business Interruption Insurance because:

(1) Its premium cost is lower for most merchants. In the comparatively few cases where its premium cost is higher, that disadvantage is outweighed by the following advantages of coverage:

(2) For all merchants it is the best form of coverage available because:

(a) Computation of the required amount of insurance is simple since it is a percentage of the difference between only two figures—annual business earnings and the sum of the annual cost of merchandise sold and materials, supplies and services purchased;

(b) It provides a choice of four percentages of Contribution (Coinsurance) at graduated rates of premium, and is therefore sufficiently flexible to meet all needs;

(c) It blankets the coverage of Payroll of Group II employees with the coverage of all other expenses and the purchaser need not determine prior to a loss which employees classify as Group II nor the annual amount of their payroll;

(d) Adjustment of loss is simplified, in that coverage is of the reduction in gross earnings less discontinuable expenses, eliminating the necessity of breaking down a claim into loss of Net Profit and and loss of necessarily continuing expenses, separately determined.

SERVICE TYPE BUSINESSES

The Gross Earnings Form in Relation to Non-Manufacturing Businesses Other than Mercantiles—The year 1953 is memorable for the adoption of the following definition of "Gross Earnings." This definition was designed to end the 13-year old controversy over the items of costs and expenses properly deductible from sales income for purposes of the application of the Contribution Clause, for service businesses—such as hotels, restaurants, theatres, bowling alleys—as well as to mercantiles.

Gross Earnings: For the purposes of this insurance, "Gross Earnings" are defined as the sum of: (a) total net sales, and (b) other earnings derived from operation of business, less the cost of (c) merchandise sold, including packaging materials therefor, (d) materials and supplies consumed directly in service(s) sold, and (e) service(s) purchased from outsiders (not employees of the insured) for resale which do not continue under contract.

Prior definitions differed by states as follows:

(1) In Midwestern states, the definition was "total net sales less cost of merchandise sold and cost of materials and supplies consumed in the service rendered by the insured,

plus other earnings derived from operation of the business," and in these states this policy form was usable for all types of non-manufacturing and mercantile businesses.

(2) In other states which fell into two groups, the definition was "total net sales less cost of merchandise sold, plus other earnings derived from operation of the business." In one such group, the Gross Earnings Form could be used on both non-manufacturing and mercantile businesses, while in the other group, use of this form was restricted to mercantile businesses, i.e., businesses of predominantly retail or wholesale occupancy where the business is the sale and storage of merchandise.

This diversity of definition and application began in 1940 when use of the Gross Earnings Form (which was adopted in 1938-1939 for businesses selling only merchandise) was extended to all non-manufacturing businesses (selling service and/or merchandise) without concurrently expanding the definition to permit the deduction from sales of costs other than cost of merchandise. As agents, brokers, underwriters, and adjusters began to realize that to permit deduction of only the cost of food and beverages sold by hotels and restaurants was unfair discrimination, and as the cost of services rendered was being deducted as "supplies" under the Two Item Form, a practice began of deducting the cost of services rendered (exclusive of labor) as part of the "merchandise" sold by a service type business. Therefore, in the case of hotels and restaurants, the deductions—in addition to the annual cost of food and beverages—included the annual replacement cost of supplies and services, i.e., linen, table and kitchen ware, water, soap, stationery for guests, garage and cleaning supplies, laundry, dry cleaning, flowers, entertainment, music, employees' uniforms, licenses and permits—all constituting the cost (exclusive of labor cost) of the service sold to guests.

The deduction was felt reasonable in light of the fact that the percentage of "Gross Earnings" to sales of 28%-

32% for mercantile businesses compared with an average of 83% for transient hotels and 44% for restaurants when only the cost of food and beverages is deducted from sales. By this comparison, the unfair discrimination against such service businesses was evident since on every $10,000 of annual sales covered under the 50% Contribution Clause, the average mercantile store was required to purchase approximately $1,500 insurance, whereas when only the cost of food and beverages was deducted, the average transient hotel was required to purchase $4,200, and the average restaurant approximately $2,200.

The difficulty which developed under the Gross Earnings Form for non-manufacturing service type businesses did not trouble service businesses classified as manufacturing because of use of machinery, since the term "Gross Earnings" in Manufacturing Risk Form No. 4 authorized deduction of cost of raw stock defined as "materials and supplies" for conversion into finished stock, or for consumption in the service rendered by the Insured. This reference to materials and supplies consumed in the service rendered was helpful in the case of laundries, dry cleaners, dyers, garages, and repair shops—classed manufacturing risks.

Theatres and Bowling Alleys—Although hotels and restaurants have been the storm center of the differences of interpretation of the gross earnings of non-manufacturing service businesses, other lines—principally theatres and bowling alleys—have also been involved.

If the narrow construction of what constitutes "merchandise" were followed, only the cost of candy, tobacco and beverages sold in theatres would be deductible from ticket sales. Nevertheless, some who argued for that interpretation, in the case of hotels and restaurants, inconsistently authorized the deduction of the expense of film rentals also—although it is obviously the cost of a service rendered—and in the same category as the cost of music and entertainment supplied to hotels and restaurants. If film rentals—which average 35-40% of sales—are not deducted (obviously they should not be deducted when the contract between theater and producer compels their payment), the "gross earnings" of the average motion picture theatre is nearly 90% of sales.

The same narrow interpretation of "merchandise" permitted the deduction of only the cost of candy, beverages and tobacco sold in bowling alleys, whereas, in the adjustment of Business Interruption losses, the expense of pin replacement and alley refinishing, and even of pin boys' wages, has been deducted—the latter because pin boys are not regular employees, but are remunerated on a "line" (game) basis. Similarly royalties or rent paid for use of pin setting or spotting machines are deductible as services purchased from outsiders for resale.

Whether the new definition of "Gross Earnings" has eliminated differences of interpretation—such as were placed on the old definitions, and were responsible for the withdrawal of the use of Form No. 3 from Eastern hotels, restaurants, theatres, and other non-maunfacturing businesses—remains to be seen.

Doubtless questions of interpretation will be raised—such as whether the cost of heat, light, and power (excluding wages of Insured's employees) manufactured by the Insured, is "the direct cost of materials and supplies consumed directly in service(s) sold" or, when purchased from a public utility under cancellable contracts, is the cost of "service(s) purchased from outsiders for resale." Since the Gross Earnings Policy Form is an alternative contract available with contribution percentages less than 80%—to offset elimination of ordinary payroll and the costs of heat, light, and power from sales under the Two Item Form —the propriety of deducting such costs under the Gross Earnings Form, under the guise of "supplies," is doubtful.

However, if the authors of the new definition intended such costs to be deductible, a specific authorization should have been included, since it can be argued with considerable force that heat and the conveniences furnished by electricity are obviously part of the services sold by stores as well as by hotels, restaurants, and theatres—whether or not the heat and electricity are purchased from outsiders.

Similarly, the cost of music and entertainment purchased by hotels and restaurants from outsiders, under cancellable contracts, is deductible—because they are services purchased for resale to guests. Certainly film rentals of theatres are deductible, depending on whether they are under contracts cancellable by fire. That the new definition of "Gross Earnings" is not immune from conflicting interpretations is another demonstration of the fact that although brevity is achieved by generalization, it is at the sacrifice of definiteness.

In any event, whatever the type of business and the definition of "gross earnings" may be, care must be exercised, when deducting borderline items of expense, to ascertain that the amount of insurance that is assumed to comply with the requirement of the Contribution Clause is also sufficient to indemnify for the actual loss sustained of net profit and the expenses that necessarily continue during the longest conceivable period of suspension of business—resulting from property damage.

The need for this precaution is obviously greatest when the amount of insurance is only sufficient to meet the requirement of the 50% Contribution Clause. The wisdom of carrying more, rather than less, than enough insurance is manifest, since Business Interruption Insurance deals with the uncertain future.

THE GROSS EARNINGS FORM IN RELATION TO MANUFACTURING BUSINESSES

Except in respect of the Contribution Clause formula and premium cost, all phases of the discussion relating to the application and advantages of the Gross Earnings Form to Mercantile businesses apply with equal force to businesses engaged in manufacturing operations. The only difference between the Gross Earnings Forms for mercantile and for manufacturing businesses (aside from the fact that the latter, like all forms designed for coverage of manufacturing plants, places limits upon the coverage of raw stock and stock in process, and denies liability for loss to finished goods) is in the Resumption of Operations Clause and in the definition of the term "Gross Earnings" in the form for manufacturing plants, which is worded as follows:

Gross Earnings: For the purposes of this insurance "Gross Earnings" are defined as the sum of:

(a) Total net sales value of production,

(b) Total net sales of merchandise, and

(c) Other earnings derived from operation of the business, less the cost of:

(d) Raw Stock from which production is derived,

(e) Merchandise sold, including packaging materials therefor,

(f) Materials and supplies consumed directly in service(s) sold, and

(g) Service(s) purchased from outsiders (not employees of the Insured) for resale which do not continue under contract.

No other costs shall be deducted in determining "Gross Earnings."

In determining "Gross Earnings," due consideration shall be given to the experience of the business before the date of damage or destruction and the probable experience thereafter had no loss occurred.

Earnings Produced at Time Product Is Manufactured— By specifying that the "total net sales value of production" instead of "total net sales" is the basis of determination of Business Interruption value, the Gross Earnings Form for manufacturing plants is not the first form to confirm what has long been a fundamental principle of Business Interruption Insurance—that a manufacturer's earnings are produced at the time his product is manufactured, and not at the time it is sold and delivered. All of the earlier standard forms provided for recovery of loss resulting from prevention of production. True, in the later forms the production ratio was dropped, but only because the comparison was between reduced production caused by the fire, and production prior to the fire, when it was realized that past production is not a reliable index of future production.

The loss adjuster was thus freed to determine the actual loss based upon the reduction in future production, taking sales into consideration if necessary. Since, but for his production of goods, a manufacturer has nothing to sell, Business Interruption Insurance indemnifies him primarily for loss of production; hence the reference to "sales value of production" in the Gross Earnings Form and in the Work sheets for that form and the Two Item and Weekly Forms, as previously presented.

As the Resumption of Operations Clause must be taken into consideration when determining "actual loss sustained" where production has been interrupted but sales continue from finished goods in storage, the reader is referred to the discussion of the revised "Resumption of Operations" Clause in Chapter 16.

Risks Which Store Finished Goods—For manufacturers selling their finished goods shortly following their production, or where production is uniformly confined to certain seasons and sales to other seasons, the amount of "sales" and the amount of "sales value of production" will be practically identical. Where, however, finished goods are accumulated in storage to be held for future sale along with the sale of goods produced at that time, the amounts represented by "sales" and by "sales value of production" differ. This fact must be taken into consideration in using a Work Sheet, the basis of which is simply "Sales."

If, for example, $100,000 is the sales value of finished goods produced in the Year X, and which are held for sale. and are sold in the following year Y, and the sales value of finished goods produced in year Y and sold in year Y is $300,-000, the "sales" in year Y are $400,000. However, the "sales value of production" in year Y is only $300,000. Therefore, with the use of a Work Sheet the basis of which is "sales," the amount of Business Interruption Insurance to be purchased would be substantially greater than with the use of a Work Sheet the basis of which is "sales value of production."

The manufacturer's profit on the finished goods manufactured in year X and sold in year Y is eliminated from the coverage of Business Interruption Insurance, but can be protected while on storage by either Merchandise Profits insurance, or under the Selling Price Adjustment Clause attached to Property Damage Insurance policies covering such goods (See Chapter 10).

Determining Sales Value of Production—Determination of the sales value of production, although involving more data than simply the amount of sales, is not difficult. With Formula X in the Work Sheet in chapter 5 as the guide, it is merely necessary to add together the annual net sales and the selling price of the finished goods on hand at the close of the twelve month period which is used as the basis, and deduct the selling price of the finished goods on hand at the beginning of the period. Where the inventories at the beginning and end of each twelve month period are practically identical, the "sales value of production" is the same as "sales."

Attention is again directed to the simplicity of the Work Sheet for the Gross Earnings Form as compared with the Work Sheets for the Two Item Contribution and the Weekly Forms.

COMPARISON OF MANUFACTURERS' PREMIUM COSTS

Although the rates determining the premium cost of the Gross Earnings Form for a mercantile or non-manufacturing business are uniform percentages of the rate per $100 of insurance on the building housing the business, and the rates determining the premium cost of the Gross Earnings Form for manufacturing businesses are also percentages of the building rate, such percentages vary according to territory as follows:

Percentage of 80% Coinsurance Rate on Building— Manufacturing Properties

Gross Earnings Form % of Contribution	Midwest States	Elsewhere except (1)
50%	90%	100%
60%	80%	90%
70%	75%	82%
80%	70%	75%

(1) In Texas the percentages are 110%, 96%, 85% and 76%. In New York City, where contents (and not building) rates are the basis, the percentages are 75%, 70%, 62%, and 55% respectively. In Canada the percentages are as shown in Chapter 11. In Pacific Coast states the 100% Contribution Clause is also available at 69% of the building rate.

As the basis for a comparison of a manufacturer's premium costs as between the Gross Earnings and the Two Item Contribution Form, the following table presents the varying percentages of the building rate for the Two Item Form:

Percentage of 80% Contribution Rate on Building

TWO ITEM FORM

	Midwest	Texas	Elsewhere except (2)
Item I	84%	80%	77%
Item II(3)	126%	120%	115½%

(2) In New York City the percentages are of the contents rate and are respectively 55% and 82½%. In Canada the percentages of the building rate are higher as shown in Chapter 11.
(3) 90 days coverage of Payroll of Group II Employees.

Since for mercantile businesses the percentage to Gross Earnings of Group II Employees payroll, heat, light and power (deductible from Gross Earnings under the Two Item Form but not under the Gross Earnings Form) rarely exceeds 45%, the majority of merchants find the Gross Earnings Form less expensive than the Two Item Form, particularly in Midwestern states.

An analysis of figures of a large number of manufacturing businesses, however, shows that payroll of Group II Employees, heat, light and power ranges up to 82% of gross earnings, and that 24% of the total number have percentages less than 30%; 60% less than 45%; and 73% less than 50%. Since 40% was the basis in determining rates charged manufacturers in other than Midwestern states, the following examples and tables disclose the reason for the substantially greater purchase of the Gross Earnings form by Midwesterners than by manufacturers elsewhere:

GROSS EARNINGS FORM

IN MIDWESTERN STATES		ELSEWHERE
$100,000	Gross Earnings	$100,000
50%	Contribution	50%
50,000	Insurance	50,000
.90	Rate	1.00
$ 450.00	Premium	$ 500.00

TWO ITEM FORM

MIDWESTERN STATES		ELSEWHERE*
$100,000	Gross Earnings	$100,000
	45% Group II Payroll	
45,000	Heat, Light & Power	45,000
$ 55,000		$ 55,000
80%	% Contribution	80%
$ 44,000	Insurance Item I	$ 44,000
.84	Rate	.77
$ 369.60	Premium Item I	$ 338.80
$ 8,400	Insurance Item II²	$ 8,400
1.26	Rate	1.155
$ 105.84	Premium Item II	$ 97.02
$ 369.60	Premium Item I	338.80
$ 475.44	Total Premium	$ 435.82

Compared with the cost of the Two Item Form, the Gross Earnings Form is less by $25.44 for Midwestern manufacturers in this example and more by $64.18 for manufacturers elsewhere.

1. *Except in New York City, Texas and Canada.
2. The amount of insurance for Item II in this example is determined by assuming 3% heat, light and power and 42% annual Group II payroll, i.e., $42,000, 25% of which for 90 days is $10,500; which times 80% Contribution equals $8,400.

Critical Ratios or Percentages—Since the percentage to Gross Earnings of Group II payroll, heat, light and power varies widely in manufacturing businesses, and the rates of premium costs vary by territories, the following tables will

100

be helpful in determining the critical percentages to gross earnings of such combined expense. For manufacturers whose percentages are less than the percentages in the tables, the premium cost of the Gross Earnings Form of the indicated percentage of contribution will be lower than the premium cost of the Two Item 80% Contribution Form, and vice versa.

Table No. 1—When Two Item Form Covers Payroll of Group II Employees for 90 days

% of Group II Payroll, Heat, Light & Power to Gross Earnings				Gross Earnings Form % of
Midwest	N. Y. City	Texas	Elsewhere*	Contribution
52%	22%	22%	30%	50%
45%	6%	15%	20%	60%
34%	3%	11%	10%	70%
25%	0%	7%	4%	80%

Table No. 2—When the Two Item Form Does Not Cover Payroll of Group II Employees

% of Group II Payroll, Heat, Light & Power to Gross Earnings				Gross Earnings Form % of
Midwest	N. Y. City	Texas	Elsewhere*	Contribution
33%	15%	13%	19%	50%
29%	5%	9%	13%	60%
22%	2%	7%	7%	70%
17%	0%	4%	3%	80%

*Except Canada

From the above it is evident that the Gross Earnings form is less expensive for a considerably higher proportion of manufacturers in the Midwest who wish to insure Ordinary Payroll of Group II Employees, than it is elsewhere. A tabulation of all manufacturers buying Business Interruption insurance shows that 40% of those in Midwestern states prefer the Gross Earnings form, compared with 16% elsewhere.

For those who do not care to insure Payroll of Group II Employees the Gross Earnings form is more expensive than coverage under Item I of the Two Item Form for many manufacturers, since most of them operate with percentages

101

higher than those shown in Table 2. But here again more manufacturers in the Midwest prefer the Gross Earnings form than elsewhere, because of the higher critical percentages, as shown in Table 2.

However, even though the Gross Earnings Form is more expensive for the manufacturer who does not want Group II Employees Payroll coverage, he will be wise to take advantage of its superior contractual conditions.

If efforts to simplify coverage for manufacturers by replacing both the Two Item and Gross Earnings forms by a single form, result in a form of the Gross Earnings type with provision for optional elimination, by endorsement, of coverage of payroll of Group II Employees, manufacturers will be able to secure coverage equivalent to Item 1 of the Two Item form but on the preferable basis of reduction in gross earnings less discontinuable expenses. In that event any comparison of premium costs between a policy written with, and a policy excluding, coverage of payroll of Group II Employees, and use of figures on the preceeding pages, will depend upon whether the rate charged when coverage of such payroll is eliminated, is the rate which has been charged for corresponding coverage under Item 1 of the Two Item form.

SUMMARY FOR MANUFACTURING BUSINESSES

Except as to premium cost for manufacturers in other than Midwestern states, the Gross Earnings Form is as superior to other forms of Business Interruption Insurance for manufacturers as it is for merchants, because:

(1) Determination of the amount of insurance needed to comply with the requirement of the Contribution Clause is simple since it is the Contribution percentage of the difference between only two figures—the annual sales value of goods produced and the cost of all raw stock from which such goods are produced.

(2) It provides a choice of four percentages of Contribu-

tion at graduated rates of premium, and is therefore sufficiently flexible to meet all needs.

(3) It blankets the coverage of Payroll of Group II Employees with the coverage of all other business expenses, and manufacturers need not determine prior to a loss which of their employees classify as Group II, nor the annual amount of such payroll nor the extent to which such payroll need be retained.

(4) Adjustments of loss claims are simplified in that coverage is of the reduction in gross earnings less discontinuable expenses, eliminating the necessity of breaking down a claim into loss of Net Profit and loss of necessarily continuing expenses, separately determined.

Typical loss adjustments under the Gross Earnings Policy Forms are reproduced in Appendix No. 4, No. 5, and **No. 6.**

CHAPTER 7

THE EARNINGS INSURANCE POLICY FORM

Early in 1954, in answer to numerous requests, the Fire Insurance companies devised a simplified form of Business Interruption Insurance for managements of small mercantile and non-manufacturing businesses—a form that was more salable than Gross Earnings Form No. 3.

Called Earnings Form No. 5, it was compiled as the result of an extensive study made by the Eastern Underwriters Association and Dun & Bradstreet.

In 1952, the Eastern Underwriters Association sent questionnaires to many agents, underwriters, adjusters, and accountants. This questionnaire asked: "What are the principal deterrents to the sale of Business Interruption Insurance?" The answers indicated a general agreement that lack of knowledge, complicated rules and forms, and the reluctance of prospective buyers to reveal the figures of their businesses were the principal deterrents.

Dun & Bradstreet made a report to the Eastern Underwriters Association, based on a survey of retailers in communities of less than 25,000 population, which disclosed that of those interviewed, only 10% carried Business Interruption Insurance; nearly two-thirds had never been solicited; all but 5% believed that property damage would not force business interruption for more than 3.15 months; and a third believed they could resume business in a satisfactory temporary location.

Based on data obtained from the retailers interviewed, this report suggested that a period of indemnity of four months would be adequate for all categories of retailers except Building Material dealers (including hardware stores), and that coverage in the amount of $8\frac{1}{2}\%$ of annual sales would provide complete protection for all retailers except those selling jewelry, furniture, and building materials.

The result of the answers to the questionnaire and the Dun & Bradstreet report was the promulgation of the following Earnings Insurance Form No. 5—for coverage of only mercantile and non-manufacturing businesses:

Insurance attaches to this item only when "Earnings" are specified on the first page of this policy and when an amount is indicated in the space provided therefor and for not exceeding said amount.

When the insurance under this policy covers Earnings, such insurance shall cover the loss of earnings sustained, less operating expenses which do not necessarily continue, during necessary interruption of business caused directly by the peril(s) insured against damaging or destroying real or personal property on the described premises during the term of this policy.

Earnings are defined as net profit plus payroll expense, taxes, interest, rents and all other operating expenses earned by the business.

This Company shall be liable for

(a) such loss during that period of time only, commencing with the date of the damage or destruction but not limited by the expiration of this policy, as would be required with the exercise of due diligence and dispatch to rebuild, repair or replace the damaged or destroyed property; and

(b) such loss during that period of time, not exceeding 2 consecutive weeks, when, as a direct result of the peril(s) insured, against access to the described premises is prohibited by order of civil authority; and

(c) such expenses as are necessarily incurred for the purpose of reducing any loss under this item (except expense incurred to extinguish a fire), not exceeding, however, the amount by which the loss under this item is thereby reduced.

This Company shall not be liable for

(a) more than 25% of the amount specified for this item in any 30 consecutive calendar days; nor for

(b) any increase of loss due to local or state ordinance or law regulating construction or repair of buildings; nor for

(c) any other consequential or remote loss; nor for

(d) more than the actual loss sustained.

In determining loss hereunder due consideration shall be given (1) to the earnings of the business before the date of damage or destruction, and to the probable earnings thereafter, had no loss occurred; (2) to the continuation of operating expenses, including payroll expense to the extent necessary to resume operations with the same quality of service which existed immediately preceding the loss; (3) to the reduction of loss which could be made possible by the Insured by resuming complete or partial operation of the described property, or by making use of other property.

The liability under this item shall not exceed a greater proportion of any loss than the insurance hereunder bears to all insurance, whether collectible or not, covering in any manner the loss insured against by this item.

The reference to "this item" is included because this form may be attached as an item to a policy, other items of which provide specific insurance on building or contents, or both.

Since the Contribution (Coinsurance) Clause in the Gross Earnings Form No. 3 had been called the chief deterrent to selling it, the clause was omitted from the Earnings Insurance form, and in its place was inserted the provision that the insured's recovery should be limited to not more than 25% (33-1/3% in the Pacific Coast edition) of the amount of the policy in any 30 consecutive calendar days.

Because of this monthly limit, instead of a Contribution Clause based on annual earnings, a merchant can purchase as little or as much insurance as he desires without disclosing to the salesman any data respecting his annual sales, costs and expenses. However, a merchant purchasing this form of coverage will wisely determine the amount of net profit he will lose, and the amount of his operating expenses that will necessarily continue during the 30 consecutive days of his highest earnings, when his business may be closed by property damage. Having determined the sum of these amounts, he should purchase a policy in an amount at least four times (three times on the Pacific Coast) such sum, so that recovery of 25% (33-1/3% on Coast) of the policy amount will reimburse for loss of net profit and the expenses necessarily continuing, if damage to or destruction of business premises and contents prevents operations during the 30 consecutive days of peak earnings.

106

This method of determining the amount of insurance which is adequate for full coverage of the sustainable loss, is advised because in case of claim for loss, (1) the actual loss sustained during each period of 30 consecutive days of business interruption will be separately determined and paid up to and not exceeding 25% (33-1/3% in the Pacific Coast edition) of the amount of the policy; (2) any shortage of recovery in one such period of 30 consecutive days cannot be included in or added to the recovery for a subsequent period; (3) any excess of insurance over the loss sustained in any such period is subsequently recoverable if interruption of business extends beyond 120 (90 in Pacific Coast States) consecutive days—subject, of course, to the percentage limit—and (4) there is no provision for prorating recovery within any period of 30 consecutive days.

Example: Assuming the maximum amount of loss of net profit and necessarily continuing expenses sustainable by a merchant, not located in a Pacific Coast State, is $2,500 during any period of 30 consecutive days, and not more than 120 consecutive days will be required to replace building and contents following the worst possible damage—the total amount of insurance required is $10,000, i.e., four times $2,500. However, if 120 days are deemed insufficient for repairing the damage, and the insured fears that 180 days may be required, he should purchase $15,000 insurance. As 25% of $15,00 0is $3,750, the excess of $1,250 over $2,500 needed for the loss sustainable in any period of 30 consecutive days, multiplied b yfour (i.e., $5,000), is available for payment of loss of $2,500 during each of the fifth and sixth periods of 30 consecutive days of business interruption.

A corresponding procedure should be followed for merchants in the Pacific Coast States, where recovery is 33-1/3% instead of 25% per 30 consecutive days, and therefore 90 days should be substituted for the 120 days in the previous example.

Who Are Prospective Purchasers? Any merchant, or

proprietor of a service type business, who is unwilling to purchase any form of Business Interruption Insurance policy that contains a Contribution (Coinsurance) Clause applying on the basis of annual earnings, or desires to exclude from coverage certain sources of earnings which may not be excluded when other forms are used, is a good prospect for the Earnings Insurance form of policy. Examples are the many small mercantile businesses—such as drug, clothing, furniture, jewelry and food stores—and services businesses—such as restaurants, hotels, boarding houses, sanitariums, funeral homes, automobile service stations, clubs, physicians' offices, etc. Other prospects are: retailers who object to coverage of earnings from sales of merchandise shipped directly to customers by wholesalers or manufacturers, and from sales of new cars. New businesses, which have not been in operation long enough to subscribe to a Contribution Clause based on future annual earnings, but are earning their expenses— whether or not a net profit is also being earned—are also good prospects, providing they are under experienced management.

Premium Cost—As the Earnings Insurance form lacks a Contribution Clause, and insurers are subject to payments in full of losses that—because of underinsurance—would be reduced by Coinsurance penalties under other Business Interruption policy forms, the rate charged for this form must exceed the rate charged for such other forms. Since the Gross Earnings form is its chief competitor, the premium cost and conditions of the Earnings form should be compared with the premium cost and conditions of the Gross Earnings Form No. 3. Whereas the rate for Form No. 3 with the 50% Contribution Clause is uniformly 80% of the 80% Coinsurance rate for Building insurance in all states, the rate for the Earnings Insurance form varies by territories—being the Gross Building Rate in Mid-Western States; the Full Contents Rate in New York City; and the following percentages of the 80% Coinsurance Building

Rate elsewhere:

200% on Masonry Buildings   } in Pacific Coast
150% on Frame (also All Steel) Buildings { Territory;

100% in Eastern and Southern States, in which the original percentage was 150%.

As the amount of insurance purchased (as well as the rate charged) determines the comparative premium costs of the two policy forms, the comparison for each purchaser will obviously depend upon the amount of recovery from an Earnings Insurance policy that will satisfy him in case of a loss. Since he may purchase, without the threat of a Coinsurance penalty, an amount he considers sufficient for the period of 30 consecutive days of average, or of peak earnings, he has a wide latitude under an Earnings Insurance policy—whereas the amount he purchases under a Gross Earnings Form No. 3 policy must be dictated by the Contribution Clause, unless he is prepared to chance a Coinsurance penalty in case of insufficient insurance at the time of a claim for loss.

It is true that the premium cost of an Earnings Insurance policy—written for an amount sufficient to indemnify the insured for a complete interruption of business during the 30 consecutive days of normally peak earnings—is lower for some merchants than the cost of a Gross Earnings Form policy would be. However, the greater total amount of insurance available in the latter form—in the event of unforeseen contingencies prolonging rehabilitation of business premises beyond the period of indemnity, or increased earnings in any period of 30 days, or both—may well prove to be worth more than the extra cost of a Gross Earnings Form policy. In such cases, increasing the amount of an Earnings Insurance policy can easily result in a premium cost greater than the cost of a Gross Earnings Form policy—because of the higher rate of the former—while its limits upon recovery per 30 consecutive days continues to place an Earnings Insurance policy at a disadvantage.

BUSINESS INTERRUPTION INSURANCE

A Loss Adjustment—In Appendix No. 8, the details of the adjustment of an actual claim for loss—sustained by a large delicatessen and food store in an Eastern city under a policy of Earnings Insurance—are presented. This adjustment not only illustrates the method of determing and paying loss sustained separately per each period of 30 consecutive days of business interruption; it also serves to illustrate a possible difference in amounts of insurance and premium costs between the Earnings and Gross Earnings policy forms. Assuming the 80% Coinsurance Rate of the building occupied by this store was .50, the premium cost of the $32,000 insurance carried would be $240 at the rate of .75 (150% of .50). Had the proper amount of insurance of $50,000 been carried under the Gross Earnings form with the 50% Contribution Clause, the premium would have been only $200—or 16-2/3% less for 56% more insurance—which could have been used, had the period of business interruption exceeded 120 days. If the insured had wanted to hold the cost of the Earnings Insurance policy to a premium less than $200, any amount he could have purchased would not have been sufficient to pay for the loss of $6,645.85 for the first period of 30 consecutive days, and would have been grossly in adequate for a loss exceeding 120 days. Had the revised Eastern Rate Rule been in effect, the premium cost of $32,000 insurance would have been $160 instead of $240, or 20% less than the cost of $50,000 insurance under a Gross Earnings Form policy.

If the store had occupied a brick building in a Mid-Western City under good public protection, where the Gross Building Rate is charged, the premium for $32,000 Earnings Form Insurance would be $213.44.

CHAPTER 8

AGREED AMOUNT CONTRIBUTION AND ADJUSTABLE PREMIUM POLICIES

Of all the clauses comprising Business Interruption Insurance policies, the Contribution (Coinsurance) Clause is of greatest importance to both Insured and Insurer. To the Insurer it is a necessary stabilizer, providing the basis for computation of price and of liability. To the Insured it is like the sword of Damocles—a constant threat. To avoid the penalty in his property insurance policies he must maintain insurance up to the specified proportion of the physical value of his property on the day of a possible future loss, a difficult feat at best.

It is no less difficult to maintain Business Interruption Insurance up to the specified percentage of his business earnings, not merely as of a single day of a possible future loss, but for a period of 12 months beginning with that day.

By watching business trends constantly the correct amount of insurance required can be maintained.

However, in a recent period of 12 months, the adjustment of over 1,000 losses disclosed Contribution Clause penalties averaging 13% of the loss sustained. Although this is a marked improvement over the average of 30% in a former ten-year period, the constant threat of a Contribution Clause penalty poses the question: How can the buyer of Business Interruption Insurance avoid it? One method is to check sales, costs and expenses frequently—periodically adjusting the amount of insurance to the future trend. Too few Insureds take the trouble to check Business Interruption requirements oftener than once annually, and some who are covered by policies written for terms longer than one year check only when the policy is renewed. Manifestly, such disregard of the Contribution Clause is likely to result disastrously in the event of a loss.

111

Since Business Interruption Insurance is not obtainable without a Contribution Clause, except under the limited form of "Earnings Insurance" described in Chapter 7 for Mercantile and Non-Manufacturing businsses, and except in a very few territories where the rate charged for a contributionless policy is prohibitively high, how can the teeth in the Contribution Clause be drawn, or at least dulled?

There are two methods—by the Agreed Amount Endorsement, and by the Premium Adjustment Endorsement.

THE AGREED AMOUNT ENDORSEMENT

An Agreed Amount Contribution Clause is simply a Contribution Clause in which the required amount of insurance is a fixed amount in dollars, instead of an amount which is a specified percentage of the value at the time of a loss. With an Agreed Amount Contribution Clause in his policy, the Insured is therefore protected against becoming a coinsurer in case of a partial loss so long as he maintains the agreed amount of insurance, even though the value of his insurable interest has increased.

The transformation is accomplished in the United States by the Agreed Amount Endorsement, which suspends the contribution percentage until a specified date, and substitutes for it the amount in dollars which is agreed upon between the Insured and the Insurer, the latter acting through the Rating Bureau of which it is a member.

As a prerequisite of approval of the agreed amount by the Rating Bureau, the Insured files with the Bureau a statement of the Business Interruption value of his business on a form provided by the Bureau which then determines the period, normally one year, during which the Agreed Amount is to be effective, the expiration date of which is inserted in the endorsement.

At the expiration of the effective period, the Agreed Amount can be continued in the same or a different amount, or it may be revised prior to the date of its expiration, by the Insured filing a new statement of value with the Bureau. Except in Midwestern states where a 5% increase is required, the Agreed Amount Endorsement is available without an increase in rate.

Eligibility—All buyers of Business Interruption Insurance are not eligible to enjoy the Agreed Amount Endorsement. Manufacturers are not eligible unless their plants qualify as "superior risks." In some states operators of mercantile and non-manufacturing businesses are eligible only if they occupy premises equipped with automatic sprinklers or are rated as fire resistive.

In some states the recently revised endorsement denies liability for a greater proportion of the loss than the values for the fiscal year preceding the date of insured's application, as declared in such application, bears to the actual values for that year.

The Insured's statement of value for the past fiscal year is of value to the Rating Bureau only as providing a basis for judging the adequacy of the Insured's estimate of his future earnings which are the basis of the agreed amount of insurance submitted by the Insured for Bureau approval. Since an auditor cannot assume the responsibility of certifying to what the future holds for any business, the Rating Bureau is faced with the responsibility of determining whether the Insured's estimate of future earnings is high enough to justify approval.

When the Insured's statement is his first, and is not certified by a reputable auditor, it is practically impossible for the Bureau to challenge its propriety. But when it is the Insured's second or later statement, the Bureau has a foundation upon which to base approval or rejection. Doubtless there have been instances where the Bureau's examination of a Statement filed for the Agreed Amount Endorsement has been perfunctory, and inadequate amounts have been approved. That is one of the risks the underwriter must face in writing Business Interruption Insurance subject to an Agreed Amount Contribution Clause.

Record of Estimates Filed—The following history of the gross earnings actually filed by a department store for the Agreed Amount Endorsement illustrates the need for alert and realistic scrutiny of statement supporting applications for approval of agreed amounts:

For Year Ending	Actual Earnings	Advance Estimate of Earnings	Agreed Amount (80% of Gross Earnings)	% Increase[1]	% Decrease[2]
3/45	$256,246	$150,000	$120,000	70%	....
3/46	290,318	177,000(a)	142,000	63%	30%
3/47		245,000(b)		....	15%
		295,000(c)	236,000	18%	....
3/48	(d)	289,000	231,000	....	....

(1) % of increase of actual over advance estimate.
(2) % of decrease of advance estimate compared with previous year's actual earnings.

(a) Approval of $177,000 deprived underwriters of premium on difference between $177,000 and $290,000.

(b) The Rating Bureau's refusal to approve $245,000 was proved to have been justified. A 15% reduction in gross earnings was improbable in view of upward trend in department store's sales and profits as publicized early in 1946.

(c) As revised (80% of which is $236,000.)

(d) On latest data available, sales and profits continued to increase, indicating that actual earnings for year ending March 1948 would be in excess of $289,000; yet the Insured would not be a coinsurer so long as the approved Agreed Amount of $231,-000 is maintained.

Estimates of Decrease in Values—In some territories, Rating Bureaus refuse to accept all statements of future Business Interruption values which are lower than the value filed for the past period of time. Under the revised midwestern rule when the future values estimated in the Insured's application do not appear reasonable, the Bureau will refuse to publish the Agreed Amount rate unless given the Insured's statement of satisfactory reason for any material reduction in expected earnings compared with past earnings. While such refusal is usually justified when retail sales and earnings are quite generally increasing, it is unjust to the occasional merchant who, because of conditions peculiar to his particular business, honestly anticipates a decrease in his earnings. In such cases, the Bureau is justified, after investigation, in accepting a statement of anticipated decreased earnings. Manifestly, during a business recession, when the earnings of many merchants are decreasing, to refuse all statements of decreased earnings would be indefensible

That it is possible for buyers of Business Interruption Insurance, written with the Agreed Amount Endorsement, to establish Agreed Amounts of Insurance, based on estimated sales, differing less than 5% from actual sales, has been demonstrated by 12 prominent department stores which, with sales aggregating approximately $9,500,000,000, during a recent 20-year period had filed advance estimates of sales only 4.2% less than the actual sales proved to be. Not until wartime conditions required them did any of the stores file mid-term adjustments in their estimates. For another group of 26 stores with sales of approximately $2,400,000,000 during varying periods of time the estimates were only 1.9% less than the actual sales. For all 38 stores the advance estimates of the Insured were only 3.8% less than the actual sales.

Disadvantages of Agreed Amount Endorsement—Good as it is, the Agreed Amount Endorsement is not entirely free of disadvantage to the Insured.

By eliminating the percentage contribution clause, it eliminates an incentive to the maintenance of an adequate amount of insurance where the Insured's Earnings are increasing, so that, in case of a catastrophe, he may not have sufficient insurance.

Furthermore, when the Agreed Amount Endorsement is attached to a policy written for a term longer than one year, the endorsement does not suspend the percentage contribution clause for the full term of the policy, and the Insured must be on the alert either to extend the period of suspension or be prepared to maintain insurance in an amount sufficient to comply with the requirement of the percentage contribution clause.

Moreover, to some Insureds, the requirement that a statement of value be filed with a Rating Bureau as a prerequisite of approval of this Endorsement is objectionable.

Advantages of Agreed Amount Endorsement—The fact remains, however, that the endorsement offers one advantage which outweighs all its drawbacks—freedom from the contribution penalty so long as the Agreed Amount of insurance is maintained during the life of the endorsement. And when the Agreed Amount Endorsement is attached to a Gross Earnings policy, the result is an ideal and most attractive contract for buyers who seek simplicity combined with freedom from contribution penalty. In only one respect—premium cost—can the Agreed Amount Endorsement be said to have a competitor, the Premium Adjustment Endorsement.

THE PREMIUM ADJUSTMENT ENDORSEMENT

Except for a few experimental policies, the issuance of Reporting Form or Adjustable Premium Business Interruption Insurance policies did not begin until 1932, when the Associated Reciprocal Exchanges of New York offered their form of Prospective Earnings Insurance to merchants. As a result of experience with that and later forms written without a Coinsurance Clause, for a provisional amount of insurance—subject to adjustment of premium based upon the insured's annual reports of earnings value—these Exchanges developed the following form, which is designed to be used for all classes of business—Retailers, Wholesalers and Manufacturers:

Insuring Clause: This policy, subject to all of its conditions and limitations, insures against direct loss of earnings on operations prevented by:

(a) damage to buildings, other structures or personal property located on premises described or to personal property located within 100 feet thereof if in the open or on vehicles;

(b) prevention of access to the described premises by order of civil authority when a direct result of damage to property in the vicinity thereof by a hazard insured against hereunder.

Limitations of time: Liability under this policy shall be limited to direct loss of earnings on operations which, had they not been prevented, would have taken place during the following periods commencing with the inception of the damage to the property in respect of which such liability arises and not limited by the expiration date of this policy:

(a) under clause 1 (a): the length of time which would have been required with the exercise of due diligence and dispatch to repair, rebuild or replace such of the described property as has been damaged;

(b) under clause 1 (b): two weeks.

"Loss of earnings" defined:

(a) The term "loss of earnings" as used in this policy means the loss to the insured disclosed by *comparing actual income and expense* (subject to such amendments as are consistent with the limitations and exclusions contained in this policy) for whatever period is affected *with estimated income and expense* for the same period assuming that there had been no loss.

(b) Such actual expense shall not include any amount representing reduction in value of any asset, tangible or intangible, caused directly or indirectly by the event in respect of which loss of earnings is claimed.

(c) Such actual expense shall include any expense incurred to reduce loss under this policy but, in the absence of prior authorization by this Company or its adjuster, not beyond the amount by which loss is thereby reduced.

Various Limitations: There shall be no liability under this policy for more than the smallest of the following amounts:

(a) the amount described in this policy as the limit of liability (notwithstanding the requirement that premium adjustment shall be based upon the full value reported even if in excess of such limit);

(b) the proportion of any loss which the amount hereby insured shall bear to the whole insurance covering the property against the period involved, whether collectible or not.

Duties of the insured: There shall be no liability under this policy for loss occasioned by the insured's failure (to the extent within his control) to:

(a) resume use of the described property or make use of any other suitable property or service whether owned by the insured or not;

(b) except as otherwise provided herein, discontinue any expense which is not essential to the resumption of business at normal volume and normal efficiency with minimum delay;

(c) make every other reasonable effort to reduce loss under this policy.

Guaranteed ordinary payroll: The insured's obligation to discontinue any expense which is not essential to the resumption of business at normal volume and normal efficiency with minimum delay shall not apply to such payroll expense as may be continued for a period of — weeks from inception of loss.

Premium adjustment: The provisional amount of insurance stated herein does not limit the liability hereunder. It is used only to compute the provisional premium, which shall be adjusted at expiration of this policy and, if the term exceeds one year, at each anniversary, in the following manner:

(a) The insured shall furnish (within sixty days after the end of the fiscal year involved and on the standard reporting blank provided by the Company) a report of earnings value for each fiscal year any part of which falls within the term of this policy, using the following agreed percentage of gross earnings in the calculation of such earnings value: —%.

(b) Earned premium shall be computed on this Company's share of such earnings value for the portion of the report year falling within the period of adjustment. The full amount of such value shall be used even if in excess of the amount stated in this policy as the limit of liability.

(c) An adjustment of premium shall be made for the difference between the earned premium and pro rata of the provisional premium for each period of adjustment.

Not reproduced are the added clauses denying liability for any increase of loss occasioned by any local or state ordinance or law regulating construction or repair of buildings, for any indirect or remote loss, and for loss until the liability of non-concurrent insurance, if any, has been exhausted. Also appraisal, loss reinstatement, subrogation, no control and electrical exemption clauses, and permits for work and materials, alterations and repairs, and vacancy or unoccupancy.

Following are the advantages to the insured claimed for this policy form, compared with other policy forms:

Clarification of coverage by stating that loss is determined "by comparing actual income and expenses—for whatever period is affected, with estimated income and expense for the same period assuming that there had been no loss."

Absence of a Coinsurance or Contribution Clause.

Placing upon the insurer the responsibility of deciding whether an expediting expense is to be incurred.

Absence of 30-day coverage restrictions on indemnity for loss due to damage to mercantile stocks, and manufacturers' raw stocks and stocks in process of manufacture.

Elimination of denial of liability for loss due to damage to a manufacturer's finished stock, thereby disagreeing with the reasoning that a manufacturer's loss of earnings is measured by the sales value of lost production.

Guaranteed coverage of ordinary payroll for four (or more, if desired, for additional charge) weeks, free of charge, without the necessity of proving that continuance of such payroll is essential to the resumption of normal business with minimum delay.

Adjustment of premium at each anniversary of the inception date of the policy, based upon the insured's report of earnings (Income less Cost of Goods Sold in the case of Retailers and Wholesalers). If more than four weeks coverage of ordinary payroll is taken by a Retailer or Wholesaler, there is added one fifty-second (1/52nd) of the annual amount of ordinary payroll for each week of coverage in excess of four. The annual report required of a manufacturer deducts annual cost of raw materials and supplies, ordinary payroll and net profit, from annual income to produce his "expense base." The earnings value on which premium is charged is the sum of Net Profit, 70% of the "Expense base," and ordinary payroll for the number of weeks of coverage. As the value used for premium adjustment purposes includes only 70% of a manufacturer's "expense base," he is relieved of paying premium on 30% of expenses other than the cost of raw materials and supplies and ordinary payroll which these Exchanges estimate will not continue in the average case in the event of loss—judging from their study of the operating statements of a number of manufacturers. However, a manufacturer's recovery for loss of necessarily continuing expenses is not limited to 70% of the "expense base."

The rates charged Manufacturers for this policy form are the same percentages of the 80% Coinsurance Building rate as are prescribed in Bureau rules for Item 1 of the two Item Form No. 2. For Retailers and Wholesalers, the rates for insurance equal to 50%, 60%, 70% and 80% of gross earnings are the same as promulgated by Rating Bureaus for Form No. 3 for the corresponding percentages of Contribution Clause. However, Wholesalers electing to carry less than 50% insurance to gross earnings may carry as little as 20% insurance to gross earnings at the rate charged for the 50% Contribution Clause. This privilege is granted Wholesalers because these Exchanges believe that the majority of Wholesalers, unlike Retailers, being able to promptly and efficiently resume operations from temporary office and storage facilities, and by having merchandise shipped by manufacturers direct to customers, are adequately protected against loss by insurance equal to only 20% of gross earnings. Where Wholesalers engage partly in retailing and processing operations or stock merchandise obtainable only in the foreign market, the policyholder's own self-interest is relied upon for election to carry more than 20% coverage —the increase being commensurate with the increased exposure to loss.

The Associated Reciprocal Exchanges also offers coverage under policies written subject to the Business Interruption Forms Nos. 1, 2, 3 and 4, described in Chapters 5 and 6 at Bureau rates, modified by an endorsement transforming them into adjustable premium contracts, and voiding the

Contribution Clauses. For the purposes of premium adjustment, the endorsement requires the Insured to furnish, within 30 days after the close of the Insured's fiscal year next preceding the expiration or anniversary date of the policy, a statement of value for the fiscal year preceding such date.

The Factory Mutuals' Forms—The Associated Factory Mutual Fire Insurance Companies of New England in 1933 were the first to issue a Premium Adjustment Contract to manufacturers through the Manfacturers Mutual Fire Insurance Company of Providence, Rhode Island. In 1939 the Cotton and Woolen Manufacturers Mutual Insurance Company of Boston issued another form.

In their latest editions, which are used by all the subscribers of the Factory Mutual Rating Bureau of Providence, these forms, which are of the Two-Item type and are used to cover mercantile and non-manufacturing, as well as manufacturing properties, are labelled T-1 and T-2. Only Form T-2 includes Coinsurance Clauses, one applying to Item 1 (which covers Net Profit and Fixed Charges other than Ordinary Payroll) operating only if prior to a loss the insured had failed to furnish the required statements of value; the other Coinsurance Clause applying to Item 2 (Ordinary Payroll Coverage) operating if the amount of insurance is less than the specified percentage of the entire ordinary payroll expense that would have been earned during the period of time (specified in the clause) following the date of loss. However, each Coinsurance Clause operates only if the agreed loss exceeds 5% of the total amount of insurance, or $10,000, whichever is the lesser.

In addition, this Group of Mutuals has a Gross Earnings type form (No. T-11) without a Coinsurance Clause, notwithstanding the insured fails to furnish the required statements of value.

All three forms provide that the maximum limit of liability for any loss (except under the Ordinary Payroll coverage of Item 2 of Forms T-1 and T-2) is the percentage (specified in the form) of the loss which would be sustained during a total interruption of business for the specified number of months following the date of loss, not exceeding the provisional amount of insurance for which the policy is written. In practice the limit of liability is placed at 25% in excess of the insured's estimate of his gross requirement.

All forms require the insured to furnish, as of the first day of the month in which the policy begins, a statement of estimated values anticipated for the following twelve months, and a similar statement at six month intervals. Under Forms T-1 and T-11 the insured is also required to file statements of actual experience during the policy period and the final premium is based thereon. Form T-2 differs from this in that semi-annual statements of estimated values are filed by the insured, the weighted average of which constitutes the basis for adjustment of premium. Under all three forms, premium is adjusted at the expiration of the policy, usually on the basis of 80% of values reported, or at any other percentage desired, from 25% to 100%, with proper adjustment of rate.

To provide for the peculiar needs of service-type businesses, such as hotels, hospitals, warehouses and public utilities, all three forms may be amended to cover "Net Operating Revenue"—which is defined to be the gross operating revenue from all sources, less all operating expenses except income taxes and such operating expenses as must necessarily continue during interruption of business.

In 1950 these Companies introduced "Unemployment Fund Insurance" which provides for endorsement of any Use and Occupancy policy not covering Payroll Insurance, to cover under a separate item the actual loss sustained by the Insured in reimbursing any State Unemployment Fund for the actual amount disbursed by such State Fund to the regular employees of the Insured who are out of gainful employment due to shut-down of the business of the Insured resulting from damage or destruction by the insured casualties. Unless a reporting type form is used, this is subject to 100% Co-insurance.

The Capital Stock Company Forms—Superior Risk Interim Binders—Meanwhile, the Capital Stock insurance companies operating through the Factory Insurance Associations were meeting competition involving properties classed "superior risks" by means of "Interim Binders," issued supplementary to Use and Occupancy policies.

One such binder covered the increased Use and Occupancy interest of the Insured, as described in the policy, to the amount of $100,000, provided that, before the tenth day of each month, the insured furnished a statement of the total of net profits and expenses earned during the preceding month, upon receipt of which the Association agreed to prepare policy or endorsement increasing or reducing the insurance in the amount of increase or decrease shown by the Insured's statement, dating from the 15th day of the preceding month.

A later form of "Interim Binder" furnished such additional insurance as was required to cover 100% of the increased Use and Occupancy value but in an amount not exceeding 25% of the sum of the annual net profit and the annual amount of fixed charges appearing in the latest statement of insurable value filed by the Insured; provided, however, that before a specified day of each third month, the Insured shall furnish a statement of actual Use and Occupancy values for the previous three months, and the estimated values for the ensuing twelve months, with an annual adjustment of premium to be based on the statements of quarterly values.

Other Early Developments—While the Factory Insurance Associations were issuing the Interim Binder on "superior risks," the Capital Stock insurance companies were studying proposals for Reporting Form coverage of ordinary risks. The conclusion was that, since the large majority of Business Interruption Insurance policies cover at only one location, and because issuance of Reporting Form Property Damage insurance policies on stocks of merchandise was at that time confined to stocks situate at two or more locations, Reporting Form Business Interruption insurance could not be written.

However, the Stock Companies eliminated the then mandatory requirement of 100% contribution under the Two Item Form, and provided 80% as the alternative, so that the purchaser of a policy carrying the 80% Contribution Clause would have a leeway of 20% to offset discontinuable expenses.

Subsequently, when the writing of Property Damage reporting Form insurance was extended to cover stocks of merchandise at single locations, the Stock companies resumed study of proposals that a corresponding Business Interruption coverage be adopted. Debate centered largely on whether the proposed contract should require periodic reports of earnings, and whether it should contain a Contribution Clause.

Since many Insureds experienced difficulty in rendering monthly reports of values of tangible merchandise, it was felt the difficulty would be greatly increased if periodic reports of the intangible values involved in Business Interruption insurance was required. A Reporting Form contract was therefore considered impracticable, and rejected in favor of a Premium Adjustment Contract, requiring only an annual report of earnings preferably based upon the Insured's preceding fiscal year.

The question whether a contribution clause should apply was not so easily settled. It was realized that business managements had been educated to think of reporting form or premium adjustment policies as contracts free of the possibility of contribution penalty because of the precedent established under Merchandise Reporting Form policies. Many Business Interruption insurance underwriters, however, opposed a contributionless contract with a high limit of liability, since it would tie up their underwriting capacity for the writing of higher rated property damage insurance covering the same premises and advocated extending the use of the Agreed Amount Contribution Clause to all classes of property and business as a reasonably satisfactory substitute.

The Canadian Clause—Meanwhile, in October, 1943, the North America Companies formally announced to Canadian agents a new premium adjustment Use and Occupancy policy to be written for 100% of values with adjustment of premium at expiration based upon the Insured's report of Use and Occupancy value earned during the preceding twelve months.

This announcement was followed, in December 1943, by the promulgation by the Canadian Underwriters Association of a Premium Adjustment Clause. In the revised editions of that clause applicable to the Gross Profits as well as the Business Interruption insurance forms, the premium is adjusted on each of the annual anniversary dates of a three-year policy; the insured is allowed twelve months after the expiration of an annual policy, (or after each anniversary date of a three-year policy) in which to file a report of value; and the rate used for annual adjustment of premium paid for a three-year policy is one-third of the three-year rate. The clause does not contain a full report (honesty) clause because the insured's reports of value must be certified by an auditor. If premium adjustment is desired in connection with Item 2 (Ordinary Payroll Coverage) of the Two Item forms Nos. 1 and 2, the entire annual ordinary payroll must be insured and the Coinsurance Clause for Item 2 amended accordingly.

The American Stock Company Endorsement—Spurred by the Canadian promulgation and increasing pressure from Insureds, agents and brokers in the United States, the Eastern Underwriters Association recommended a Premium Adjustment Endorsement which was first promulgated by the

Middle Department Rating Association in September, 1945.

Because that endorsement included a mandatory 100% Contribution Clause, which increased by 25% the amount of insurance required under the Two Item Form, and by 100% the amount required under the Gross Earnings Form, it has been superseded by an Endorsement which was first promulgated by the Illinois Inspection Bureau on September 15, 1947.

Profiting by the cold reception accorded the Endorsement promulgated in 1945, the 1947 Form was and continues to be designed to be used only with the Gross Earnings Form, and with a choice of either 50%, 60%, 70%, 80%, or a higher percentage, of Contribution Clause, at the regular rates applicable thereto. A minimum provisional and final retained premium of $200.00 or $500.00 per account according to local rule, regardless of term of policy, is required and in no event shall the total earned premium be less than 50% of the premium without any premium adjustment.

Whereas the 1945 Endorsement increased premium cost by 25%, the only increase in premium cost of the 1947 Form is that due to the withholding by the Insurer of 10% of return premium resulting from the adjustment of premium.

Such increase ranges from 1.1% of the actual earned premium when the value reported is 10% less than the amount on which the provisional premium was paid, to 5% when the value reported is 33-1/3% less, and to 1% when the value reported is 50% less.

The endorsement may not be attached to a policy to which the Agreed Amount Endorsement is attached.

Cancellation or reduction in the amount of the policy at the request of the Insured except on an anniversary of the inception date of the policy, voids the endorsement.

The endorsement contains a Full Reporting Clause, whereby the Insured's recovery in case of loss shall not exceed that proportion which the last reported gross earnings filed prior to the loss bears to the actual gross earnings during the period covered by the report.

126

The "last report," in case of loss occurring under an annual policy, or during the first year of a three-year policy, is the report which the Insured is required to furnish on the inception date of the endorsement. It consists of the Gross Earnings for the latest preceding fiscal year for which figures are available. In case of a loss occurring during the second or third year of a three year policy, the "last reported value" is of the Gross Earnings reported for the fiscal year preceding the year in which loss occurred.

In case the reader questions the provision that the Insured's recovery for a loss may not exceed the percentage of Gross Earnings specified in the Contribution Clause and which, but for the loss, would have been earned during the 12 months following the date of loss, attention is called to the fact that the Insured has a choice of four or more percentages of contribution.

Consequently, if the Insured purchases coverage subject to the 50% Contribution Clause and, therefore, his premium is adjusted on the basis of 50% of the Gross Earnings he reports to the Insurer, manifestly the maximum recovery to which he is entitled should not exceed the same 50% of the Gross Earnings.

In short this misunderstood provision simply provides that the Insured shall recover loss on the same basis on which he pays premium. If the Insured has reason to anticipate that, in case of a prolonged suspension of business, his loss of net profit plus necessarily continuing expenses will amount to 60%, 70%, 80% or even some higher percentage of annual gross earnings, the Insured should purchase a policy written subject to the higher percentage of contribution which fits his requirements, so that both premium and loss will be paid accordingly.

If, for example, Insured feels that his loss may amount to 150% of annual gross earnings, he should maintain and pay for insurance equal to 150% of annual gross earnings and take the 150% contribution clause. The regular contribution rate credits will be allowed for 60%, 70%, and 80% contribution clauses but, for any contribution clause of a percentage higher than 80%, the maximum obtainable rate credit is the credit allowed for the 80% contribution clause.

Advantages and Disadvantages—Fundamentally, all Reporting Form or Premium Adjustment policies of insurance, whether providing Time Element or Property Damage Coverage, are to the Insured's advantage, since they are designed to limit premium cost to the premium applying to the amount of insurance actually needed.

Manifestly, contracts written without a contribution requirement are more to the Insured's advantage than those containing a contribution clause. However, the disadvantage of a contribution requirement can be largely surmounted by the initial purchase of overinsurance (the greater the amount, the less the probability of contribution penalty), with the Insured having the assurance that premiums paid for unused insurance will be returned.

Effect of Increased or Decreased Earnings—While Premium Adjustment Business Interruption policies increase the detail and the cost of handling, which is a disadvantage to the Insurer, there is one phase which is definitely to the disadvantage of Insured or Insurer, depending upon the Insured's business conditions.

Business Interruption insurance is designed to indemnify for loss of future earnings whereas, under all established forms of premium adjustment contracts, premium cost is based upon past earnings, which are the only earnings any Insured can report accurately. As a result, when the Insured's earnings are on the upgrade, the Insurer receives premium based upon the lower earnings of the past, but is liable for loss on the basis of the higher earnings of the future, which extend beyond the expiration date of the insurance.

Conversely, when the Insured's earnings are on the down grade, the Insured pays premium on the higher earnings of the past, but is indemnified in case of loss on the basis of the lower earnings of the fuutre which extend beyond the expiration date of the insurance.

Although consideration has been given to methods by which such disparity could be overcome (for instance, by adjusting premium on the average of the sum of the earnings during the term of a policy and the earnings of, for example, six months following expiration of the policy), all forms completely ignore the disparity. During the years during which the Stock Companies were developing Premium Adjustment contracts, the disparity has been to the Insured's advantage, since earnings of practically all lines of business were increasing, and it was doubtless deemed expedient to ignore the disparity.

It has also been argued that the disparity is no greater than it is under a policy written without premium adjustment, when, because the Insured's earnings are increasing, the amount of insurance is increased by endorsement near the expiration of a policy. The Insurer then receives premium on the increased amount for only the short unexpired term of the policy, but is nevertheless exposed to loss on the higher amount of insurance during the period of business suspension following the expiration date of the policy. The disparity is of course much more likely to occur when the Premium Adjustment Insurance of an Insured is not retained from year to year by the same Insurer.

The provision that the Insured's final report of value shall cover the time "from the close of the Insured's last fiscal year to, *or beyond,* the expiration or cancellation date of the policy," is only intended for application where it is impracticable for the Insured to furnish figures for a period which terminates on the exact date of the expiration or cancellation of the policy.

That it is not intended to require a report for a substantial or significant period subsequent to the date of expiration or cancellation of the policy is evidenced by the fact that a mandatory and lengthy period of time "beyond" is not specified.

While the Insurance Companies have generously ignored the disparity referred to, even though it has been to their disadvantage, will Insureds also be willing to ignore it, if and when the tide of business earnings turns, and they realize that their premiums are being adjusted on the higher earnings of the policy term, whereas the indemnity they receive for loss resulting from business suspension extending beyond the policy term will be on the basis of reduced future earnings?

To meet the need of the Coal Mining Industry, the conditions of Premium Adjustment Endorsement are incorporated as part of the special West Virginia Coal Properties Business Interruption Form No. 7-A described in Chapter 16 under the caption "Special Conditions Applicable to Mining Risks."

PREMIUM ADJUSTMENT ENDORSEMENT vs. AGREED AMOUNT CONTRIBUTION ENDORSEMENT

Since both these endorsements are designed to mitigate one or more of the disadvantages to the Insured of the percentage type of contribution clause, this discussion would not be complete without a comparison such as the following, which applies only when these endorsements are used by Capital Stock Fire Insurance Companies.

Premium Adjustment Endorsement	Agreed Amount Contribution Endorsement
Available to Manufacturing, Non-Manufacturing and Mercantile businesses of both Superior and Non-Superior Classifications; and only in connection with the Gross Earnings Policy Form except in certain coal mining states.	Available only in connection with the Gross Earnings and Two Item Contribution Policy Forms to (1) all Mercantile and Non-Manufacturing businesses except where local rules limit eligibility; (2) to all manufacturing businesses occupying plants classified "Superior."

130

Final premium cost should not exceed the cost of the Agreed Amount Endorsement.
Minimum Premium required.

Final premium cost substantially less than cost of Premium Adjustment Endorsement, except in Midwestern states under some circumstances. Minimum premium not required.

Requires compliance with a Contribution Clause based upon a percentage of value for the 12 months beginning with date of loss—a value which may fluctuate.

Requires compliance with a Contribution Clause based on a fixed amount agreed upon between the Insured and the Insurer.

Requires overinsurance, or periodic checking of amount of insurance, to avoid contribution penalty; but unearned excess of paid premium is returned to Insured when premium is adjusted at expiration of policy.

Neither overinsurance nor periodic checks of amount of insurance are necessary. No possibility of contribution penalty so long as the agreed amount of insurance is maintained and Rating Bureau approval of the amount has not expired. No return of unearned premium is obtainable for unused portion of agreed amount of insurance.

Threat of contribution penalty combined with assurance of return of unearned premium tends to induce maintenance of an abundant amount of insurance.

Possibility of insufficient insurance to pay actual loss sustained if Insured's earnings had increased substantially and agreed amount was not increased.

If the Insured's earnings are decreasing the Premium Ajustment Endorsement is preferable because a contribution penalty is improbable and premium paid for overinsurance is returned to Insured; whereas under the Agreed Amount Endorsement no return premium is obtainable unless the agreed amount is reduced.

If the Insured's earnings are increasing the Agreed Amount Endorsement is preferable because it avoids a contribution penalty so long as the agreed amount of insurance (although less than the required percentage of value) is maintained, and the Endorsement has not expired; whereas under the Premium Adjustment Endorsement a contribution penalty is possible.

The Premium Adjustment Endorsement and Re-negotiated Government Contracts—In the event Government contracts for supplies required by our armed forces are again negotiated because of developments in the international situation, and such contracts are re-negotiated as defense and war supplies contracts were during World War II, with the objective of requiring contractors to refund the excess profits realized therefrom, the existence of a Business Interruption Premium Adjustment Contract (which was not generally available during the recent war) will provide the basis for adjusting the paid premium in accordance with the Insured's actual earnings after re-negotiation of his Government contracts. Such premium adjustment will probably be coupled with provision for advance partial payment of claims, deferment of final payments until re-negotiation of contracts has been completed, and application of Contribution clauses to the value determined by the re-negotiation process.

Chapter 9

MULTI-LOCATION DIRECT AND CONTINGENT COVERAGES

Blanket Business Interruption Coverage—When business operations conducted in a building are dependent upon the operations conducted in one or more other buildings, Business Interruption Insurance should be written to blanket all such buildings and their contents because of what is known as their "interdependency."

When the blanketed buildings are all situated at one location, the coverage is properly referred to as "blanket" but, in practice, the term "Blanket Business Interruption Insurance" is commonly used to refer only to Business Interruption Insurance when written blanket over the business premises situated at two or more locations. This is permissible provided all such premises are owned or operated by the Insured, or if such premises, if not so owned or operated, contain property owned by the Insured and coverage is limited to loss resulting only from damage to the Insured's property.

If, for example "X," a manufacturer of automobiles, operates Plants "A," "B" and "C," manufacturing engines in "A," bodies in "B" and assembling cars in "C," and contracts with the operator of Plant "D" to manufacture carburetors using materials owned by "X," all four plants are properly covered by Blanket Business Interruption Insurance. But if "X" does not own the materials used to manufacture carburetors at Plant "D," then Plant "D" is not eligible for inclusion in the blanket coverages of "X."

Since, however, Plants "A," "B" and "C" are dependent upon Plant "D," Manufacturer "X" may purchase "Contingent Business Interruption Insurance" on Plant "D" which furnishes materials, parts or services essential to the construction of the automobiles manufactured by "X." Such contingent coverage is designed to indemnify "X" for loss of earnings resulting from suspension of the manufacture of automobiles at Plants "A," "B," and "C" due to the failure of Plant "D" to deliver carburetors because property damage at Plant "D" suspended production.

Moreover, the operator of Plant "D" may also purchase Contingent Business Interruption Insurance on Plants "A," "B," and "C" to indemnify against loss of his earnings should "X" be unable to accept delivery of carburetors because property damage at the plants of "X" prevents production.

When Is Blanket Coverage Required?—Any manufacturer or merchant who, like "X," owns or operates buildings and/or contents at two or more locations, may purchase Business Interruption Insurance written blanket over all such locations. If such locations are operated interdependently, blanket coverage is manifestly essential, since property damage at one location will cause more or less interruption of business or production at all locations immediately or eventually.

If some or all of such locations are operated independently of each other, they may also be covered by blanket Business Interruption Insurance because of common ownership or operation. However, too many blanket Business Interruption policies are being written over independently operated locations, each of which could be covered specifically.

Advantages and Disadvantages of Blanket Coverage—As to coverage, there are at least two advantages to the Insured when independently operated locations are blanketed—one policy covering all locations, instead of one policy specifically covering each location, and the fact that insurance applicable to each location is limited only by the amount of blanket insurance instead of being limited by the lesser amount specifically applying thereto when each location is covered by a separate policy or by a separate item of a schedule comprising a number of items.

However, in the event of claim for loss, the Insured must

open the books of all locations not involved in the claim to determine whether or not the requirement of the Contribution Clause has been met, whereas, when each location is specifically covered, only the books of the damaged or destroyed location need be checked.

Moreover, when two or more locations (except warehouses, garages and offices which do not constitute the principal business of the Insured) are blanketed, a percentage of contribution higher than the minimum must apply. For the varying percentages consult manual of rules; in most territories the increase for the Gross Earnings Form is from 50% to 70%, while for the Two Item Form the increase is from 80% to 90%.

It is questionable whether these disadvantages of blanket insurance are always offset by the advantages.

Comparative Cost of Blanket Coverage—As to premium cost, blanket coverage can be of advantage or disadvantage to the Insured, depending upon circumstances. It will be advantageous when a location carrying a high specific rate occupies an area smaller than the average, and therefore depresses the average rate as computed by the floor area method. It will be disadvantageous to the Insured when a location carrying a high specific rate occupies an area larger than the average, and therefore increases the average rate.

Since the requirement that a higher percentage of contribution be used when two or more locations are blanketed applies alike to Insured whose locations are operated independently and to Insured whose locations are operated interdependently, there is unfair discrimination. As between Insured "A" who operates two or more theatres independently of each other, and Insured "B" who operates two factories interdependently, it is unfair discrimination to require "B" if he carries needed blanket coverage to carry the same high percentage of insurance to gross earnings as "A" (who does not need blanket coverage over independent locations). If "B" factories were all at one location, they could be covered by the Gross Earnings Form with only 50% Contribution Clause or by the Two Item Form with only the 80% Contribution Clause.

The requirement of a higher percentage of contribution when two or more locations are blanketed means that the purchaser must buy $12\frac{1}{2}$% more insurance to comply with the 90% Contribution Clause (without credit in rate therefor) at a $12\frac{1}{2}$% increase in premium, when the Two Item Form is bought, and 40% more insurance to comply with the 70% Contribution Clause at a 16-2/3% increase in premium taking the regular credit in rate for that clause, when the Gross Earnings Form is used.

While unquestionably the operator of independently operated locations should be encouraged to cover each location specifically, by being penalized in premium cost when such locations are blanketed, the operator of interdependently operated locations should not be penalized. He purchases the only form of coverage (blanket coverage) by which such locations are properly covered, whether he has ten interdependently operated buildings all located within one city block, or ten interdependently operated buildings or plants each in a different city.

However, the inclusion in blanket coverage of garages, offices and warehouses used in connection with the insured's plant and not constituting the principal business of the insured, are not construed to be additional locations even though not situated at the Insured's main location.

AVERAGE RATES FOR BLANKET COVERAGE

Floor Area Method—For reasons explained in the discussion of Average Rating methods in Chapter 13, average blanket property damage insurance rates computed on the basis of property values are never used in determining average blanket Business Interruption Insurance rates, since the distribution of property values is presumed not to coincide with distribution of Business Interruption values.

Even where blanketed locations are independently operated and, therefore, their individual Business Interruption "values" are obtainable, such values are not used to compute an average rate, except in Pacific Coast states. Invariably, elsewhere, whether operations be independent or interdependent, average blanket Business Interruption Insurance rates are computed by the "Floor Area Method": The total floor area of the operating sections (warehouse excluded) of each location is multiplied by its specific Business Interruption rate, and the sum of the products is divided by the total floor area of the operating sections of all locations.

Value Method—The Value Method (multiplying the Business Interruption "value" of each location by the specific rate of the location, and dividing the sum of the products by the aggregate Business Interruption "Value" of all locations) would produce more equitable results in all cases where locations are operated independently of each other, and the value at each location is definitely ascertainable. But unless rating bureaus undertake to determine whether locations are truly independent, a responsibility they are presently unwilling to shoulder, use of the Value Method would invite adjusted estimates applying to interdependently operated locations, reviving the abuses which forced the adoption of the Floor Area Method.

BLANKET COVERAGE WHEN WRITTEN INTERSTATE

Blanket Business Interruption is as available to cover two or more locations in two or more States as it is available to cover two or more locations in the same city. When the locations covered under a policy are in the territories of two or more rating bureaus, the bureau in the territory where the largest operating area is located has jurisdiction over the blanket policy as to form and rate. That bureau secures the specific rates and floor areas of locations outside

137

its territory from other rating bureaus, and computes the average blanket form rate by the Floor Area Method. In some territories when the insured has property such as dies or patterns at a plant or plants not owned or operated by the insured, and blankets his plant with such dies and patterns, the average rate is the rate of the insured's plant, plus 10% of the highest Business Interruption rate of any plant where such dies or patterns are covered.

Master Policies—Since each state has a Resident Agency Law, requiring that all policies covering property located therein shall be written by a resident agent, and requires payment of a tax on all premiums applying to such policies, every master policy covering in two or more states should be written at the home office of the insurance company, and be supported by an "underlying policy" for each state, written by a resident agent thereof. Therefore, a clause similar to the following is attached to the master policy:

"For the convenience of the Insured, this one policy is issued covering properties in various states. It is understood, however, that separate policies underlying this policy have been or will be issued through resident agents residing in each state specified in which Resident Agency Laws are in effect. It is also under stood and agreed that the said Underlying Policies are not to be considered as additional insurance, but duplicates only, under which no liability attaches. IN CASE OF LOSS, it is understood and agreed that it shall be adjusted in accordance with the terms and conditions of the Standard Policy of the state in which loss occurs."

Following is the corresponding clause attached to each Underlying Policy:

"It is hereby understood and agreed that in consideration of the issuance of this Company's Master Policy No...................... for the convenience of the Insured, no liability attaches under this Underlying Policy notwithstanding any phraseology therein which may be construed to the contrary. And whereas this Underlying Policy is issued for the purpose of complying with the Resident Agency Law of a State in which the said Master Policy covers in part, it is further understood and agreed that the amount of liability and the premium consideration appearing in this Underlying Policy are the estimated pro rata proportion of the amount and premium in the said Master Policy applying in the said State."

Master Policies covering interstate should not be written by a local agent in one state because he is not authorized to write insurance covering outside the territory designated in his commission of authority, and accounting difficulties are avoided when such policies are written in the Insurance Company's Home Office.

When policy is written to cover dies and patterns owned by the insured and located at an out-of-state plant not owned by the insured, blanket with the insured's plant, loss due to damage to such dies and patterns is deemed equivalent to contingent coverage and issuance of an underlying policy is unnecessary.

Countersignature endorsements in lieu of underlying policies. Manuals of rules should be consulted to ascertain whether contersignature endorsements signed by a resident agent for each state covered by a master policy, may legally be substituted for Underlying Policies.

Average Blanket Rate Example—The following example illustrates the entire procedure, beginning with the computation of an average blanket rate of $1, determined by the rating bureau having jurisdiction over State "A" because the largest processing occupancy area is located in that state. It shows how the master policy's premium of $2,500 is apportioned between State "A," "B," and "C," and between Locations Nos. 1, 2, 3, and 4. The two locations in State "C" can be blanketed or scheduled in the underlying policy issued for State "C." If locations Nos. 3 and 4 are in different cities, the Floor Area Method is also used for apportioning countersigning commission paid to local agents.

Computation of Average Rate by Floor Area Method

	Area	Rate	Product
Location No. 1 in State A	50,000	$0.40	$200
Location No. 2 in State B	30,000	1.00	300
Location No. 3 in State C	10,000	3.50	350
Location No. 4 in State C	10,000	1.50	150
	100,000		1,000

$1,000 divided by 100,000 sq. ft. equals $1.00 average rate

Blanket Insurance: $250,000 @ $1.00 = $2,500.00 Premium

Underlying Policies

	% of Area	Amount	Rate	Premium
For State A—Location No. 1	50%	$125,000	$ .40	$ 500
For State B—Location No. 2	30%	75,000	1.00	750
For State C—Location No. 3	10%	25,000	3.50	875
For State C—Location No. 4	10%	25,000	1.50	375
	100%	$250,000		2,500

If the amount of the master policy is increased or reduced the amounts of the underlying policies are revised in accordance with the original apportionment. But if the rate of one or more locations is revised, or a new location is added or an original location is eliminated from the coverage of the master policy, the average blanket form rate must be recalculated and the amount of insurance and premium reapportioned between all underlying policies.

CONTINGENT BUSINESS INTERRUPTION INSURANCE[1]

Contingent Business Interruption Insurance is the coverage applicable where the Insured desires to be indemnified for the loss he sustains if business premises not owned or operated by him, but upon which his business is dependent in whole or in part, are prevented by property damage from operating. Because published rules are ambiguous they may be incorrectly construed to authorize issuance of Contingent Business Interruption policies applying to contributing or recipient plants owned or operated by the Insured. The

---

[1]See Chapter 15 for Contingent Extra Expense Insurance.

intention of the rules is to authorize such policies to apply only to contributing or recipient plants which are not owned or operated by the Insured.

Following are the various forms of Contingent Business Interruption Insurance which are hereinafter discussed.

1. Contributing Properties Coverage.

2. Recipient Properties Coverage.

3. Off-premises Power, Light, Heat, Gas and Water Supply Coverage.

4. Selling Agents' Commissions Insurance.

5. Income from Personal Services Coverage.

(1) CONTRIBUTING PROPERTIES CONTINGENT BUSINESS INTERRUPTION INSURANCE

This is bought by the Insured dependent upon business premises which are not owned or operated by the Insured (referred to in the contract as "Contributing Properties") for supplies of materials, parts and services which will be interrupted if the premises of contributing properties sustain property damage. This coverage is written under a separate policy—not in the same policy in which the Insured's direct Business Interruption insurance is written.

Amount of Contingent Insurance—When the Insured's entire business is 100% dependent upon the materials, parts, or services supplied by the "Contributing Properties," the amount of Contingent Insurance should be identical with the amount of direct Business Interruption Insurance carried by the Insured and under the same type of policy form (Two Item or Gross Earnings).

If only a portion of the Insured's business (for instance, one department) is dependent upon "Contributing Properties," the amount of Contingent Insurance may properly be less than the amount of direct insurance, since the Contribution Clause in the Contingent Coverage policy form requires the maintenance of the insurance equal only to the Business Interruption value dependent upon the materials, etc., supplied to the Insured by the "Contributing Properties."

Since the great majority of buyers of Contingent Business Interruption Insurance require the same amounts of direct and contingent insurance, the question is sometimes asked, "Why may not both coverages be written under one policy and blanketed?"

The objection to most underwriters is the difficulty in underwriting two forms of liability under one policy, even though they are specifically covered under separate policy items, and the difficulty of computing a correct premium when the two forms of coverage are blanketed. In time, underwriters may become reconciled to such difficulties, and a rating procedure may be evolved which will produce a compensatory premium for the blanketing of both insurable interests. That "Contributing" Properties are frequently factories which are unattractive subjects of insurance, as compared with Insured's own business premises, and are not under the control of the Insured, are factors contributing to the present separation of coverages.

Multi-Location Blanket Coverage. Since contingent loss occurs at the insured's locations, notwithstanding property damage causing such loss occurs at the contributing property, the coverage is classed blanket, requiring a minimum of 70% Contribution Clause if the Gross Earnings type form is used, and 90% if the Two Item type form is used, when two or more locations of the insured are blanketed. The blanketing of two or more contributing properties is not classed as Blanket Coverage requiring 70% (or 90%) Contribution Clause provided only one location of the insured is covered.

Differences of Contributing Properties Form—Contributing Properties Contingent forms differ from the direct coverage forms for manufacturing properties in two important respects. They do not deny liability for loss sustained due to damage to finished stock of the contributing properties, and do not limit coverage on the raw stock of contributing properties to 30 days.

The finished stock of Contributing Properties is not excluded since it is composed of the materials and/or parts upon which the Insured's business is dependent.

The raw stock used by a contributing plant to produce such finished stock is covered for the full time the damaged or destroyed materials would have operated the contributing plant, and not for only 30 days, since the replacement of such materials is not within the control of the Insured.

The exigencies of wartime forced and educated American manufacturers to use sub-contractors to an unprecedented extent in order to produce the supplies urgently needed by our armed forces, and to do it with maximum possible speed.

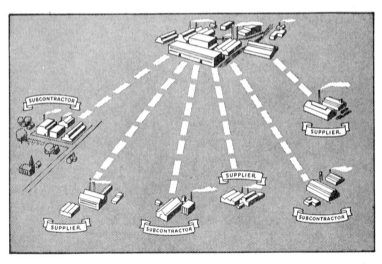

This diagram illustrates graphically why many manufacturers need Contingent Business Interruption Insurance on the plants of sub-contractors and suppliers.

For instance, one corporation manufacturing war materials reported that between April, 1939, and October, 1941, the number of sub-contractors engaged in special manufacturing tasks contributing to the production of the devices it manufactured for our armed forces increased from 36 to more than 360. In addition, 400 other manufacturers were daily shipping important parts to its assembly lines.

In its 1941 report to stockholders, another manufacturer (known here as the John Doe Company) reported that more than 400 sub-contractors were supplying it with parts of war munitions, ranging from delicate machinery operations to castings weighing more than 40 tons. While the illustration above is a reproduction of the diagram which illustrated the John Doe Company's report, it is also a graphic presentation of the situation of many manufacturers today who, in addition to carrying Business Interruption Insurance on their own plant, should also carry Contingent Business Interruption Insurance on the plants of the sub-contractors and suppliers upon whose products they are dependent. Moreover, every sub-contractor and supplier shown in the illustration is a subject for Contingent Business Interruption Insurance covering the plant of the John Doe Company which he has contracted to supply with materials and parts.

(2) RECIPIENT PROPERTIES COVERAGE

Recipient Properties Contingent Business Interruption Insurance, although purchased much less often than Contributing Properties coverage, is needed by the manufacturer who is a sub-contractor supplying the materials or parts to the prime contractor, whose plant is referred to in the policy form as the "Recipient Property," i.e., the property that receives the product of the Insured.

Contingency Insured Against—The contingency insured against under Recipient Properties coverage is the inability of the prime contractor, because of property damage to his "recipient property," to receive the materials or parts manufactured by the Insured (the sub-contractor), thus causing a suspension or interruption of production at the Insured's plant, and a consequent loss of earnings.

Every sub-contractor and supplier is ordinarily a subject

144

for Recipient Properties Contingent Business Interruption Insurance.

In the same John Doe Company's report, the company stated that it had also served as a sub-contractor to other manufacturers, making, for example, magnetos and superchargers, etc., for aircraft manufacturers, and parts for firms which, in turn, were manufacturing other parts for the John Doe Company. In this situation, a manufacturer needs both forms of Contingent Business Interruption insurance—Contributing Properties and Recipient Properties.

How Policies Are Written—Both Contributing Properties and Recipient Properties coverages may be written to cover one or more Contributing or Recipient Plants which are specifically mentioned by name and location in the policy form; or they may be written to cover unnamed plants when the Insured cannot specifically name the plants on which he requires coverage. Even when the names and locations of all covered plants are disclosed in the policy, Contingent Business Interruption Insurance is a form of insurance most underwriters avoid unless every plant is an acceptable risk. But when the identity of the covered plants is not disclosed, buyers should not be surprised when their offerings meet with cold reception from underwriters, who cannot be expected to risk substantial sums on unknown properties with unknown physical and moral hazards.

In some territories in an attempt to overcome the underwriter's reluctance to write Contingent Business Interruption Insurance on unidentified properties, the Insured's recovery for loss sustained at any one such location was formerly limited to 5% of the total amount of insurance. This limit has been revised to one-half of one percent of the policy amount for any one month of business suspension, thus introducing a desirable time element. When coverage is extended to unnamed contributing properties, the possibility exists of the earnings value thereof to the Insured being included in the basis of the application of the Contribution Clause.

Not the least of the underwriter's objection to Contingent Coverage on unnamed locations has been the possibility that the rate charged for such coverage could be lower than the rate that would be charged if all locations were named in the policy. Such absurd result, possible under the former inflexible formula, is impossible under the present formula which is discussed in Chapter 13. Manuals of rules prescribing the rates charged under varying conditions and in different territories should be consulted, bearing in mind that the rating bureau having jurisdiction over the territory in which the Insured's plant is located has jurisdiction over the Contingent Business Interruption Insurance policy form and rates notwithstanding the contributing or recipient plants are located in other territories.

Multi-Location Blanket Coverage. Since contingent loss occurs at the insured's locations, notwithstanding property damage causing such loss occurs at the recipient property, the coverage is classed blanket, requiring a minimum of 70% contribution clause if the Gross Earnings type form is used, and 90% if the Two Item type form is used, when two or more locations of the insured are blanketed. The blanketing of two or more recipient properties is not classed as Blanket Coverage requiring 70% (or 90%) Contribution Clause provided only one location of the insured is covered.

Underlying Policies—Even though the Contributing and/or Recipient Properties covered are located in another state, underlying policies are not necessary. The policy is issued in the Insured's state; the Insured's loss occurs there (even though the property damage which causes the loss occurs in another state), and the premium tax is paid to the Insured's state.When the Insured's plants are located in two or more states underlying policies are issued. Then the premium paid should be apportioned to the underlying policy

146

issued for each of the states in which an Insured's plant is located, using the floor area method.

(3) OFF PREMISES POWER, LIGHT, HEAT, GAS AND/OR WATER SUPPLY COVERAGES

This form of Contributing Properties Contingent Business Interruption Insurance is designed primarily for the coverage of loss resulting from the interruption of supply of power, light, heat, gas, or water from a public utility or privately operated plant located outside the Insured's premises. It is customarily endorsed upon the Insured's policy of direct Business Interruption Insurance for a flat premium charge of .02 or .025 per $100 per annum (depending upon the territory) for Fire insurance coverage of public utility sources of power, light, heat, or gas, and 50% (100% in some Southern states) of the Business Interruption rate of the supplying plant when it is not operated by a public utility. Additional Fire insurance charges of .02 for coverage of outside source of water supply, and from .01 to .025 for coverage of outside transmission lines are also prescribed. The corresponding charges for coverage against the perils covered by the Extended Coverage Endorsement vary by territories because of the varying degrees of the windstorm peril.

Duration of Power Failures—Of all the public utility services, manufacturers are chiefly concerned lest electric power fail resulting in suspension of machinery operations and consequent loss of earnings. Because of excellent power intercommunication facilities in most sections of the United States, interruptions of power supply due to property damage to power generating plants, sub-stations, transformers and/or transmission lines, have been comparatively brief, but such interruptions can be costly in loss of earnings.

A tabulation of many such interruptions the country over discloses that 15% were for 24 minutes or less 20% were for one hour or less, 40% were for three hours or less, 10% were between three and eight hours, 12% between eight and

24 hours, 20% between 24 and 60 hours, 10% for "several days" and one suspension continued for "several weeks."

When it is realized that the additional premium paid by a merchant or manufacturer for coverage against interruption of power and light due to fire damage to the machinery of a public utility electric generating station at the annual premium rate of .02 per $100 of Business Interruption Insurance carried, will be a total loss to the Insurer if the suspension of production due to failure of power supply exceeds 30 minutes of an eight hour working day, the wisdom of purchasing the "off-premises power plant coverage" is apparent. Moreover when tornadoes and hurricanes demolish smokestacks of power plants and raze miles of poles and transmission lines, and Business Interruption coverage against such contingencies is obtainable for the very reasonable additional premium presently charged, the wisdom of purchasing comprehensive Fire and Extended Coverage off premises power-plant and transmission lines coverage is also evident. A few examples of off premises utilities losses follow.

● On a dark, rainy afternoon in January, 1936, a short circuit in the Hell Gate Station of the New York Edison Company caused the failure of the alternating current supply of a large part of the area between 59th and 129th Streets, New York City, and in southern Westchester County, depriving 400,000 consumers of service for various periods up to 11 hours. In December, 1937, a short circuit in the cable box of one generator in the power station supplying the 60 cycle system of the Buffalo Niagara Electric Company caused differential relays to disconnect both generators. The oil fire which resulted discharged a considerable amount of smudge throughout the station, which had to be cleaned up before power could be restored. A large number of Buffalo industrial consumers using old motors in the 50 cycle system were without current six to eight hours. Only the consumers on the 25 cycle system were unaffected.

● In October, 1944, a leak in a liquefied natural gas storage tank of the East Ohio Gas Company in Cleveland caused an explosion and fire, resulting in discontinuance of gas supply of the National Bronze and Aluminum Foundry Company which, because it was forced to shut down for 36½ hours, recovered a substantial sum under the "Off Premises Power Endorsement" attached to its Business Interruption Insurance policies.

● The importance of Business Interruption coverage of water supply is demonstrated by the experience of a Pennsylvania Steel Company in 1937, when maliciously caused explosions damaged concrete water supply tunnels, shutting down the steel mill during the five days required for repairs.

Following are a few of the Business Interruption Insurance losses recovered for interruption of business due to lack of power because of damage to electric transmission lines by the 1954 hurricanes:

$6,217.85 by a Knitting Mill shut down for four days;
$1,230.30 by a Shoe Factory shut down for 25 hours;
$ 435.00 by a bakery closed for three days;
$ 223.78 by a restaurant down for two and one-half days;
$ 117.57 for one day interruption of business during the August hurricane and $390.04 for one day's interruption during the October storm by a beauty parlor which for these two claims recovered nearly seven times the premium paid for Extended Coverage and Off Premises Power Coverage for 300 days.

All of which indicates that manufacturers and merchants dependent upon public service electric power and light will wisely carry Business Interruption Insurance extended to cover off premises sources of electricity.

(4) SELLING AGENTS COMMISSIONS INSURANCE

The individual or firm engaged in selling all or part of the output of a factory, in consideration of a commission on the amount of each sale when the goods are delivered, commonly known as a Selling Agent, Factor, or Broker, has an insurable interest in such factory which can be insured under a special form of Contingent Business Interruption Insurance known as "Selling Agents Commissions Insurance." Such insurable interest may not now be covered, as formerly, under the Contributing Properties Contingent Business

149

Interruption Insurance policy form at the low rate prescribed therefor. In fact that Form denies liability for loss of selling commissions.

Like the Contributing Properties contingent form discussed in Subdivision 1 of this chapter, the Selling Agents Commissions form does not deny liability for loss sustained by the Insured due to destruction of or damage to finished stock at the factory the output of which he sells, nor does it limit to 30 days the coverage of the Insured's loss due to damage to or destruction of raw materials of the Contributing Property. Also like the Contributing Properties form, and for the same reason, the Selling Agents Commissions form may properly insure commissions earned from the sale of the output of one or more factories in one or more states and, since the Selling Agent's loss is sustained in the state in which his business is domiciled and in which his policy is issued and to which the premium tax is paid, an Underlying Policy need not be issued for any other state in which a Contributing Plant is situated.

(5) CONTINGENT LOSS OF INCOME FROM PERSONAL SERVICES COVERAGE

Where an individual is an employee of, or in some other capacity is dependent upon a particular business for his income, such as salary, commissions, bonus, or participation in profits, he may purchase a special standard form of Contributing Property Contingent Business Interruption Insurance variously known as "Loss of Personal Income Insurance" or "Contingent Loss of Income for Personal Services" insurance. This special form indemnifies such individual for loss of income if the premises of the business from which he receives income is damaged or destroyed, resulting in interruption of that business and the consequent reduction in, or complete stoppage of, the income of the insured.

Uses of Coverage—This special form has been purchased

chiefly by managers of chain stores and other businesses, compensated partly by salary or drawing account and partly by participation in the profits of the business where the business is not protected by Business Interruption Insurance. It also can be used to protect one member of a partnership when other members refuse to protect the business by Business Interruption Insurance, but of course when so used, it will protect only the income of the insured. Commission salesmen, dependent upon the uninterrupted production of goods by their employers or their employers' suppliers, are prospects for this form. Salesmen or organizations selling the output of a factory are also prospects, but are preferably protected by separate Selling Agents Commission Insurance. Inventors desirous of protection against loss of royalties payable by manufacturers of their inventions, and stockholders desiring to insure against loss of dividends on stock issued by a business that does not carry Business Interruption Insurance, are also prospects for Personal Income insurance.

CHAPTER 10

STOCK COVERAGES

For the purposes of Business Interruption Insurance, there are four kinds of stock—raw, in process, finished, and mercantile, which are defined as follows:

"**Raw Stock**"—Materials and supplies in the state in which the Insured receives them for conversion into "finished stock," including supplies consumed in such conversion.

"**Stock in Process**"—Raw stock which has undergone any aging, seasoning, mechanical or other process of manufacture at the location described in the policy, but which has not become "finished stock."

"**Finished Stock**"—Stock manufactured by the Insured, and ready for packing, shipment or sale.

"**Stock**"—When used in mercantile and non-manufacturing properties forms, refers to merchandise kept for sale. When described in manufacturing properties forms as "retail stock" and "wholesale stock" the reference is to goods manufactured by the Insured and ready for sale on the mercantile premises blanketed with the Insured's factory.

"**Merchandise**"—When used in manufacturing properties forms refers to goods which are not the product of the Insured's manufacturing operations but which are other goods kept for sale by the Insured.

Because of the different kinds of stock, all Business Interruption policy forms are divided into two groups: (1) Mercantile and Non-Manufacturing Properties forms, and (2) Manufacturing Properties forms, each distinguished by the manner in which it treats the coverage of stock.

The forms for mercantile and non-manufacturing properties which formerly covered "stock" for 30 days gratis, and could be endorsed to grant unlimited stock coverage for an additional premium now provide unlimited coverage of stock.

The forms for manufacturing properties, reproduced in this book, deny liability for loss due to damage to or destruction of "finished stock" and cover "merchandise" for an unlimited period but cover "raw stock," and "stock in process" gratis for only 30 days, subject to endorsement increasing the time of each coverage for an additional premium determined by the number of additional days purchased. The method of computing the additional premium is described in Chapter 13.

However, as loss experience has disclosed need for the 30 day limitation in comparatively few industries, and the trend is toward simplification in forms, it is probable that the forms for manufacturing properties will be revised to cover both raw stock and stock in process without the 30 day limitation, Manuals of Rules and forms should be checked to determine whether such revision has been promulgated.

RAW STOCK

Originally, raw stock was covered for whatever period of time the damaged or destroyed raw materials would, but for the fire, have furnished operating conditions for the factory, with the stipulation that the insurance shall not be liable on account of raw stock unless or until actual curtailment of production shall have occurred through the Insured's inability to produce suitable materials to take the place of those damaged or destroyed.

Later, the extent of coverage was simply expressed as being for "that period of time for which the damaged or destroyed raw stock would have made operations possible." When that phraseology was found inadequate, the following became standard, and is now employed in all policies:

Raw Stock: If raw stock, while on the premises described, is damaged or destroyed during the term of this policy by the peril(s) insured against so as to necessitate an interruption of business, this policy is extended to cover loss during such additional time, if any, as the shortest period described in (a) or

BUSINESS INTERRUPTION INSURANCE

(b) or (c) below exceeds the time during which this Company is liable under Section of (see note) this form:

(a) The time for which said raw stock would have made operations possible;

(b) The time required, with the exercise of due diligence and dispatch, to replace or restore said raw stock;

(c) 30* consecutive calendar days.

If forms are revised to eliminate the 30 day restriction and this Raw Stock Clause is deleted, nevertheless in conformity with the fundamental contractual condition that recovery is for not exceeding "actual loss sustained" due to damage or destruction, the Insured's recovery for loss to raw stock will continue to be only for the period of time for which the raw stock would have made operations possible, or for the time required to replace or restore the raw stock, whichever is the shorter time.

Examples of Raw Stock Coverage—The following examples illustrate the extent of raw stock coverage under various circumstances. All examples assume that three months are required to repair or replace the Insured's building(s), machinery and equipment which have been damaged or destroyed. In Examples (A) and (B) the Insured's recovery is regulated not by the Raw Stock Clause but by the fundamental provision of the contract that recovery is for "actual loss sustained."

EXAMPLE A:

If the destroyed raw stock would have made operations possible for only two months but for the fire, and more than two months are required to replace it, the Insured's total recovery is limited to two months because the factory would have been forced to shut down in any event at the end of two months for lack of raw

NOTE: The Section number inserted here is the number of the opening paragraph of the form in which liability is assumed for the length of time required to rehabilitate the buildings, structures, machinery or equipment, subject to the period of indemnity, if any, for which the policy is written.

(*) The 30 day period may be increased by endorsement for an additional premium. If forms are revised to eliminate the 30 day limitation and this Raw Stock destruction will continue, as now, to be only for the period of time for which the raw stock would have made operations possible or for the time required to replace or restore the raw stock, whichever is the shorter time. This will be in conformity with the fundamental condition of the contract that recovery is for not exceeding the "actual loss sustained".

154

stock, and therefore the loss sustained during the third month required to repair or replace the building(s), machinery and equipment is not chargeable to the fire.

EXAMPLE B:

Another illustration of the operation of the "actual loss sustained "principle of the policy is provided where the destroyed raw stock would have made operations possible for only one month, and two months are required to replace it. Since the factory would not have been able to operate during the second month because of lack of raw stock, the Insured's loss during the second month is not chargeable to the fire, and his recovery is limited to the loss sustained during the first and third months of the time required to repair or replace the buildings, machinery and equipment.

EXAMPLE C:

If the raw stock would have made operations possible for five months, and cannot be replaced in less than four months, the Insured's recovery is for three months to replace buildings, machinery and equipment, plus the 30 days granted by the Raw Stock Clause. Had the 30 day limitation been deleted, the recovery would have been for the full four months required to replace, which might add 1 day in the case of a 31 day month.

EXAMPLE D:

If the raw stock would have made operations possible for four months, and cannot be replaced in less than five months, the Insured's recovery is also for three months to replace the buildings, machinery, and equipment, plus the 30 days granted by the Raw Stock Clause. Had the 30 day limitation been deleted, the recovery would have been for the full four months required to replace, which might add 1 day in the case of a 31 day month.

EXAMPLE E:

But if the raw stock cannot be replaced in less than five months and it would have made operations possible for more than five months, or vice versa, the Insured's recovery under the Raw Stock Clause is limited to three months plus 30 days unless the policy has been endorsed extending the 30 days to 60 days or more, for an additional premium. Had the Raw Stock Clause and the 30 day limitation been deleted, the recovery would have been for whatever the period of time in excess of five months the destroyed raw stock would have made operations possible, or is required to replace it, whichever is the shorter time. The reader is referred to Chapter 2 for descriptions of actual raw stock losses.

STOCK IN PROCESS

Prior to 1924, forms for manufacturing properties provided for the coverage of "stock," which was defined to mean "materials or raw stock entering into the production of goods." When an increasing number of losses occurred involving claims for the time required to replace raw materials in various stages of manufacture, aging or seasoning, and disagreement developed as to whether policies written to cover "stock" should be construed to be liable for the length of time required to remanufacture, age, or season raw materials to the state in which they stood when destroyed, standard forms were revised late in 1924 to differentiate between "raw stock" and "stock in process."

The latter was defined as it is in present day policy forms, and was excluded from coverage unless liability for its reproduction be specifically assumed by endorsement attached to policy for an additional premium determined by the number of days of coverage specified by the Insured.

This was the genesis of the method presently followed of permitting manufacturers to "write their own ticket" as to the amount of both raw stock and stock in process coverage received, with this difference: Today the coverage of 30 days is uniformly granted without charge, and additional premium is payable only when more than 30 days' coverage is specified. The only exception to this procedure has been in the "Specified Time Form" standard in Pacific Coast States—see Chapter 11. If and when the Two Item and Gross Earnings forms are revised to cover stock in process for more than 30 days, the following clause will doubtless be deleted as unnecessary.

Standard Stock in Process Clause—Following is the

"Stock in Process Clause" presently in all standard manufacturing properties policy forms. If the 30 day restriction is eliminated this clause will undoubtedly be deleted as unnecessary relying upon the "Actual Loss Sustained" condition of the standard form.

Stock in Process: If stock in process, while on the premises described, is damaged or destroyed during the term of this policy by the peril(s) insured against so as to necessitate an interruption of business, this policy is extended to cover loss during such time, if any, in addition to the time for which this Company is liable under Sections 2 and 6 of this form, as would be required with the exercise of due diligence and dispatch to replace said stock in process or to restore it to the same state of manufacture in which it stood at the date of damage or destruction, except that such additional time shall in no event exceed 30* consecutive calendar days.

NOTE. Section 2 applies to Buildings Equipment and Merchandise; Section 6 to Raw Stock. *The 30 days can be extended by endorsement for additional premium.

A Comparison—Comparison of the "Stock in Process" and "Raw Stock" Clauses discloses this difference:

By the "Raw Stock Clause," the time that raw stock replacement is covered is in addition to the time required to repair or replace buildings, machinery and equipment, provided either the time the destroyed raw stock would have made operations possible, or the time to replace the raw stock, exceeds the time required to repair or replace buildings, machinery and/or equipment.

Under the "Stock in Process" clause, the time of coverage is in addition to the time for which the insurer is otherwise liable. Therefore, the 30 days of gratis stock-in-process coverage, or the days of coverage (beyond the gratis coverage) purchased by the Insured for an additional premium, begin at the expiration of the time for which the Insurer is liable because of damage to or destruction of buildings, machinery, equipment *and raw stock*, thereby recognizing that the remanufacture or reconditioning of stock-in-process to the same state in which it stood at the date of the loss, cannot, in the majority of cases, begin until buildings, machinery, equipment *and raw stock* have been restored and ready for resumption of operations.

Examples of the industries requiring more than 30 days coverage of "stock in process" are tanneries (because of hides in process in vats), woodworkers (because of lumber in process of seasoning), breweries (because of beer in process of aging).

Distillers of whiskey and spirituous liquors do not require "stock in process" coverage, because their products are customarily defined to be "finished stock" when ready for aging, barreling, bottling, or sale.

If such products were defined as "stock in process" while being aged in bonded warehouses, the purchase of many months or years of additional "stock in process" coverage would be necessary. When defined as "finished stock," they are coverable by the special standard whiskey and wine market value clauses attached to property insurance policies. Descriptions of actual "stock in process" losses are included in Chapter 2.

Molten Material (Glass and Metal) Clauses require mention in connection with a discussion of "stock in process." By these clauses, in consideration of a 10% increase in rate in the majority of states, Business Interruption loss in some states is covered if caused by accidental leakage or escape of molten material from containers thereof, whereas in other states, loss is covered if caused by heat only from molten material accidentally discharged from equipment, provided damage to equipment was not caused by a specifically excluded peril.

In the first mentioned states, the clause denies liability for loss for the time (or labor) required to remove the escaped molten material or to restore the container and contents to the state in which they stood just prior to the leakage or escape, whereas in the other states, liability is denied for any additional time that operations could not be resumed because of presence of the discharged and solidified material, or the necessity of repairing the fault which permitted the accidental discharge.

Originally all clauses provided coverage as described for the first mentioned group of states, denying liability "for loss during the time and for the labor required to remove the escaped material and to restore the 'container'." Due to prolonged controversy in connection with claim filed for loss resulting from a New England blast furnace explosion, respecting whether the breached foundations of the furnace were part of the "container," the clause was revised only in the first mentioned states, omitting the word "container," and denying liability for the additional time operations could not be resumed because of the necessity of repairing the fault, regardless of the location thereof.

Both types of clause are mentioned here because loss for the time required to remove escaped molten materials (such as molten glass and metal) although realistically "stock in process," after theyhave solidified, is not covered under either clause; nevertheless, the clauses are of value to the policyholder because they assume liability for loss caused by property damage resulting from radiation of heat from escaped molten materials as though such loss were caused by a hostile fire. Whether this extension of coverage coupled with denial of liability for loss for the time required to remove solidified materials which impede resumption of operations, is worth a 10% increase in rate, is for the policyholder to decide, taking his circumstances into consideration.

FINISHED STOCK

Recovery by manufacturers under Business Interruption policies for loss sustained resulting from destruction of their finished stock is denied, because Business Interruption insurance deals with the future, whereas finished stock is the product of the past, and a manufacturer's profit is earned at the time he manufactures his finished stock.

The loss a manufacturer sustains when his finished stock is destroyed is coverable by separate merchandise profits insurance, or by property insurance written subject to a selling or market price clause where and when rating bureaus permit such clauses, or by the "Combined Manufacturing and Mercantile Operations Endorsement" hereinafter described.

If "finished stock" were covered by its manufacturer's Business Interruption Insurance and also by merchandise profits insurance, or by a selling price clause attached to property insurance policies, the Insured would be in the position of claiming double recovery of loss of profit.

Coverage of Combined Manufacturing and Mercantile Operations—Where a manufacturer does a combination manufacturing and mercantile business, selling from his manufacturing premises merchandise which he did not manufacture, his earnings from the sale of such merchandise are covered by manufacturing properties forms. Formerly such coverage was obtainable only by means of a "Combined Manufacturing and Mercantile Operations Endorsement" attached to manufacturing properties forms. That endorsement has been replaced in some territories by a new form of "Combined Manufacturing and Mercantile Operations Endorsement". This new form of endorsement is for attachment to Manufacturing Properties Forms Nos. 2 and 4 blanketing the Insured's manufacturing operations at certain locations and mercantile sales operations at the same or other locations, each specifically identified in the endorsement.

This new endorsement is designed to provide either the manufacturer who also directly operates mercantile premises for the sale of his finished product and goods of others, with blanket coverage of factory and mercantile premises, or the manufacturer and his separate affiliated or subsidiary sales corporations with blanket coverage of factory and mercantile premises written in their joint names, thus providing a combination of direct and contingent coverages. This is accomplished by revising the denial of liability for damage to "finished stock" to apply only to finished stock which is not intended for sale by the described mercantile stores of the Insured and by creating the terms "retail stock" and "wholesale stock" to refer to goods manufactured by the Insured which are ready for and intended for sale by said described mercantile stores, and by covering such goods during the time, in addition to the time required to replace buildings and equipment, required to replace such "retail stock" and "wholesale stock."

(See Chapter 13 for description of the special rating formula applicable to this Combined Manufacturing and Mercantile Operations Endorsement).

If coverage blanketing factory and mercantile premises is written under a manufacturing properties form without this "Combined Manufacturing and Mercantile Operations Endorsement" attached thereto, the denial of liability for loss resulting from damage to "finished stock" applies to such stock on mercantile premises as well as on factory premises.

MANUFACTURING vs. NON-MANUFACTURING

The lack of agreement among Rating Bureaus as to whether certain lines of business are manufacturing or non-manufacturing for the purposes of Business Interruption policy forms, and the lack of uniform and realistic definitions of manufacturing and non-manufacturing properties contribute to the confusion.

Definition of Manufacturing Properties—Although the difference between the manufacturing properties and non-manufacturing and mercantile properties forms is chiefly in their treatment of the various kinds of stock, all rating bureaus, except those on the Pacific Coast, define manufacturing properties to be those using machinery other than machinery used for building service only, or for auxiliary processes in connection with a mercantile or non-manufacturing occupancy.

161

This definition has produced some queer classifications. For instance, many Bureaus classify chicken hatcheries and greenhouses as non-manufacturing, notwithstanding they convert raw stock into stock in process, and finally into finished stock. All Bureaus classify laundries and dry cleaning plants as manufacturing because they use machinery, although they merely perform a service on customers' materials, and have no "raw stock" of their own to convert into finished stock.

Since a machine is a device by which force (an active power) is applied, and since "raw stock" can be converted into "stock in process" and finally into finished stock" without the use of machinery, it is evident that to classify a business as "manufacturing," simply because it uses machinery is not realistic.

Pacific Coast Definition of Manufacturing Property—The Pacific Coast definition of a manufacturing property or plant is an improvement over that of other territories since, in addition to specifying use of machinery, it includes any plant engaged principally in the "application or transformation of mechanical, electrical, thermal, or chemical energy," and/or where there is a "change in the form or composition of materials resulting from the application of either hand or machinery processes."

Bearing in mind that the chief difference between manufacturing and non-manufacturing forms is their different treatment of the various kinds of stock, manifestly the simple and realistic definition of a manufacturing property would be—"one that converts raw materials into finished stock by means of aging, seasoning, mechanical or other process of conversion."

PROFITS AND COMMISSIONS INSURANCE AND SELLING PRICE CLAUSES

Any discussion of Business Interruption Insurance is not complete without reference to Profits and Commissions insurance, and Selling Price clauses which are attached to property insurance policies. By means of them, manufacturers can insure against loss of profits on their "finished stock" which is excluded from their Business Interruption policies, and commission merchants can employ Profits and Commissions insurance to insure against loss of their commissions on stock, sold or unsold, while in storage.

Ineligible Classes for Profits and Commissions Insurance —Except in a few territories, merchants other than commission merchants may not secure Profits and Commissions insurance on their merchandise, since their loss is best covered by Business Interruption Insurance, which indemnifies for loss of continuing expenses as well as profits during the time buildings, equipment and merchandise are being replaced, which may extend for the time normally required for several or more turnovers of merchandise, whereas Profits and Commissions insurance indemnifies for loss of profits on only the one turnover of merchandise involved in the loss.

Merchants may not, in any territory, have a Selling Price clause attached to their property insurance policies, unless such clause is restricted to apply to stock which is sold but not delivered to purchaser. As in the case of Profits and Commissions insurance, the Selling price clause indemnifies against loss of profits on only the one turnover of goods involved in a fire, whereas Business Interruption Insurance indemnifies against loss during the period of time which may and frequently does exceed the time required for one turnover of goods.

Coverage—In Midwestern states, the single standard Profits and Commissions policy form covers actual loss sustained of profits and/or commissions on finished merchandise sold or unsold, with the proviso that, if the Insured is able to continue sales by the use or acquirement of other merchandise, his recovery shall be limited to the actual loss resulting from actual loss of sales and/or reduction in the amount of profits and/or commissions derived from actual sales.

In the majority of other states, there are two Profits and Commissions policy forms. No. 2 is similar to the Midwestern form. Form No. 1 differs considerably in that it limits recovery to the same percentage of the prospective profits and commissions that would normally have been realized from the sale of merchandise, as the percentage of final property loss on the stock to the companies insuring the stock, after the completion of any salvage handling operations.

Form No. 1 is therefore an unsatisfactory purchase for the owner of goods which may be profitably salvaged by the insurance companies writing the property insurance thereon since, for example, if they pay the Insured a total loss and recover 60% by salvaging the goods, the Insured receives only 40% of its profit loss from the companies writing the profits insurance under Form No. 1.

Under Form No. 2, and under the Midwestern form, this Insured would receive 100% of the loss of profit, less any profit realized as the result of continuing sales of substitute goods.

Under the Selling Price clause, however, there would be no deduction for profit realized as the result of such continuing sales, since the full selling price would be recovered, less only the discounts and unincurred charges to which the goods would have been subject had no loss occurred, the payment of which the Insured is relieved when the goods were destroyed.

Interstate Form—In June, 1947, the former Interstate Underwriters Board adopted for use in Interstate Reporting Form policies a new form of Selling Price clause for the coverage of a manufacturer's finished stock. This clause provides for recovery of the factory price, plus freight and handling charges, less all discounts and unincurred expenses, less also "any markup for wholesale distribution and retail sales."

Many manufacturers who sell at wholesale and/or retail do not have a "factory price" and, where a manufacturer has a "factory price" (which presumably means his manufacturing costs plus only manufacturing profit), the deduction therefrom of any mark-up for wholesale distribution or retail sales will reduce his recovery to a figure less than the "factory price."

This type of Selling Price clause has therefore attracted considerable criticism. In fact, many rating bureaus have not adopted it. The prevention of recovery of a manufacturer's wholesaling or retailing profits is in conflict with the conditions of the Profits and Commissions Insurance policy form, which is standard in all territories.

Uses of Profits and Commissions Insurance—Profits and Commissions Insurance is most frequently written to protect manufacturers against loss of profits on the finished goods they manufacture. It may also be written to protect commission merchants against loss of commissions earned on the sale of merchandise which is destroyed before it can be delivered to purchasers.

When so written, it should not be confused with "Selling Agents Commission Insurance," which is designed for the agent who contracts to sell the output of a factory and buys such insurance to protect against his loss of commissions, not only in case the finished goods of the factory are destroyed before delivery to the agent's customers, but also against his loss of commissions on the products which the factory is prevented from manufacturing during the time it is wholly or partially shut down by property damage —see Chapter 9.

Special Market Value Clauses for Cotton Seed Oil Mills— As cotton seed is not obtainable during a considerable period of time following the cotton ginning and seed buying seasons, a special market value clause has been available to oil mill operators in some territories, whereby cotton seed, also peanuts, soy beans, or any other oil bearing seed, are valued in case of loss thereto, at the market price of the potential finished products thereof, less all discounts or unexpended cost of processing and less all other unincurred expenses to which such seed would have been subject had no loss occurred. Since the potential profit from the sale of oil or other finished products of the raw seed covered by this clause is also the profit that would be included in the basis of application of the Contribution Clause in Business Interruption Insurance if carried, oil mill managements have not purchased such insurance, preferring to rely upon the recovery obtainable under the Special Market Value Clause in case their raw stock (seed) be destroyed. In so doing, however, they were unprotected against loss of earnings in case of prevention of production of finished products due to damage to or destruction of their machinery process divisions, i.e., their oil mills. Therefore, for such managements as desire protection against loss of potential profits, whether caused by destruction of irreplaceable seed, or of machinery process divisions, or both, an alternative form of Market Value Clause was made available in 1954 in some territories for use only when Business Interruption Insurance is also maintained, whereby recovery in case of loss of seed is on the basis of market price of the potential finished products **less profit** and less discounts, unexpended processing cost and unincurred expenses.

The use of this Clause eliminates the objectionable double coverage of profit when both Property Insurance on seed subject to the described special Market Value Clause, and Business Interruption Insurance are carried. Since, however, Business Interruption Insurance does not indemnify for loss sustained beyond the time required for replacing property damaged or destroyed, and loss may occur at the time seed is irreplaceable, oil mill operators are unable under standard forms to secure the complete coverage needed due to their seasonal operations until the period of indemnity in Business Interruption forms is extendable beyond the time to replace (refer to discussion of "Period of Indemnity" in Chapter 11).

CANADIAN METHODS: SPECIFIED TIME POLICIES

Since Canadian methods of writing insurance against loss of earnings are in many respects similar to methods followed in the United States, and as American underwriters and producers frequently write insurance on Canadian properties, this book would be incomplete without a description of Canadian methods.

Differences in Canadian Forms—Business Interruption Insurance is written throughout the Dominion of Canada in much the same way it is written in the United States. In addition, "Profits Insurance" is written under Time Element coverage policy forms similar to the Consequential Loss policy forms which originated in Great Britain. The form known in the United States as "Profits and Commissions Insurance" is referred to in Canada as "Stock Profits and Commissions Insurance." Both Business Interruption Insurance and Profits Insurance as written in Canada may be written subject to periods of indemnity less than 12 months in a manner similar to the Specified Time Business Interruption policy forms available in the Pacific Coast states, which are described in the concluding section of this chapter.

Business Interruption Insurance is written in Canada under the Two Item Contribution Forms Nos. 1 and 2, and Gross Earnings Forms Nos. 3 and 4 for non-manufacturing and manufacturing properties respectively, and under the Earnings Insurance (no coinsurance) Form for mercantile and non-manufacturing properties only, as are standard in the United States. The weekly form, which was available on all types of Canadian properties, was withdrawn on January 1, 1949, except for Insureds using it prior to that date.

Both Tuition Fees and Extra Expense Insurance are written as in the United States.

In addition, three Profits Insurance Forms are available—the former "Turnover" and "Estimated Results" Profits forms (which, although withdrawn from Manuals of Rules may continue to be used by the Insureds covered by them prior to January 1, 1949) and the new "Gross Profits form," effective January 1, 1949.

RATES

Percentages are of the 80% Coinsurance building rate, or of the no-coinsurance building rate where a coinsurance rate does not apply.

Policy Form	Mercantile and Non-Manufacturing Unsprinklered	Sprinklered (a)	Manufacturing Unsprinklered	Sprinklered (a)
Two-Item				
Item I	82½%	110%	93½%	110%
Item II	Item I rates, plus 50%			
Gross Earnings—Quebec				
50% Contribution	80%	125%	121%	143%
60% Contribution	70%	108%	109%	129%
70% Contribution	65%	100%	98%	116%
80% Contribution	60%	92%	91%	109%
Gross Earnings—Ontario				
50% Contribution	80%	107%	121%	143%
60% Contribution	70%	100%	109%	129%
70% Contribution	65%	87%	98%	116%
80% Contribution	60%	80%	91%	108%
Gross Earnings— British Columbia				
50% Contribution	80%	80%	100%	100%
60% Contribution	70%	70%	90%	90%
70% Contribution	65%	65%	82%	82%
80% Contribution	60%	60%	75%	75%
100% Contribution	55%	55%	69%	69%
Gross Profits Form				
Item I	95%	95% Brit. Col. 127% Elsewhere	107½%	107½% Brit. Col. 127% Elsewhere
Ordinary payroll Endorsement—90 days Coverage	Item I Rates, plus 50%			
Earnings Form without Contribution Clause	150%	150%	Not applicable to Manufacturing Properties	

(a) Except for superior properties.

Stock Coverages—Stock in mercantile and non-manufacturing properties is included gratis for 30 days' coverage, and a 25% increase in rate is charged for unlimited coverage. The coverage of "Raw Stock" of manufacturers is unlimited except when otherwise provided by specific promulgation. "Stock in Process" is covered and rated as in the United States.

Contingent Coverages—Whereas in the United States rate charges for coverage of outside sources of power and of Contributing and Recipient Properties are published in all manuals of rules, in Canada the rate charges are specifically quoted by the Rating Bureaus upon receipt of application.

Underground Coverage at Mining Properties is not permissible. **The Agreed Amount Coinsurance Clause** is not permissible because a **Premium Adjustment Clause** is available under all Business Interruption forms except the Weekly Form. As in the United States, the Contribution clause continues in effect in conjunction with the Premium Adjustment clause, and a return premium is allowed when the amount of the policy exceeds the amount of Business Interruption value filed by the Insured following the expiration date of the policy. The return premium allowed may not exceed 50% of the premium paid by the Insured. The Canadian Premium Adjustment Clause was promulgated for Capital Stock Companies in December, 1943, two years before a corresponding clause was promulgated in the United States.

Period of Indemnity—See discussion under this heading under Profits Insurance methods.

GROSS EARNINGS FORM NO. 4
FOR MANUFACTURING PROPERTIES

This policy form (which has been standard in the U. S. since 1945 and is described in the concluding portion of

Chapter 6) was not adopted in Canada until January 1, 1949. With the objective of producing a ratio of premium cost for this form comparable to the cost of the Two Item Contribution Form, similar to the ratio produced by the rating formula used in the Eastern, Southern, and Pacific Coast states, the Canadian Underwriters Association adopted the following rating formula, in which the percentages shown are of the 80% Coinsurance building rate:

	Unsprinklered	Sprinklered
50% Coinsurance	121% (x)	143%
60% Coinsurance	109%	129%
70% Coinsurance	98%	116%
80% Coinsurance	91%	108%
For comparison, rates for the Two Item Contribution Form are as follows:		
Item I	93.5% (x)	110%
Item II	Item I Rate plus 50%	

The differential between 93.5% and 121% is approximately the 30% differential in the Eastern, Southern and Pacific Coast states, while the corresponding differential in Midwestern states is only 7%. Since 40% of manufacturers buying Business Interruption Insurance in Midwestern states are buying the Gross Earnings form in preference to the Two Item Contribution form, as compared to 16% in other states, the prospects are that not more than one in six Canadian manufacturers will prefer the new Gross Earnings form, since Canadian manufacturers are doubtless just as cost conscious as are American manufacturers.

Indeed, the ratio will probably be lower in Canada because the new Gross Profits form is also available, presenting a choice of three forms, instead of two, as in the United States. To the Insured already covered by the old Estimated Results form, which may be renewed, there is a choice of four forms!

CANADIAN PROFITS INSURANCE METHODS

"Turnover" and "Estimated Results" Forms—The writing of Time Element Profits insurance policies was standardized in Canada in 1927 by the promulgation of policy forms similar to the British form of Consequential Loss policy, devised in 1899 by Ludovic Mac L. Mann of Glasgow, Scotland.

These forms of policies, known as "Turnover" and "Estimated results" forms, were based on the principle that loss of earnings arises solely and directly from the reduction in sales ("turnover"), which results in a loss of net profit in the proportion that the business lost bears to the volume of business ordinarily transacted, aggravated by an automatic increase in the ratio of fixed charges and the payment of additional expenses incurred to minimize the Insured's loss. The yardstick used to measure the loss was therefore expressed in terms of "turnover" or "sales."

Both the Turnover and Estimated Results Profits forms contained a 100% Coinsurance Clause, which provided that the loss paid shall not exceed the "ascertained percentage" of the shortage in Turnover due to the fire, the comparison being on the basis of the previous year's experience in the Turnover Basis form, and on the basis of the probable experience following the fire in the Estimated Results form. Both forms provided for the listing of the charges and expenses the Insured elects to insure. This privilege was likely to prove dangerous to the Insured when only expenses necessarily continuing for long periods of business suspension were specified, resulting in failure to recover for expenses that continue during short, but not long, periods of suspension.

Finished Goods of the Insured who is a manufacturer were not excluded from the coverage (as they are under Business Interruption policies), because reduction in sales was the basis of the Insured's recovery under the Profits forms and indemnity continued until sales were restored to normal. However, the Insured recovered only the proportion of net profit and of the Insured's specified fixed charges that would have been earned on that part of the finished stock on hand that, but for the fire, would have been sold during the period of business suspension.

Period of Indemnity—A chief attraction of the Canadian Profits forms is the elimination of the provision (which is present in all Business Interruption forms) that indemnity ceases at the expiration of the period of time required with the exercise of due diligence to rebuild, repair or replace the damaged or destroyed property.

Manifestly, this extension of coverage, which is responsible for the increase in the rates for Profits forms compared with those for Business Interruption forms, is important to merchants and manufacturers

(1) whose volume of sales will not return to normal as soon as replacement or damaged or destroyed property is completed,

(2) are likely to lose customers and/or irreplaceable contracts, or

(3) occupy rented premises and, since they depend upon location for sales volume, may experience reduction in sales if business must be resumed in other rented but less favorably located premises.

Warehouses storing seasonal products or used household furniture, businesses unable to secure seasonal stock following completion of rebuilding operations, and seasonal hotels which lose patronage for the balance of their season following rehabilitation of physical damage, are examples of businesses preferring the Profits to the Business Interruption Insurance policy forms.

If means were available for extending the period of coverage under all Business Interruption Insurance policy forms in the United States and Canada beyond the time required for physical rehabilitation, there would probably be little demand for the Canadian Profits forms, and many lines of business in the United States would secure a more complete and necessary coverage. If a precedent for such extension of time coverage is needed, it is at hand in the well established Tuition Fees Insurance policy form and in the Louisiana Public Storage Warehouse and Pacific Coast Seasonal Stock Endorsements. As ways and means of extending the Period of Indemnity are under study as this book goes to press, manuals of Rules should be checked for possible revisions in this direction.

Under the old Canadian Profits forms, the normal period of indemnity was 12 months. Under Canadian Business Interruption policies, a 12 month period of indemnity became standard in December, 1941, because of war conditions, but was eliminated late in 1944. Subsequently the 12 month period became mandatory when the Premium Adjustment Clause applies, also when coverage is blanket over two or more locations, unless a period longer or shorter than 12 months is endorsed on policy. Under both Canadian Gross Profits and Business Interruption policies, except those written under the Gross Earnings form, periods of indemnity shorter than 12 months are available at the following reductions in rate.

8 months Period of Indemnity—Deduct $7\frac{1}{2}\%$
6 months Period of Indemnity—Deduct $12\frac{1}{2}\%$
4 months Period of Indemnity—Deduct 20%

Since the Periods of Indemnity shorter than 12 months apply in the event of partial as well as total suspension of business, and the amount of insurance required by the coinsurance clause is on the annual basis, the following table is presented to show the small increase in premium, compared with the considerable increase in the period of time coverage, received when the 12 month Period of Indemnity is purchased:

Increase in Period of Indemnity		Increase in Time Coverage	Increase in Premium Cost
From	To		
4 mos.	6 mos.	50%	9.4%
4 mos.	8 mos.	100%	15.6%

4 mos.	12 mos.	200%	25.0%
6 mos.	8 mos.	33-1/3%	5.7%
6 mos.	12 mos.	100%	14.0%
8 mos.	12 mos.	50%	8.1%

In short, when, for example, a 200% increase (from four to twelve months) in the period of time can be purchased for only 25% increase in premium cost, or a 100% increase (from 6 to 12 months) for only 14% more premium, it is imprudent for any merchant or manufacturer to purchase a Period of Indemnity less than 12 months, considering that the policy deals with the uncertain future.

The Period of Indemnity may be increased to 15, 18, 21 or a maximum of 24 months without increase in rate but the amount of insurance must be increased in the same ratio and the coinsurance clause will apply to the extended period.

Premium Adjustment is available in connection with all forms but manuals of rules should be checked with respect to the permissible percentages of coinsurance, policy term, and Period of Indemnity when the Premium Adjustment Endorsement is attached to a policy. When the policy covers the Insured's ordinary payroll under a separate item, no return of premium is allowed in respect thereto. To secure premium adjustment in connection with ordinary payroll, it is necessary to insure the entire annual ordinary payroll as a specified fixed charge. As in the case of Business Interruption policies, the return premium may not exceed 50% of the premium paid by the Insured.

NEW GROSS PROFITS POLICY FORM

This policy form was adopted effective January 1, 1949, to supersede the Estimated Results Profits form, although Insureds covered under the latter are permitted to continue its use at an increase in rate over the Gross Profits Form.

The new form is modeled along the lines of the Gross Profits form adopted by the Consequential Loss Committee of the Fire Officers Committee of London for use in Great

Britain after January 1, 1939. In this form, as compared with the Estimated Results form, the term "Gross Profits" is substituted for "Profits"; the term "Rate of Gross Profit" replaces "Ascertained Percentage"; "Insured Standing Charges" replaces "Specified Fixed Charges"; but the terms "Turnover" and "Net Profit" are retained.

Under the new form, the Insurance Company agrees to pay, in respect of Item I of the form, the amount of loss resulting from interruption of business in accordance with the following provisions:

Item No.   Sum Insured
1. Gross Profit $

The insurance under item 1 is limited to loss of Gross Profit due to (a) Reduction in Turnover and (b) Increase in Cost of Working and the amount payable as Indemnity thereunder shall be:

(a) *In Respect of Reduction in Turnover:* The sum produced by applying the Rate of Gross Profit to the amount by which the Turnover during the Indemnity Period shall, in consequence of the fire, fall short of the Standard Turnover,

(b) *In Respect of Increase in Cost of Working:* The additional expenditure (subject to provision No. 2 below) necessarily and reasonably incurred for the sole purpose of avoiding or diminishing the reduction in Turnover which but for that expenditure would have taken place during the Indemnity Period in consequence of the fire, but not exceeding the sum produced by applying the Rate of Gross Profit to the amount of the reduction thereby avoided,

... less any sum saved during the Indemnity Period in respect of such of the Insured Standing Charges as may cease or be reduced in consequence of the fire,

... provided that if the Sum Insured by this item be less than the Sum produced by applying the Rate of Gross Profit to the Annual Turnover, the amount payable shall be proportionately reduced.

Definitions.—The following terms wherever used in this contract shall be construed to mean:

Gross Profit.—The sum produced by adding to the Net Profit the amount of the Insured Standing Charges, or if there be no Net Profit the amount of the Insured Standing Charges less such a proportion of any net trading loss as the amount of the Insured Standing Charges bears to all business Standing Charges.

Net Profit.—The net trading profit (exclusive of all capital receipts and accretions and all outlay properly chargeable to capital) resulting from the business of the insured at the premises after due provision has been made for all Standing and other charges including depreciation.

Insured Standing Charges (See Note at end of Form)

Turnover.—The money paid or payable to the insured for goods sold and delivered and for services rendered in course of the business at the premises.

Indemnity Period.—The period beginning with the occurrence of the fire and ending not later than . . . months thereafter during which the results of the business shall be affected in consequence of the fire.

Rate of Gross Profit.—The rate of Gross Profit earned on the Turnover during the financial year immediately before the date of the fire

Annual Turnover. — The Turnover during the twelve months immediately before the date of the fire

Standard Turnover. — The Turnover during that period in the twelve months immediately before the date of the fire which corresponds with the Indemnity Period

To which such adjustments shall be made as may be necessary to provide for the trend of the business and for variations in or special circumstances affecting the business either before or after the fire or which would have affected the business had the fire not occurred, so that the figures thus adjusted shall represent as nearly as practicable the results which but for the fire would have been obtained during the relative period after the fire.

Provided that:

1.—If during the Indemnity Period goods shall besold or services shall be rendered elsewhere than at the premises for the benefit of the business either by the insured or by others on his behalf the money paid or payable in respect of such sales or services shall be brought into account in arriving at the Turnover during the Indemnity Period.

2.—If any Standing Charges of the business be not insured by this policy then in computing the amount recoverable hereunder as Increase in Cost of Working that proportion only of the additional expenditure shall be brought into account which the sum of the Net Profit and the Insured Standing Charges bears to the sum of the Net Profit and all Standing Charges.

3.—The Liability of the Company shall in no case exceed the total sum insured hereby or such other sum or sums as may hereafter be substituted therefor by endorsement signed by or on behalf of the Company.

4.—This Company shall not be liable for any loss due to fines or damages for breach of contract for late or non-completion of orders, or for any penalties of whatever nature.

5.—If at the time of any fire there be any other insurance or insurances covering the loss or any part of the loss covered by this Policy, the Company shall be liable only to pay or contribute its rateable proportion of the loss.

6.—On the happening of any fire in consequence of which a claim is or may be made under this policy, the Insured shall with due diligence do and concur in doing and permit to be done all things which may be reasonably practicable to minimize or check any interruption of or interference with the business or to avoid or diminish the loss.

7.—This Company shall be liable for actual loss sustained, as covered hereunder, during the period of time, not exceeding two weeks after date of fire, while access to the premises described is prohibited by order of civil authority, but only when such order is given as a direct result of fire in the vicinity of said premises.

NOTE: The "Standing Charges" generally insured by listing in the blank space provided in this Form, are the following:

Rent, Taxes, Interest on Debentures on Bonds, Directors' fees, Auditors' fees, Interest on Mortgages, Loans, Bank Overdrafts, and other borrowed capital, Salaries to Permanent Staff, Wages to foremen and skilled employees whose services would not be dispensed with should the business come to a standstill, Traveling Expenses, Advertising, Insurance Premium, Depreciation of Plant and Machinery not damaged by the fire, Upkeep of Automobiles and/or Horses, Lighting, Heating, Power, Pumping and Ventilation, Printing, Stationery and Postages, Agency Contracts and Expenses, Expenses of Branch or Local Offices, Royalties, Delivery and other services under contract, Miscellaneous Standing Charges (not exceeding 5% of the total amount payable in respect of specified insured standing charges).

If all of an Insured's Standing Charges are not insured the amount recoverable under Item 1 (h) "In Respect of Increase in Cost of Working" is proportionately reduced see Clause 2 of this Form and the example hereinafter presented.

If desired, a second item may be added to cover Ordinary Payroll in a manner similar to the second item of the Estimated Results Profits form and the Two Item Contribution Business Interruption Insurance form.

Rates for Gross Profits Form
Percentages are of the 80% Coinsurance Building Rate

	Unsprinklered	Sprinklered
Manufacturing Properties Item I	107.5%	Estimated Results
Mercantile and Non-Manufacturing Properties Item I	95%	Profits Form Rates

For Ordinary Payroll Item — Item I rate (without deduction for Short Period of Indemnity) plus 50%

It will be noted that in the case of unsprinklered properties, the rates for the new Gross Profits Form are considerably lower than Estimated Results Form rates.

Since the terms "Gross Profits" and "Gross Earnings" are practically synonymous, the promulgation of the new Gross Profits Form raises the question—how does it differ from the Gross Earnings Business Interruption form?

The Gross Profits Form indemnifies for the loss determined by applying the rate of gross profit to the shortage in turnover (income) less discontinuable expenses, plus increase in cost of working incurred to reduce the shortage in turnover which is subject to the 100% Coinsurance Clause.

The Gross Earnings Business Interruption form indemnifies for the loss determined by the reduction in "gross earnings" less discontinuable expenses, plus expenses incurred to reduce the shortage in gross earnings which expenses are not subject to the application of coinsurance clause.

The Gross Profits Form has the advantage of (1) indemnifying for loss sustained beyond the date of physical rehabilitation up to the expiration of the Period of Indemnity and (2) indemifying for loss of sales resulting from destruction of a manufacturer's finished goods whether or not production was prevented, since this form does not deny liability for a manufacturer's loss due to destruction of his finished stock. The Gross Earnings Form has the following advantages—it (1) is available with a choice of four percentages of coinsurance 50%, 60%, 70% and 80% whereas 100% coinsurance is mandatory under the Gross Profits Form; (2) exempts expediting expenses from the application of coinsurance whereas the corresponding coverage of "Increase in Cost of Working" provided in the Gross Profits Form is subject to 100% coinsurance; and (3) may be written without a Period of Indemnity and when so written the amount of insurance can be completely exhausted by the payment of loss sustained by the Insured, whereas the Period of Indemnity in the Gross Profits Form limits the Insured's recovery to such Period.

For an illustration of the operation of the Gross Profits Form the reader is referred to the adjustment of an actual loss presented in Appendix No. 7. In that case all standing charges were insured although not fully, accounting for the application of the coinsurance clause to the loss of "Increase in Cost of Working". If, for example, the total of all Standinf Charges had been $75,000, which plus Net Profit of $8,581.70 would have meant a gross profit of $83,581.70 instead of $68,247.70, the Insured's recovery for "Increase in Cost of Working" would have been as follows:

By Clause No. 2 $\dfrac{\$68,247.70}{\$83,581.70} \times \$4,500 = \$3,674.25$

By the Coinsurance Clause

$\dfrac{\text{Amount of Insurance} \dots \$60,000}{\text{Gross Profit} \dots \$68,247} \times \$3,674.25 = \$3,230.03 -$ Item I(b)

The immediately preceding computation illustrates the application of the 100% coinsurance clause reading—"provided that if the Sum Insured by this item be less than the Sum produced by applying the Rate of Gross Profit to the Annual Turnover, the amount payable shall be proportionately reduced."

All rules and regulations, including those relating to Periods of Indemnity and the Premium Adjustment Endorsement, applicable to Business Interruption and Estimated Results Profits policies, apply to the new Gross Profits policy form.

British Columbia Specified Time Forms—Since the Province of British Columbia and the Yukon Territory are the only sections of Canada having Specified Time forms and, as such forms are identical with the Specified Time forms standard in Pacific Coast states, the reader is referred to the discussion which follows.

SPECIFIED TIME FORM IN PACIFIC COAST STATES, BRITISH COLUMBIA AND THE YUKON TERRITORY OF CANADA

The "Specified Time Forms" (No. 7 for Mercantile and

Non-Manufacturing Properties and No. 8 for Manufacturing Properties) derive their name from the two provisions they contain specifying:

(1) Maximum period of time to which the Insured's recovery for loss sustained is limited, and

(2) The number of days to which his recovery, at specified sums per day, for the expenses of heat, light and power, payroll of department heads not under contract, and labor payroll, is limited.

To a limited extent Canadian policies written subject to periods of indemnity short of 12 months may also be termed specified time policies. However, the coinsurance clause in Canadian policies written subject to short periods of indemnity requires the maintenance of insurance equal to the coinsurance percentage of the annual earnings value, and therefore **reduced** rates are granted in consideration of the short periods of recovery. The coinsurance clause in Pacific Coast Specified Time forms, on the other hand, requires the maintenance of insurance equal to the same percentage of the annual Business Interruption Insurance value that the number of months of time coverage elected by the Insured bears to 12 months, so that **increased** rates are required.

For example, when the Insured elects to specify a limit of six months' recovery for a partial or total suspension of business, the coinsurance percentage is 50%, and if four months specified time is elected, the coinsurance percentage is 33%.

In both Specified Time Forms, the Insurance Company assumes liability for the actual loss sustained by the Insured, consisting of.

Item I. The net profits on the business which is thereby prevented;

Item II. Fixed charges and expenses, only to the extent to which they would have been earned had no fire occurred, as follows: Salaries of indispensable employees, superintendents, executives and of employees under contract, taxes, interest, rents, royalties, insurance premiums, advertising, special contracts, dues, subscriptions, directors' fees, accounting expenses, legal expenses and fees, all other fixed charges and expenses not including expenses (if any) listed under Item III, and......................

(Any item enumerated under Item II may be excluded from, or additional fixed charges or expenses may be added to the coverage.)

Item III. Such other expenses, if any, as listed below only to the extent to which they would have been earned if no fire had occurred;

(a) Light, heat and power:

$..................per day for..................days, a total of $..................

(b) Payroll of department heads not under contract:

$..................per day for..................days, a total of $..................

(c) Labor Payroll:

$..................per day for..................days, a total of $..................

(Any item enumerated under Item III may be excluded from the coverage.)

2. It is a condition of this contract that the length of time of suspension for which loss may be claimed:

(a) Shall not exceed........percent (......%) of 365 calendar days;
(Insert same percent as inserted in contribution clause.)

(b) Shall not exceed such length of time as would be required with due diligence and dispatch to rebuild, repair or replace such property herein described as may have been destroyed or damaged;

(c) Shall commence with the date of the fire and not be limited by the date of expiration of this policy.

3. *"Contribution Clause."* It is expressly stipulated and made a condition of this contract that, in the event of loss, this company shall be liable for no greater proportion thereof than the amount hereby insured bears to .... percent of the total of the net profits (Item I) and charges and expenses (as specified in Item II) which would normally have been earned during the period of twelve (12) months immediately following the fire, plus 100% of the total amount specified under Item III.

4. This company shall not be liable under this policy as to net profits for more than the net profits prevented by the total or partial suspension of business nor for charges and expenses in excess of those which must necessarily continue during a total or partial suspension of business, and then only to the extent to which such charges and expenses would have been earned had

no fire occurred; nevertheless this company shall be liable for such expenses as may be incurred for the purpose of reducing any loss under this policy, not exceeding, however, the amount in which the loss is so reduced.

5. In determining the amount of net profits and charges and expenses that would have been earned had no fire occurred, whether for the purpose of ascertaining the amount of loss sustained or in the application of the contribution clause, due consideration shall be given to the experience of the business before the fire and the probable experience thereafter, had no loss occurred.

6. *Resumption of Operations:* If the insured, by resumption of complete or partial operation of the property herein described or by making use of other property, could reduce the loss hereunder, such reduction shall be taken into account in arriving at the amount of loss hereunder.

7. *Special Exclusions:* This company shall not be liable for any increase of loss which may be occassioned by any local or state ordinance or law regulating construction or repair of buildings or structures, nor by the suspension, lapse or cancellation of any lease or license, contract or order, nor for any increase of loss due to interference at the described premises by strikers or other pesons with rebuilding, repairing or replacing the property or with the resumption or continuation of business; nor shall this company be liable for any other consequential loss or remote loss.

The foregoing is the wording of the essential portion of Non-Manufacturing Properties Form No. 7. The Manufacturing Properties Form No. 8 differs therefrom only by the addition of a Raw Stock limitation and the Finished Stock Exclusion Clause.

Coverages for Raw Stock—In Form No. 8, for manufacturing properties, unlimited coverage of raw stock may be included by specific mention (for an increased rate in the case of certain kinds of stock). "Raw stock" is defined to mean the materials and supplies in the state in which the Insured receives them or which have undergone any aging, seasoning, mechanical or other process of manufacture but which have not become finished stock.

When raw stock is covered, the Insurer's liability for loss resulting from its destruction is limited to that period of time for which the amount destroyed would have made operations possible had the fire not occurred, but not exceeding the "specified time" applying under the policy. It will therefore be noted that stock in process is treated the same as raw stock, and the Insured has the alternative of no stock coverage whatever, or full stock coverage at an increased rate if his raw stock is not readily obtainable in the open market or is seasonal.

Differences from Other Forms—Specified Time forms differ from other Business Interruption forms in that:

(1) They provide that the length of time of business suspension for which loss may be claimed shall not exceed a specified percentage (elected by the Insured) of 365 calendar days, such percentage being any one of 10 percentages ranging between 25% (the permissible minimum) and 100%;

(2) They provide for coverage of only the particular fixed charges and expenses which the Insured elects to insure as specified in Items II and III of the form, the latter item providing particularly for coverage of the expense of light, heat and power, payroll of department heads under contract, and labor payroll, each for a specified sum per day, and for a specified number of days;

(3) They contain a contribution clause the percentage of which is the percentage of specified time, to which is added 100% applying to the expenses specified as covered under Item III, and

(4) They provide for coverage of raw stock and stock in process without limit of time other than the basic specified time, i.e., the period of indemnity for which the policy is written.

Specified Time Form Rates—Pacific Coast States of Arizona, California, Montana, Nevada, Utah, Idaho and Alaska —The rates charged for the ten specified periods of indemnity as presented in the following tables are percentages of the 80% coinsurance building rate (termed the "base rate") except that when an 80% coinsurance rate does not apply, the no coinsurance (flat) rate is the basis. The percentages are grouped by the following building construction classes—

Class A: masonry on steel frame.

Class B: masonry on reinforced concrete frame, monolithic reinforced concrete, or masonry walls, floors and roof and steel or reinforced concrete columns.

Class C: ordinary floor and roof construction with brick, stone or concrete block walls.

Class D: frame, veneered, corrugated iron or iron clad on wood or steel frame, or a building inferior to Class C.

(1) Manufacturing Properties:

Contrib. Cls. on Policy	Class A-B	Class C	Class D & All-Steel
100%	84%	84%	84%
92%	91%	89%	88%
83%	100%	95%	92%
75%	110%	102%	97%
67%	122%	109%	102%
58%	139%	120%	109%
50%	158%	130%	116%
42%	184%	142%	123%
33%	225%	155%	132%
25%	280%	168%	140%

No policy shall be written with less than 25% Contribution clause.

(2) Non-Manufacturing Properties:

Contrib. Cls. on Policy	Class A-B	Class C	Class D & All-Steel
100%	78%	78%	78%
92%	85%	83%	81%
83%	93%	88%	85%
75%	102%	95%	90%
67%	113%	101%	94%
58%	129%	111%	101%
50%	147%	121%	107%
42%	171%	132%	114%
33%	209%	144%	122%
25%	260%	156%	130%

In the States of **Oregon and Washington,** the percentages range from 157% for 25% contribution, to 84% for 100% contribution on manufacturing properties, and from 146% for 25% contribution to 78% for 100% contribution on non-manufacturing properties.

In the **Canadian Province of British Columbia,** the Specified Time Form may be used only in renewing the few remaining policies written subject to that form. In such cases the minimum permissible percentage of contribution is now 50%. The percentages of the building rate charged range from 129% for 50% contribution to 102% for 100% contribution for manufacturing properties, and from 116% to 90% for mercantile and non-manufacturing properties.

Although the amount of insurance required by the contribution clause in the Specified Time forms is the percentage of the annual value that the specified time bears to 12 months, whereas the amount of insurance required in connection with the short periods of indemnity in Canadian Business Interruption and Profits policies is determined by the annual contribution percentage of the annual value, regardless of any short period of indemnity in the policy, the comparisons between the increases in time coverage and the increases in premium cost under the two systems are similar, Canadian occupants of non-fire resistive buildings having the advantage, as the following tables disclose:

Specified Time Form Cost Comparisons
For Arizona, California, Montana, Nevada, Utah, Idaho and Alaska

Construction Class	Increase in Period of Indemnity From	To	Increase in Time Coverage	Increase in Specified Time Forms	Premium Cost Canadian Period of Indemnity
A-B	4 mos.	6 mos.	50%	7%	9.4%
	4 mos.	12 mos.	200%	13%	25. %
	6 mos.	12 mos.	100%	6%	14. %
Class C	4 mos.	6 mos.	50%	27%	9.4%
	4 mos.	12 mos.	200%	64%	25. %
	6 mos.	12 mos.	100%	30%	14. %
Class D	4 mos.	6 mos.	50%	33%	9.4%
	4 mos.	12 mos.	200%	94%	25. %
	6 mos.	12 mos.	100%	45%	14. %

Increase in Period of Indemnity		Increase in Time Coverage	Oregon* Wash- ington*
From	To		
4 mos.	6 mos.	50%	34%
4 mos.	12 mos.	200%	113%
6 mos.	12 mos.	100%	60%

*Regardless of construction of building.

Although, with the exception of fire resistive constructed properties, the comparisons under the Specified Time forms are not as favorable as those under the Canadian periods of indemnity, they are nevertheless impressive. For example, a 200% increase (from 4 to 12 months) in the time during which loss is recoverable can be purchased for only 64% increase in the premium cost of the California occupant of a brick building of non-fire resistive construction, and 94% if the building is of frame construction.

The California occupant of a fire resistive building can secure a 200% increase in time for only 13% increase in premium cost!

With the inducement of such cost differentials coupled with the uncertainties the future always holds in respect of time required to rebuild, repair and replace damaged or destroyed buildings and their contents, because of shortages of materials and disturbed labor conditions, the periods of indemnity under Specified Time Forms far short of twelve months should attract only businessmen willing to gamble with heavy odds against them.

THE TEXAS EXPERIMENT

In 1935, the Texas Board of Insurance Commissioners, to meet the demand for policies written for short periods of indemnity, which had resulted in filings by individual companies of policy forms designed to provide insurance for limited periods of business suspension, promulgated Specified Time forms, identical with the Pacific Coast forms, at percentages of the no-coinsurance building rate, ranging from

150% for the 25% Coinsurance Clause for three months coverage, to 70% for the 92% Coninsurance Clause for eleven months coverage.

The experience with the Specified Time forms having proven unsatisfactory, due both to their ambiguity as to the application of the Contribution Clause to fixed charges and expenses, and to the inadequacy of the short periods of indemnity in the face of wartime shortages of materials and equipment, these policy forms were withdrawn in 1943. However, as a concession to the existing holders of policies written subject to such forms, the privilege of using the Two Item Contribution Policy form, with a 30% or 50% Contribution clause at 120% and 100% respectively of the no-coinsurance building rate, was promulgated for coverage under Item I of that form.

In 1945, when the 80% coinsurance replaced the no-coinsurance building rate as the base rate, the rates for 30% and 50% contribution under Item I of the Two Item Contribution form were revised to the following respective percentages of the 80% coinsurance building rate— 130% and 100% for mercantile and non-manufacturing properties, and 140% and 110% for manufacturing properties. For 100% and 80% contribution, the rates promulgated were respectively for mercantile and non-manufacturing properties 60% and 70%, and for manufacturing properties 70% and 80%, of the 80% coinsurance building rate.

Thus Texas became and continues to be the only area in the United States and Canada in which the Two Item Contribution Form is available with a choice of four (30, 50, 80 and 100) percentages of contribution.

The Pros and Cons of Specified Time Forms—Because "East is East and West is West, and never the twain shall meet" has been the situation with respect to the Specified Time Business Interruption forms since they were adopted on the Pacific Coast in 1928, the following pros and cons are presented to aid the reader to understand the features in controversy.

No. 1—PRO—Since Business Interruption Insurance is "time insurance," the Insured should be permitted, for a consideration in premium rate, to buy it in an amount sufficient only for the time he estimates his business can be interrupted by property damage. Many small merchants have purchased the Specified Time form with a short period of indemnity in preference to other forms requiring an amount of insurance they believe to be excessive for their needs. Proponents of the Specified Time Form can point to the combined experience of several loss adjustment bureaus which adjusted a total of 2135 Business Interruption claims in excess of $5,000 during the four years 1953-1956 inclusive, of which 40% were for less than two months, 65% were for less than four months, and 80% were for less than six months. The aggregate of the amounts paid in the group adjusted for less than six months was 64% of the total paid for all losses during the four years.

CON—Specified Time forms tend to promote competition between salesmen based on their differing estimates of time required to rehabilitate the buyers' premises. Whether or not such competition is responsible for inadequate periods of indemnity, the tendency of Insured to be optimistic and to economize in premium payments is likely to result in the purchase of inadequate amounts of insurance, followed by dissatisfaction of Insured in case of losses of unforeseen duration, and ill will toward salesmen and Insurers.

These forms introduce an element of gambling into Business Interruption Insurance, and produce confusion by greatly multiplying the number of choices of coverage open to the buyer. Since short periods of indemnity restrict recoveries for partial as well as total suspensions, the Insured with a 3 Months Specified Time Policy, who sustains a 50% loss for six months, can recover for only three months.

The absence of a period of indemnity under other than Specified Time forms permits recoveries of both partial and total suspension losses up to the amount of insurance for which premium was paid, and provides the factor of safety and the catastrophe coverage which are essential when dealing with earnings losses extending into the uncertain future.

One loss will suffice to illustrate the consequence of short periods of indemnity under the Specified Time form. A Hollywood restaurant, covered for a specified time of 3 months with a 25% Coinsurance Clause, was destroyed by fire. Because of unfavorable weather conditions, unforeseen difficulties attending replacement of special decorations, and controversy over lease conditions, eight months elapsed before business was resumed. The Insured recovered only 40% of their loss whereas, by the payment of 20% more premium for an eight months period of indemnity, 100% of the loss would have been recovered. Obviously this was the result of poor salesmanship, over-optimism, the Insured's misguided desire to economize, or a combination of all three.

No. 2—PRO—Ten percentages of coinsurance are available under the Specified Time form ranging from 25% for a three months period of indemnity, to 100% for a 12 month period of indemnity. One of the advantages to the insured is escape from the coinsurance penalty in case of a partial loss where, for example, the 25% Coinsurance Clause is complied with on an annual basis, but the amount of insurance is less than the amount required for the particular three months during which business is suspended, because the Insured did not purchase insurance sufficient for the busiest consecutive three months.

CON—This is one of the disadvantages to the underwriter. If, for example, the annual value is $120,000, and a partial loss occurs during the Insured's busiest period of three months, when the value is $40,000 (instead of the average of $30,000), the underwriter pays the full amount of the loss, although he has only 75% insurance to full value for the three months involved.

However, the Insured's recovery for a partial loss in an amount disproportionate to recovery in case of total loss can occur under all forms of property insurance. In this example, the Insured would recover only $30,000 were the loss total to the $40,000 value for the three months.

No. 3—PRO—The Specified Time Form provides a means of specifically insuring certain items of expense elected by the Insured for coverage whereas, under other contribution policy forms, insurance based on the coverage of all expenses (excepting only heat, light and power and ordinary payroll under the Two Item Form) is mandatory.

CON—Even the most ardent supporters of the Specified Time form deplore its ambiguity as to the application of the Contribution Clause to charges and expenses.

The conflicting interpretations arise because Item II of this form provides for the coverage of certain specified "fixed" charges and expenses elected by the Insured, and "all other fixed" charges and expenses, not including expenses (if any) listed under Item III; and Item III provides for specific coverage of (a) light, heat and power, (b) payroll of department heads not under contract, and (c) labor payroll, each for a specified sum per day for a specified number of days elected by the Insured.

The Contribution Clause applies to net profits, and to the "charges and expenses as specified in Item II," plus 100% of the total amount specified under Item III.

The differing interpretations arise because the coverage is of "fixed" charges and expenses, and because the extent to which items of business expense necessarily continue and therefore can be said to be "fixed" frequently depends upon the extent and duration of business suspension. A certain item of expense which necessarily continues in the event of a short and/or partial suspension of business may be unnecessary and therefore discontinuable in case of a long and/or total suspension of business.

Therefore one interpretation, the one accepted by the majority of loss adjusters and underwriters on the Pacific Coast, is that the Contribution Clause applies only to the charges and expenses that are necessarily continuing, i.e., "fixed" in the event of a total suspension, and, therefore, if the amount of insurance is based upon the annual amount of those items of expense, the Insured will recover, without coinsurance penalty, the full amount of a partial loss, including recovery of expenses which, though necessarily continuing, are not in the basis of coinsurance application because they are discontinuable in the event of a total suspension.

Another interpretation is that expenses that necessarily continue during a short or partial suspension are also "fixed" and, since they are therefore included in the basis of coinsurance application, the Insured is subject to a coinsurance penalty unless the annual amounts of practically all charges and expenses are included in the application of coinsurance.

This difference of interpretation cannot arise under the Two Item and the Gross Earnings Contribution Business Interruption forms, which require that the annual amount of all expenses, whether or not continuing, excepting only ordinary payroll and heat, light and power expense under the Two Item Form, be included in the basis of the application of their Contribution Clauses.

No. 4—PRO—Item III of the Specified Time form provides means of insuring (a) heat, light and power expense, (b) payroll of department heads not under contract, (c) labor payroll, each for a specified sum per day of business suspension for a specified number of days, however few the Insured may desire, with 100% contribution applied accordingly.

The Two Item Business Interruption form requires the expense of heat, light and power and payroll of department heads to be insured for 80% of the annual expense and, if ordinary payroll is insured, requires 80% of that expense to be insured for at least 90 days.

The Gross Earnings form requires all these items to be insured for the minimum of 50% of the annual expense.

CON—This feature of the Specified Time form is admittedly of advantage to the Insured who is shopping for the least possible coverage and the lowest premium cost. It is not for the Insured seeking coverage of a catastrophe loss which may be sustained at some future time, the conditions of which cannot be accurately forecast. The specified sums per day for the specified maximum number of days may be very inadequate.

This feature is obviously objectionable to underwriters who are thereby faced with total losses under the elected items of coverage without commensurate compensation.

No. 5—Pro—Businesses requiring amounts of Business Interruption Insurance beyond the capacity of admitted domestic insurance companies, when based on a 12 months period of indemnity, can purchase primary insurance under the Specified Time form with short periods of indemnity without danger of coinsurance penalty, supplemented by insurance written by non-admitted companies on an excess of time basis.

CON—The Specified Time form is not the only policy providing primary coverage as the basis for excess insurance. Other forms can serve as such primary coverage, with the excess insurance written to pay loss sustained in excess of the amount of loss recoverable after the coinsurance penalty has been suffered.

The purchase of Excess insurance to pay on an excess of time basis which is fixed, admittedly may present less difficulty than the purchase of excess insurance written to pay the loss sustained above the amount recovered from the primary insurance which may be less than anticipated because of the operation of coinsurance and other clauses, and therefore may throw a greater loss upon the excess insurance than the underwriter anticipated.

No. 6—PRO—The Specified Time form coverage of a manufacturer's raw stock and stock in process for the full period of indemnity, without extra charge except for raw stocks that are seasonal or not readily obtainable in the open market, is an advantage in some industries, such as lumber, compared with the 30 day gratis coverage under other forms, and the extra premiums charged for coverages exceeding 30 days.

CON—This feature of the Specified Time form is admittedly of advantage to manufacturers, but it is not necessarily inherent in a form of the Specified Time type. It could again be adopted for other Business Interruption forms from which it was eliminated in favor of the 30 day gratis coverage (which may be extended for an additional premium) because all manufacturers do not need full coverage, and to increase the premium cost of all manufacturers because of the few who require full coverage is unfair discrimination.

CHAPTER 12

WARTIME METHODS

Since shortages of time, materials and labor created tremendous difficulties in connection with the National Defense Program of 1940 and the subsequent Wartime Program, it is necessary to review the events of 1940-1945 in relation to our national economy to understand the effect of wartime conditions upon Business Interruption Insurance in the United States.

Historical Background—The war between Great Britain and Germany began officially on September 3, 1939. Thereafter, Germany invaded Poland and other countries, entering Paris in June 1940, joining forces with Italy and Japan in September 1940.

Meanwhile, the United States took the first step toward arming itself for any eventuality by creating a National Defense Council in May, 1940. Geared for only normal peacetime production, American Industry began the tremendous job of manufacturing desperately needed aircraft and other munitions for national defense. An alerted nation rolled up its sleeves.

The Selective Service Act was passed and drafting of manpower began. London suffered its worst air raid in May, 1941. Germany invaded Russia the following month, and the United States pledged support to Russia to the extent of $1,000,000,000 Lend Lease aid. Then came Pearl Harbor, December 7, 1941, and declaration by the United States of war with Japan, Germany and Italy.

Meanwhile, to assure ample supplies of vital raw materials and tools for defense industries, the Federal Government created the Defense Supplies Corporation and the Office of Production Management. More than 1,600 factories for manufacturing aircraft and other munitions were being constructed or enlarged.

Because of shortages of essential and critical materials, and to assure that such materials as were available be rationed and channeled to factories with Government contracts for Army and Navy needs, a Priority or Preference Rating System was set up. Ratings expressed in a continuous series of AAA to B-8 indicated the relative importance and urgency of various uses of materials in the national defense economy. Munitions manufacturers were given "A" ratings, and various civilian uses were classified in the "B" series, according to their importance.

Prime contractors were furnished rating certificates which could be extended to their subcontractors, of which there were many thousands, thus spreading defense work and speeding up production. One large prime contractor in New York utilized the facilities of more than 1,000 subcontractors located in many states.

Among the essential and critical materials were alcohol, aluminum, asbestos, camphor, chromium, copper, cork, hides, iodine, jute, manganese, mercury, mica, nickel, opium, paper, petroleum, platinum, quinine, rubber, silk, steel, sugar, tanning extracts, tin, tugsten, wheat, wool and zinc.

Conservation Order L-41—Learning from the experience gained in administering the original priority regulations, the Federal Government issued the famous Conservation Order No. L-41 in April, 1942. As participation in the war effort increased, this Order became more and more restrictive.

For instance, on September 2, 1942, the Order was amended to prohibit the reconstruction of any building which had been damaged or destroyed after September 7, 1942, by fire, flood, tornado, earthquake, Act of God, or the public enemy, unless its immediate reconstruction was necessary for the prosecution of the war or the protection of public health or safety, and unless the reconstruction was specifically authorized by the War Production Board, after receipt of an application giving all the facts justifying reconstruction.

As the war program claimed more and more goods for

military purposes, civilians experienced increasing shortages in many of the materials they customarily used. The
American people learned that, in a choice between military
and civilian goods, the choice was for military requirements.
Retailers and householders felt the pinch of priorities. Supplies of household articles, such as kitchen utensils, washing
machines, refrigerators, were strictly curtailed. Business
offices experienced difficulty in buying typewriters, adding
machines, metal filing cabinets and desks.

Since time was of the essence of the National Defense and,
later, the War Program, and since the Priorities System was
designed to prevent shortages of vital materials and to decrease the time required to manufacture equipment for the
armed forces, and inasmuch as time is also of the essence
of Business Interruption Insurance, priorities affected the
size of earnings losses and the underwriting of Business
Interruption Insurance.

Insurance companies were increasingly reluctant to write
Business Interruption Insurance particularly without proportionate participation in the Property Damage Insurance
on the same property, which produces greater premium income per dollar of liability for loss. Business Interruption
Reinsurance was obtainable only with great difficulty.

Limitations of Period of Indemnity—Where employed to
facilitate the rehabilitation of a war supplies factory following property damage, priorities reduced Business Interruption losses. Where a priority rating was not obtainable following property damage, substantially increased Business
Interruption losses resulted. It was therefore natural that
alarmed underwriters studied ways and means to minimize
the effect of Priority Regulations upon Business Interruption Insurance.

The first step was taken in August, 1941, when (except
in the Midwestern states) a Period of Indemnity of 12
months was inserted in all Business Interruption forms,
providing that claim for any loss, whether it be partial or

197

total, be limited to the loss sustained during the 12 months following the occurrence of a fire.

Provision was made for increasing the Period of Indemnity in multiples of 3 months, i.e., to 15, 18, 21, 24 or more months, (nevertheless limited to the time required to repair, rebuild or replace) by an endorsement which also increased the basis of contribution to correspond, thereby proportionately increasing the amount of insurance needed to comply with the requirement of the contribution clause. Concurrently, coverage of replacement of a manufacturer's raw stock was limited (except in Midwestern states) to 30 days, unless extended by endorsement for an additional premium. In Midwestern states, the rate charged was increased 30% when replacement of raw stock was covered.

Controversy arose respecting the correct interpretation of the provision in all Business Interruption forms that the Insurance Company "shall not be liable for any loss which may be occasioned by any ordinance or law regulating construction or repair of buildings."

Some claimed that the reference to a "law" is sufficiently broad to include Federal directives such as Priority Regulations, others claiming that the reference is only to local ordinances controlling the rebuilding of such damaged or destroyed buildings as are located within Fire or Zoning Limits of a municipality.

This difference of opinion among loss adjusters, underwriters, agents, brokers and buyers of Business Interruption insurance, coupled with the increasing threat of Priority Regulations to the loss ratio, resulted, in March, 1943, in the promulgation in all except two states (Indiana and Missouri) of the following Priorities Exclusion Clause, to be attached to all new and renewal Time Element forms of insurance policies (Business Interruption, Rents, Extra Expense, Leasehold Interest), unless the Insured paid double the normal rate.

198

PRIORITIES EXCLUSION CLAUSE

"In consideration of the rate and premium at which this policy is written, it is a condition of this insurance that this Company shall not be liable for any loss resulting from additional time required to rebuild, replace, or repair any property herein described as a consequence of any law, Governmental order, provision or directive, regulating, prohibiting or restricting, directly or indirectly, construction, the acquisition of machinery, equipment, material, labor, or other means required for the replacement or repair of any property damaged or destroyed."

Three Types of Policies—The promulgation of this Priorities Exclusion Clause resulted in the existence of three types of outstanding policies:

(1) Policies written at normal rates without the exclusion clause before the clause was promulgated.

(2) Policies written with the exclusion clause at normal rate.

(3) Policies without that clause, written at double rates subsequent to the promulgation of the clause.

Time Element Assumption Endorsement—The question then arose—does the same interpretation, respecting the extent of liability for an increase in loss due to the enforcement of priority regulations, apply to policies in both groups (1) and (3)? This question was definitely settled in June, 1943, by the promulgation of the following Clause to be attached to all policies written at double rates without the Priorities Exclusion Clause.

TIME ELEMENT ASSUMPTION ENDORSEMENT

"In consideration of the rate and premium at which this policy is written, it is a condition of this insurance that notwithstanding any provision of the policy excluding liability for loss caused by order of any civil authority or any provision in the policy or form attached thereto excluding loss which may be occasioned by any ordinance or law regulating construction or repair, this Company shall be liable, subject to all other conditions and limitations of the policy, for loss resulting from additional time (not exceeding the maximum limit of time, if any, specifically stated in this policy) required to rebuild, replace, or repair property herein described as a consequence of any law, governmental order or directive which regulates, prohibits or restricts construction, the acquisition of machinery, equipment, or other means required for the replacement or repair of property damaged or destroyed; but in no event shall this Company be liable for any delay which may be caused, directly or indirectly, by any local law or ordinance regulating construction or repair.

"This Company shall not be liable for a greater proportion of any loss than the amount of insurance under this policy bears to the whole amount of insurance, whether valid or not and whether collectible or not, applying to any part of the liability assumed under this policy whether or not other insurance covers or excludes in whole or in part liability assumed by this endorsement."

Following the promulgation of this clause buyers of Business Interruption Insurance who feared that the enforcement of Priority Regulations would increase the period of suspension of their business due to property damage, chose the Time Element Assumption Clause and paid double rate, while buyers who were engaged in manufacturing essential war materials, or while manufacturing civilian goods chose to chance a shortage of recovery in the event of loss rather than pay double rate, accepted the Priorities Exclusion Clause.

This situation continued until, following VE Day, May 8, 1945, and VJ Day, August 14, 1945, the Priorities Exclusion Clause and the double rate charge were abrogated as of August 21, 1945, and the Time Element Assumption Clause was permitted to be attached to all Business Interruption and other Time Element policies without increase in rate, a pro rata reduction to the normal rate to be allowed on all outstanding policies written at double rate. In 1950 policy forms were revised to deny liability for any increase in loss occasioned by "local or state" ordinances or laws eliminating the need for the Time Element Assumption Clause.

Postwar Shortages—Although Conservation Order L-41 was revoked effective October 15, 1945, Business Interruption Underwriters were not permitted to relax. In the face of widespread demand for civilian materials and equipment for which the nation had starved, severe shortages became manifest, resulting in March, 1946, in the promulgation from Washington of the Veterans Emergency Housing Program Order, diverting all essential materials from deferable and less essential construction to the construction of the large number of housing accommodations needed for returning veterans. Underwriters of Business Interruption Insurance covering the premises of businesses not engaged in supplying housing needs, including related mechanical equipment, were then faced with the prospect of increased losses due to the enforcement of the Veterans Emergency Housing Order, but without benefit of the double rate which had been abrogated in August, 1945.

Although this order was revoked June 30, 1947 strained relations with Russia resulted in the threat of renewed shortages due to increased efforts to improve the size of the nation's stockpile of many critical strategic materials. Meanwhile the European recovery program (Marshall Plan) was being promoted, Congress enacted a new Selective Service Act authorizing the drafting of both persons and industry to fill the needs of the armed forces, which resulted in the adoption in 1950 and 1951 of a system of priority ratings for manufacturers producing equipment and supplies for such forces.

Elimination of "Twelve Months Period of Indemnity"— Even though the combined results of these developments were to accentuate the prospects of increasing shortages of materials, supplemented by the threat of a labor shortage as the nation's labor force, already strained to the utmost, was depleted by the requirements of the armed forces, and notwithstanding Business Interruption Insurance underwriters had therefore reason to again fear increased losses due to delays in rehabilitating damaged or destroyed business premises, the New England Fire Insurance Rating Association

201

on July 30, 1948, eliminated the "Twelve Months Period of Indemnity" from all policy forms, followed by similar action by the other Fire rating bureaus which had adopted that restriction as a wartime measure in August, 1941.

Since the Twelve Months Period of Indemnity was in effect during four war and three post-war years, it is of considerable interest and value to record the following figures, taken from the experience of one of the large loss adjustment organizations, disclosing the comparison between the number and amount of the losses extending to 12 months and over, and the totals for all losses adjusted where the individual loss exceeded $5,000.

	Total Adjusted		12 Months or Over	
	Number	Amount	Number	Amount
12/7/41 to 1/11/45	197	$ 5,957,256	4	$ 127,984
In 1945	98	3,252,937	2	381,693
In 1946	112	4,519,257	12	1,438,191
In 1947	118	6,845,935	9	2,904,393
	525	$20,575,385	27	$4,852,261

It will be noted that only 5% of the total number of losses in excess of $5,000 that were adjusted were for suspensions of 12 months or more and that, of the total number adjusted during the war years 1941-1945, only 2%, representing only 5½% of the total amount paid, were for 12 months or more; moreover, that 9% of the total number adjusted in the post-war years of 1946 and 1947, before the Twelve Months Period of Indemnity was withdrawn representing 38% of the total amount paid, were for business suspensions of 12 months or more. During the years 1949-1951 only 2% of the number of losses representing 8% of the total amount paid, were for 12 months or more.

It therefore appears that the Twelve Months Period of Indemnity was of greater use during the post-war years than during the period of wartime conditions, in fear of which it was adopted.

Since the Priorities Exclusion and Assumption Clauses, prescribed in 1943 and withdrawn in 1945, had a greater effect upon the size of claims paid during the period of wartime controls and shortages than did the Twelve Months Period of Indemnity, manifestly the Priorities Clause method of mitigating the effects of wartime rationing and controls, coupled with increased rates charged for unlimited coverage, is the preferable method of adjusting the writing of Business Interruption Insurance to wartime conditions.

One objectionable feature of the Twelve Months Period of Indemnity to the Insured was the requirement that the denominator of the contribution fraction, be increased in proportion to any increase in the period of indemnity. Taking into consideration the substantial salvage in discontinuable expenses in the case of business suspensions of 12 months and longer, the Insured required to maintain insurance equal to the contribution percentage of 15 or 18 or 24 months' earnings could not hope to recover 100% of the amount of insurance he was thus forced to maintain.

For discussion of extension of the Period of Indemnity beyond the date rehabilitation of damaged property is completed, the reader is referredto Chapter 11 "Canadian Methods."

CANADA

War Changes in Canada—Canada was at war with Germany 27 months before the United States officially entered the conflict and, by a prodigious mobilization of her resources and manpower, nearly trebled her industrial capacity to produce ships, aircraft, tanks and munitions of war, thereby rising to second place among the exporting nations of the world, with four-fifths of her exports made up of war goods.

Although the effect upon Business Interruption Insurance of priority and other Government regulations and restrictions was as great as the effect of corresponding regulations in the United States, the only modifications of Canadian Business Interruption Insurance procedure were (1) incorporation of a Twelve Months Period of Indemnity in every new and renewal policy not written subject to a Period of Indemnity shorter than 12 months; (2) withdrawal of the term rate multiple privilege, thereby limiting policies to annual terms so as to permit annual review of premium rates; and (3) revision of that portion of the Special Exclusions Clause which referred to "ordinance or law regulating construction or repair of buildings" to read—"ordinances or laws requiring different construction from that of the property destroyed."

By this revised phraseology, priority regulations were eliminated from consideration although, in the United States, a Priorities Exclusion and a Priorities Assumption Clause were required, the latter in consideration of the payment of double the normal rate.

The mandatory Twelve Months Period of Indemnity was withdrawn in August, 1944, and concurrently the three year term privilege was restored except for policies written subject to the Premium Adjustment Clause. The revised phraseology referring to ordinances or laws requiring different construction from that of the property destroyed has become the established wording for all Time Element insurance policies in Canada.

Chapter 13

RATING METHODS

The Basis of the Rates—Manifestly the rate charged for a policy of Business Interruption Insurance should measure the probability and severity of loss, and produce a volume of premium income for underwriters adequate to cover losses, expenses and a reasonable profit.

Although Business Interruption losses result from damage to objects such as buildings, equipment, or materials, and Property Damage rates measure probability and severity of loss to such objects, Property Damage rates alone are not an adequate measure of Business Interruption loss, since they do not take the time element into consideration. Property Damage rates are therefore merely the foundation upon which Business Interruption rates are constructed.

Theoretically, the Business Interruption rate of one building, or a group of buildings, should be less than or exceed its property damage rate, depending upon whether the Business Interruption loss is expected to be less than, or more than the property loss per dollar of value. In practice, however, Business Interruption rates are very rarely higher than property damage rates applying to the same property, a condition which, while indefensible as respects some properties when individually considered, meets with general approval since, over a long period of time and as respects innumerable properties, the loss ratio (the ratio of losses paid to premium income) of Business Interruption Insurance has been lower than the loss ratio of Property Damage insurance.

Numerous instances could be cited of the illogical results produced by the present methods of determining Business Interruption rates. For example, Property Damage insurance covering a single building, because of effective sub-divisions into fire sections, is subject to only a 25% loss, but

Business Interruption Insurance covering the same building is subject to a substantially higher percentage loss because of the time required to rehabilitate the damaged or destroyed section.

Similarly, a plant consisting of four well separated buildings of equal physical value suffers only a 25% loss to Property Damage insurance when one building is destroyed but, because that building housed a bottleneck process, suffers a substantially higher percentage of loss to Business Interruption Insurance.

On the other hand, the destroyed section of another similar single building, or the destroyed building of another plant of four well separated buildings, might suffer a physical property loss of a greater percentage to Property Damage insurance than the percentage of loss to Business Interruption Insurance because the destroyed section, or building, was of little importance in the production of earnings.

Nevertheless, the operators of both the single buildings and both the plants in these examples can enjoy the same rate per $100 of Business Interruption Insurance purchased. When we ponder such inconsistencies and, while criticizing the rating system that produces them, nevertheless tolerate the results, we do so not only because of the satisfactory loss ratio and the operation of the law of averages which alone justify the means, but also because experience has taught us to be satisfied with the simple rating system that has been evolved.

Evolution of Rating System—For whatever value they may have to the student and others interested in the evolution of Business Interruption Insurance rates, the principal developments in the rating system are here recorded.

In the beginning, rates were "open," i.e., each underwriter quoted the rate he believed to be adequate or was constrained by competition to quote. As sales multiplied and the need for regulation grew, rating bureaus adopted the simple procedure of determining Business Interruption rates by means of fixed percentages of the Property Damage insurance rate on buildings, discriminating between mercantile and manufacturing properties, between buildings of fire resistive and ordinary construction, and between properties equipped and not equipped with automatic sprinkler protection.

The First and Only Analytic Rating Schedule—As the volume of Business Interruption Insurance increased and critics of the percentage method argued convincingly that, since business premises differ as to details capable of increasing or reducing Business Interruption losses, an analytic rating schedule was adopted in the form of the "System for the Measurement of the Use and Occupancy Hazard," first promulgated in Midwestern states in 1917, and largely the product of the rating genius of the late J. V. Parker, then manager of the Western Actuarial Bureau.

Since this schedule, which was subsequently adopted in all other territories, is now obsolete, it is here described for its historic value, and as a record of the fact that a scientific attempt was made over a long period of time to determine the price of Business Interruption Insurance by means of an analytic rating schedule. The particular edition of the schedule described is the one in effect when it was withdrawn in Midwestern states in June, 1929.

"SYSTEM FOR THE MEASUREMENT OF THE USE AND OCCUPANCY HAZARD"

Manufacturing Properties—The schedule prescribed two "Basis Rates," both based upon the 80% Coinsurance rate of the building and its additions, or of the group of buildings rated as a single fire risk.

Where 50% or more of the floor area was of fire resistive construction, the basis rate was 80% of the building rate; where less than 50% was fire resistive, the basis rate was 70% of the building rate. In each case the basis rate was for the Per Diem Policy form, the final rate being convertible into rates chargeable for the Weekly and Contribution forms. Charges or credits, determined by the following percentages of the basis rate, were added to the basis rate:

For **Machinery,** add 50% if not obtainable in the domestic market (meaning the market found in the United States or markets connected thereto by rail), or 20% if obtainable in the domestic market but only as made on special order.

For **Process,** add 20% if the various stages of the manufacturing process are so interdependent that the process must be continuously carried on, so that the crippling of a single machine or process in any section would cause an interruption of the process (power plant machinery not to be considered in applying this charge). If the process includes the picking of the stock, 20% additional was charged when the stock picked was in whole or in part cotton.

For coverage of replacement of **Raw Stock,** 50% was added if stock was obtainable only during certain seasons, or was not readily obtainable in the open market, doubling the charge when the building being rated was used principally for storage of raw stock.

For favorable sources of **Power,** the following deductions were authorized:

(a) If machines in machinery divisions are separately operated by individual motor drive supplied with current generated in a separate fire division____ 10%

(b) If two or more groups of machines in machinery divisions are separately operated by motor drive supplied with current generated in a separate fire division _____ 5%

(c) If there are two or more independent sources of power, each of sufficient capacity to operate the plant, and so located in reference to each other that both sources will not be normally subject to damage by the same fire_____ 10%

If credit is given under either (a) or (b), reduce credit under (c) to 5%.

No reduction under (c) to be made when all sources of supply are from the outside.
Credits under (a) and (b) are not cumulative.

When a plant was not a single fire risk, each building was rated by the foregoing schedule. Where there was an interdependency between different buildings, 20% was added to the Use and Occupancy rate of all buildings (except power houses and finished goods warehouses), and all buildings were grouped into four classes: (A) Power Plant; (B) Buildings with process requiring machinery; (C) Buildings with handwork process only, and (D) Storehouses.

If there was more than one building or fire division in any one of the classes A, B, C, or D, the rate for Use and Occupancy on the class was obtained by multiplying the Use and Occupancy rate of each building or fire division by the total floor areas of such building or fire division, and dividing the sum of these results by the total floor area of all buildings and fire divisions in the class.

When the Insured occupied only a part of a building, the floor area actually occupied was considered in determining its contribution to an average Use and Occupancy rate.

To obtain the rate for use and occupancy for the entire plant, the rate for each class was multiplied by the percentage indicated in the following table, showing apportionment according to classes of buildings included. The sum of the resulting percentages was the Use and Occupancy rate for the plant.

Average rates for blanket Use and Occupancy insurance covering on different risks or plants not interdependent were prohibited, even if they were owned and/or operated by the same Insured.

Table of Percentages

Machinery Process								
Power Plant..........A	30	31	35	0	38	0	0	0
Buildings ....B	50	53	59	80	62	95	0	85
Handwork Process								
Buildings C	15	16	0	15	0	0	75	15
Storehouses .... D	05	0	06	05	0	05	25	0
	100%	100%	100%	100%	100%	100%	100%	100%

Any class C building or section having a total floor area not exceeding 5%, and any class D building or section having a total floor area not exceeding 20% of the total floor area of all class A, B, C and D buildings for which an average rate was being computed, was disregarded. When this resulted in the elimination of all the buildings, the above table was applied as if there were no building of that class.

If processes of different plants under same ownership were interdependent, 20% was added to the Use and Occupancy rate of each plant, and the blanket rate over all plants was obtained by multiplying the Use and Occupancy rate of each plant by the total floor area of such plant, and dividing the sum of the results by the total floor area of all plants.

Non-Manufacturing Properties—As in the case of Manfacturing Properties, the Schedule prescribed "Basis Rates," depending upon whether 50% or more, or less than 50%, of the floor area was of fire resistive construction. Where the policy was written to cover only building, machinery and equipment, the basis rate was based upon the 80% coinsurance building rate. Where coverage of stock was included, the basis rate was based upon the 50/50 average of the 80% coinsurance building and contents rates.

Average rates for use and occupancy insurance covering on or in different fire divisions were obtained by multiplying the Use and Occupancy rate of each division by the total floor area of such division, and by dividing the sum of these results by the total floor area of all divisions. Warehouses were not considered in arriving at the average rate unless the rate of any or all warehouses exceeded the rate of the main building or buildings.

When the foregoing analytic rating schedule was withdrawn in June, 1929, in the Midwestern states, the Rating Bureaus returned to the simple method of taking a fixed percentage of the building rate, without regard to type of building construction.

Warehouses of non-manufacturing properties were treated as they were treated under the schedule. The raw stock charge in the schedule was continued but reduced to 30%. Average rates for properties consisting of more than one fire division were (as they are today) computed by the floor area method, i.e., by multiplying the rate of each division of a non-manufacturing property or of only each machinery process division of a manufacturing plant, by the total floor area of such division, and dividing the sum of the results by the total floor area of all such divisions, ignoring power houses and heating plants of manufacturing plants except when the factory is entirely dependent upon its power plant; then 10% of the rate of the power plant was added to the average rate only if the rate of the power plant exceeded 110% of the individual rate of all process divisions.

The action of the Midwestern states in abandoning the analytic schedule was eventually followed in other territories, although the substitution of the simple percentage method was delayed in Eastern states until 1937 because a general reduction in Business Interruption rates on manufacturing plants was feared, due to the high level of rate which had been produced by the indiscriminate application by some Rating Bureaus of some of the charges in the schedule.

The reasons for the withdrawal of the analytic rating schedule can be attributed to:

1. The lack of uniformity among rating bureaus in the interpretation and application of the charges and credits, particularly the 20% charge for interdependency of processes, which some bureaus inflicted in every case while others employed it with discrimination, resulting in considerable friction between Bureaus, agents and brokers,

2. The dissatisfaction with the results obtained by the "Table of Percentages" method of computing average rates,

3. The necessary promulgation of a specific Business Interruption rate on every manufacturing plant, and

4. To a large number of test applications of substitute methods which demonstrated that a level of rates practically the equivalent of that produced by the use of the analytic schedule could be produced by the simple percentage method without the addition of charges and credits.

So ended the only attempt by means of a schedule to modify the basic Property Damage rate of a building or plant by penalizing conditions likely to increase, and rewarding conditions likely to reduce, Business Interruption Insurance losses.

The complaint heard now and then that Business Interruption Insurance rates are unscientific will doubtless continue to be voiced by those unfamiliar with the history of the development of Business Interruption rating procedure. But students of underwriting and rating will agree that the differences between business premises, and between cycles in the national economy are so many and varied in respect to the effect of the time element on Business Interruption losses, that a schedule sufficiently refined to recognize all possible variations would be so cumbersome as to be highly impracticable.

So long as the simple straight percentage method presently used to determine Business Interruption rates produces a volume of premium income sufficient to pay losses, expenses and a reasonable profit, it should be adequate. Should it fail at any time to achieve that objective, a simple readjustment of the percentages of the Property Damage rate will suffice.

Stock Coverage Rating Methods—Basically, premiums charged for Business Interruption Insurance have always been determined by rates applying to the coverage of buildings, machinery and equipment, with higher rates provided when stock is included in the coverage of the policy.

This procedure stems from the choice of covering or not covering stock which was originally available to buyers of Business Interruption Insurance, and from the fact that stock is the principal requirement that a merchant or manufacturer continually purchases in a market which is affected by seasonal conditions, transportation facilities, supply and demand, which singly or in combination determine the speed with which stock can be replaced if destroyed.

Various methods of determining the higher rates charged when stock is covered have been tried. One method has been to use the 50/50 average of the building and stock property damage rates in place of the building rate alone, as the basis for the application of the percentage method. Another method is to increase the building, machinery and equipment coverage rate by a fixed percentage. The Analytic Schedule employed the 50/50 average method for mercantile and non-manufacturing properties, and a percentage loading for manufacturing properties. The present procedure is based upon the gift to the Insured of 30 days coverage of raw and in process stocks and a charge for coverage in excess of 30 days; and the gift of full coverage of mercantile stocks.

The present charge for coverage of raw and in process stocks in excess of 30 days is 10% of the policy rate (exclusive of charge for off premises power coverage) for each additional 30 day period of coverage purchased, subject, in some territories only, to a maximum of 25% for an unlimited additional period.

It should be noted that wherever the term "stock" is used in the foregoing description of rate treatment, allowance must be made for the different kinds of stock used, depending upon the nature of the Insured's business. As discussed in greater detail in Chapter 10, the term "stock" as applied to mercantile properties refers to the merchandise sold including packing material, whereas in manufacturing properties there are three kinds of stock—"raw," "in process" and "finished," the latter being excluded from the coverage of Business Interruption Insurance.

The charges mentioned, since they are made for each day of coverage purchased by the Insured in excess of the 30 days granted free of charge, carry out the purpose of underwriters that each Insured purchase as much stock time coverage as he desires, thereby recognizing the widely varying conditions affecting the replacement of "raw stock" and the reproduction of "stock in process," and relieving the rating bureaus of thenecessity of indiscriminately prescribing a fixed charge.

If, as predicted in Chapter 10, the 30 day restriction is eliminated, it is probable that rates published for factories normally requiring prolonged periods of time to replace their raw stocks, or stocks in process, damaged or destroyed, will include charges designed to pay underwriters for the abnormal prospects of loss.

Average Rates—Floor Area and Other Methods—The various methods that have been employed to compute an average Business Interruption Insurance rate for blanket coverage of differently rated units or fire divisions, have used property values, Business Interruption values, floor areas, the numerical or arithmetical average of specific rates, and the table of percentages which was part of the analytic rating schedule.

The latter was abandoned when that schedule was abandoned. The numerical or arithmetical method (the sum of the specific rates divided by the number of rates) has been used in some territories only in computing Contingent Business Interruption rates when two or more Contributing properties are blanketed.

Except in Pacific Coast states, Business Interruption Insurance "values" are not used since they are trustworthy only when the blanketed units or divisions are operated independently of each other and therefore have a specific "value." Property values are not used because they are seldom identical with earnings values whether or not the blanketed units or divisions are operated independently of each other. The only universally surviving method is the "Floor Area Method" whereby the total floor area of each differently rated unit or division is multiplied by its specific Business Interruption Insurance rate and the sum of the products is divided by the total floor area of all the units or divisions.

Although the "Floor Area Method" has been criticized for producing inequitable average rates in some instances, it must be conceded that it cannot be abused as the Value Method has been and can be abused. Statements of distribution of Business Interruption values have been and can be unscrupulously adjusted so as to produce lower average rates than are earned and, moreover, in the case of interdependently operated locations, it is manifestly impossible to assign a Business Interruption value to each location except by means of estimates, when the estimator is tempted to magnify the value at low rated locations, and vice versa.

Under the Floor Area Method, however, the basis, i.e., the floor area of each building, is a fixed and easily determinable figure, determined by a disinterested Rating Bureau, which is not susceptible to alteration or disagreement. Moreover, there is, in most cases, a definite relation between the floor area of a building and the importance to the whole of the operations conducted therein. Of course there are exceptions but, on the whole, the Floor Area Method has stood the test of time, particularly in connection with computations of average blanket rates covering interdependently operated locations.

Comparison of Floor Area and Value Methods—Assuming the distribution of the floor areas and the Business Interruption rates of three buildings interdependently operated by a business are as follows, the average rate of a Business

Interruption Insurance policy written to blanket the three buildings is .39, using the rates assumed in this example.

Building	Floor Area		Rate		Area Premium
A	50,000	×	.20	=	$100
B	30,000	×	.30	=	90
C	20,000	×	1.00	=	200
	100,000				390
					.39 average

Assuming the property values were as follows, the average Business Interruption Insurance rate would be .366 if computed by the Property Value Method, as follow:

Building	Property Value		Rate		Premium
A	$300,000	×	.20	=	$600
B	200,000	×	.30	=	600
C	100,000	×	1.00	=	1000
	$600,000				2200
					.366 average

If the average rate were computed on the basis of Business Interruption "values" resulting from the liberal use of imagination respecting the earnings value of each building operated interdependently with the other buildings, where the estimator succumbs to the temptation to assign highest "values" to the lowest rated buildings, the result **could** be an average rate of .281 computed as follows:

Building	Earnings Value		Rate		Premium
A	$500,000	×	.20	=	$1000
B	250,000	×	.30	=	750
C	50,000	×	1.00	=	500
	$800,000				2250
					.281 average

These examples are designed to show that, while property values can fluctuate with values of materials and equipment, and both property values and earnings values can fluctuate with the imagination or design of the person estimating such values, the floor areas are fixed and not open to disagree-

216

ment, and produce average rates that discriminate fairly between Insureds requiring blanket coverage.

In the same way and for the same reason that the Floor Area Method is used to compute the average rate of a policy blanketing units or divisions of the Insured's business premises situated at one location, it is also used to compute the average rate of a policy blanketing the premises of the Insured situated at two or more locations in the same or different cities and states, as described in Chapter 9.

Average Rate for Blanket Coverage of Manufacturing and Non-Manufacturing or Mercantile Properties—In the majority of territories, when Business Interruption Insurance is written to blanket Manufacturing and Non-Manufacturing and/or Mercantile Properties, the rate and area applying to any Non-Manufacturing and/or Mercantile property is included in the computation of the blanket coverage rate by the Floor Area Method only if the rate of such property exceeds 110% of the Business Interruption rate of the manufacturing properties. In such event the blanket coverage rate shall not exceed (a) 150% of the rate applying to the manufacturing properties, nor (b) the rate applying to the manufacturing properties increased by 10% of the highest Business Interruption rate applicable to any Non-Manufacturing or Mercantile Property included in the blanket coverage.

This formula is evidently intended to apply when the Insured's business is predominantly manufacturing both as respects earnings and area occupied, preventing low rated non-manufacturing or mercantile locations from depressing the blanket rate below the rate of the manufacturing location. But when the Insured's business is predominantly non-manufacturing or mercantile, both as respects earnings and area occupied, the formula can produce a substantially reduced premium cost when a large mercantile establishment is blanketed with a small low rated manufacturing plant, as the following examples demonstrate:

217

	Rate		**Area**		
Store	.60	×	100,000′	=	600
Factory	.20	×	5,000′	=	10
			105,000′		610

Average rate by Floor Area Method................................ .58
150% of Factory Rate... .30
Factory rate .20 increased by 10% of .60....................... .26

Since the lowest rate applies, under this formula the Insured secures insurance at the rate of .26, which would cost .60 if only the store were covered by the policy, or .58 if the Floor Area Method were followed.

In the territories having the new form of Combined Manufacturing and Mercantile Operations Endorsement designed to blanket the Insured's manufacturing operations at certain locations and mercantile sales operations at the same or other locations, as described in Chapter 10, the rate for such endorsement is the highest of two rates, one computed by the floor area method applied to covered warehouses wherever located as well as to processing areas, the other computed by the floor area method applied only to processing units of the covered manufacturing plants.

Special Rating Schedules for Coal Mining Properties— In the coal mining states of Virginia and West Virginia, the "Table of Percentages" method of computing average Business Interruption rates continues to apply to coal mining properties. By this method all structures of a mining property are grouped into three classes, as follows:

Class "A"—Power House, Sub-stations, Hoist House at shaft or slope mines, Boiler House when used in connection with Power or Hoist House.

Class "B"—Tipple, Washer, Head House and Drum House.

Class "C"—Fan House.

In the process of computing an average rate for the Two Item Contribution form, 93.5% of the 80% coinsurance property rate of each structure of a shaft or slope mine is first found. If the property being rated is a drift mine, where hoisting apparatus for conveying coal to the surface of the ground is not required, 77% is used in place of 93.5%.

If there is more than one structure in any of the three classes, the class rate is determined by adding together the rates of the different structures in the class, and dividing the result by the number of structures in the class.

The rates for the three classes are then averaged by means of the following "Table of Percentages," the sum of the products being the average rate:

Class A_____Class rate × 35%
Class B_____Class rate × 50%
Class C_____Class rate × 15%
_____
100%

Underground Coverage—Since the Business Interruption form excludes underground coverage, the rates applying to underground fans and sub-stations are excluded from the computation of the average rate. If the policy is extended to cover underground property by either of the standard form endorsements available for that purpose, additional rate charges are as prescribed in the Manual of Rules of the state Rating Bureaus. (See Chapter 16.)

In the **midwestern coal mining states,** the same "Table of Percentages" method was used prior to December, 1937. Since then, average rates for coal mining properties have been determined by the same method used for manufacturing properties, disregarding fan houses, hoist houses, pump houses, sub-stations and other auxiliary buildings.

When there is more than one machinery process division, the average rate is determined by the floor area method, using only ground floor areas and excluding areas occupied by open trestles. When strip mining operations involve only the use of power shovels, the Business Interruption rate of the entire operation is the rate of the highest rated shovel.

219

Underground coverage is available but state Manuals of Rules should be consulted for wording of endorsements and additional rate charges. (See Chapter No. 16.)

In **Pennsylvania,** the Table of Percentages Method was abandoned for the simple procedure of determining the average rate by taking 77% of the Business Interruption rate of the breaker or the tipple, as the case may be, for insurance under Item I of the Two Item Form. Manifestly this method, compared with the Table of Percentages method, produces a higher average rate when the rate of the breaker or tipple is the highest rate of any structure covered by the policy, and a lower average rate when it is the lowest rate. Underground coverage is available—(see Chapter No. 16).

Rating Treatment of Miscellaneous Properties—To this point, the discussion of Business Interruption Insurance rates has been concerned only with buildings, their contents, and supplies required for a Mercantile or Manufacturing business. Occasionally, Business Interruption Insurance rates must also be determined for equipment such as outside hoisting, conveying or drilling apparatus, radio broadcasting towers and antennae, and metal smoke stacks.

When, infrequently, insurance is written to cover separately any one of such items of equipment, the rate charge is determined by the percentage of 80% Coinsurance property insurance rate applying to the equipment, according to the form of policy purchased.

But when, as is usually the case, they are bottlenecks in the operation of a business, and are therefore properly covered blanket with the buildings and other property of the business, it is necessary that the blanket coverage rate include a charge designed to reflect their relative importance as cogs in the Insured's business operations.

Originally, attempts were made to apply the Floor Area method to determine the blanket coverage rate but since such items of equipment are without floor area, it was necessary to assign floor areas to them arbitrarily. For instance, it was assumed that the floor area of a pair of radio broadcasting towers and the antennae they supported, was the ground area between lines drawn connecting the base of the towers. When such attempts produced absurd results the system of flat charges which is presently in effect in the majority of states was adopted, the charges purporting to be proportionate to the full Business Interruption Insurance rate of the item of equipment considering the estimated time for replacement in the event of destruction.

Manuals should be consulted for such charges, which will be found to vary by territory, particularly as to charges for Windstorm coverage, since such forms of equipment are especially vulnerable to damage by windstorm.

RATING TREATMENT OF CONTINGENT COVERAGES

1. **Contributing and Recipient Properties Coverages—** When Contingent Business Interruption Insurance (see Chapter 9 for analysis) is written to apply to only one named Contributing or Recipient Plant not owned or operated by the Insured, the former rate charge of 100% of the Business Interruption Insurance rate of such plant has been reduced to 50% to recognize both the probability that other facilities will be available to reduce the loss, and the favorable loss frequency.

When Contingent Business Interruption Insurance is written to apply to two or more named Contributing or Recipient Plants, the rating formula in most territories provides that the rate be 50% of the highest direct Business Interruption rate applying to any of the named plants under a comparable type of policy form and contribution clause, without regard to stock coverage. This formula eliminates the possibility which existed under former formulas, that the rate for contingent coverage be less than 50% of the rate for direct coverage on the highest rated named plant.

However, since unnamed plants may be included in the coverage without change in rate, the formula does not prevent the rate charged from being considerably lower than the rate of the highest rated **unnamed** plant (which may exceed the rate of the highest rated named plant) is believed to be offset by the limitation upon the Insured's recovery due to loss occurring at such unnamed plant, to one half of one percent of the policy amount per month of business interuption (see Chapter 9.)

Regardless of the location of the Contributing or Recipient plants in states other than the state in which the Insured's plant is situated, the rates prescribed by the Rating Bureau having jurisdiction over the territory in which the Insured's plant is located, are the required Contingent Coverage rates.

2. Off Premises Power, Light, Heat, Gas and/or Water Contingent Coverage—(See Chapter 9 for analysis.) When direct forms of Business Interruption policies, written to cover property situated within the Insured's premises, are extended by endorsement to cover Public Utility or privately operated sources of electric power, light, heat, gas or water, located outside of the Insured's premises, the rates prescribed by the various Rating Bureaus for the extension of coverage are flat charges which are practically uniform, differing materially only as to Extended Coverage and Windstorm Coverage because of the territorial differences in the degree of the Windstorm hazard. The system of flat charges superseded the original system whereby 50% of the Business Interruption rate of the covered off premises Power Plant was the rate charged for Contingent Coverage applying thereto.

3. Selling Agents Commissions and Income from Personal Services Contingent Coverages—(see Chapter 9 for analysis).

The rates charged for these coverages vary by territories.

Usually the rate for Selling Agents Commissions Insurance is the rate for Gross Earnings Business Interruption Insurance with a choice of four percentages of contribution, while the rate for Loss of Personal Income Insurance is the 80% Contribution Clause rate for the building in some states; for the contents in others; and the Two Item Form rate plus 10% in other territories if the business is mercantile or non-manufacturing, or 25% if manufacturing, the latter increase being designed to compensate for the contingent coverage of "finished stock." Loss of Personal Income Insurance deserves a higher rate than Selling Agents Commission Insurance because of possible greater loss recoveries.

Automatic Sprinkler Equipped Properties—The methods of determining Business Interruption rates described in the preceding pages apply to sprinkler equipped as well as to non-sprinklered properties, except as to details, varying by territories, which apply to "superior risks," i.e., properties of such excellence of construction, protection, surveillance. occupancy and maintenance, as to justify preferential treatment and rates below the level of ordinary property.

Among the details of "superior risk" treatment are use of the blanket building and contents instead of the building rate as the base rate to which the Business Interruption rating factors are applied; unlimited gratis coverage of raw stock and stock in process replacement; and use of the Agreed Amount in lieu of a percentage contribution clause.

CHAPTER 14

UNDERWRITING BUSINESS INTERRUPTION INSURANCE

When applied to Business Interruption Insurance, the term "underwriting" refers to the process of determining, (1) whether the management and the premises of a business applying for Business Interruption Insurance is an acceptable risk for such coverage and, (2) the extent to which the funds of the Insurer should be risked to provide such coverage for the applicant.

Decisions under both sections of the process are the responsibility of the underwriter who is an employee of the Insurer, but the commissioned policy-writing Agent of the Insurer is not relieved of responsibility under (1) nor under (2) to the extent he is informed respecting the underwriting policies of his principal. Neither is the Broker, who is primarily the Insured's representative, relieved of all responsibility under (1), nor unconcerned respecting the result produced under (2).

In short, both Agents and Brokers are concerned with the art or science of underwriting. Moreover, the Insured is not without interest in the underwriting process, since it determines his ability to buy Business Interruption Insurance.

Primarily, this chapter is designed to acquaint Agents, Brokers and Insureds with the underwriting process to assist them to understand the reasons motivating the Insurer in discriminating between offerings of Business Interruption Insurance, both as respects acceptance and rejection, and the size of the amount of insurance accepted.

For the purposes of this analysis, the following frequently used terms are here defined:

Risk—the property which is the object of insurance.

Loss Estimate or Loss Expectancy—the probable amount of loss estimated or expected by the underwriter, expressed as a percentage of the amount of insurance on the risk.

Basic Line—the amount of insurance which the underwriter is prepared to lose on the risk being underwritten.

Net Line—the portion of the amount of insurance on a risk which the underwriter is willing to retain for the account of the insurance company.

Gross Line—the sum of the net line and the amount of reinsurance, if any, ceded by the reinsured insurance company to one or more reinsuring companies.

Reinsurance—the portion of the amount of insurance written by the reinsured (ceding) company which exceeds its net line, and is ceded by it to the reinsuring company or companies.

Acceptability—If the Insurer is offered Business Interruption Insurance on a risk on which he is committed for Property Damage Insurance, the underwriter determines the acceptability of the risk for property damage insurance, both as a subject for insurance and the amount of the basic line, through a process appraising the quality of the building construction, private and public fire protection, the degree of combustibility and susceptibility to damage, considering the hazards inherent in the risk and in the character of the contents of the building, the nature and proximity of property exposing the risk, the quality of the management and the loss history.

If the acceptability of the risk and its basic line have not been determined, it is necessary that both be determined by appraising the features above, just as though property damage insurance were being underwritten.

In short, both the acceptability of, and the basic line applicable to the risk for which Business Interruption Insurance is being underwritten, must be determined before the process of deciding whether the risk is one upon which the underwriter is justified in accepting Business Interruption insurance begins.

Generally speaking, a risk upon which property damage insurance is acceptable is also acceptable for Business Interruption Insurance, but there are exceptions which will be explained.

Exceptions to Acceptability—Since earnings, including profits are the subject of insurance, the careful underwriter investigates the degree of the Insured's business activity and prospects, taking into consideration locality, competition, supply of materials, power and labor, shipping facilities, and the salability of the Insured's product or merchandise. Even though the earning of a net profit is not a condition necessarily precedent to the eligibility of a risk to Business Interruption insurance, and the policy covers only to the extent that the amount claimed in the event of loss would have been earned had no loss occurred, a careful underwriter will be favorably influenced by evidence that the risk is being profitably operated, with good prospects, and unfavorably influenced if the reverse obtains.

Assuming that the underwriter is satisfied that he is justified, to this point, in accepting Business Interruption Insurance on the risk under investigation, he must then determine its Business Interruption loss estimate before he can decide the amount of Business Interruption Insurance, i.e., the net line, he can accept. In doing so, many factors, each involving the time element, will affect his decision, as follows:

1. Is the Insured's business seasonal? If so, how are the merchant's sales, and the manufacturer's sales and production, distributed by seasons? A total loss may result if operations are suspended for the entire operating season.

2. Does the Insured operate other properties? If so, where are they located? What is the function of each? Are they operated independently of, or interdependently with, the

risk being underwritten? If they are operated independently, do their operations duplicate those of the risk being underwritten, and/or can they assist in reducing the amount of a Business Interruption loss? If they are operated interdependently with the risk being underwritten, full information respecting the degree of interdependency should be secured, for use in case they are covered blanket with the risk being underwritten.

3. Are the Insured's operations dependent upon materials, parts of products, power, heat, gas, water or other necessities furnished by other concerns? If so, where are the sources of supply located? What is the function of each?

4. Are there competitors of the Insured from whom assistance can be secured in the event of suspension of the Insured's operations because of property damage, thereby reducing the amount of Business Interruption Insurance loss?

5. What effect is the climate likely to have upon the time to rehabilitate the risk in the event of property damage?

6. Is the risk located within the fire limits of a municipality, because of which it may not be rebuilt if damaged in excess of a specified percentage of value or size, except of a superior type of construction requiring additional time?

7. Is the construction of the building such as to require prolonged time for repair or reconstruction?

8. Are processes or machines in duplicate? If in duplicate, are the duplicate processes or machines in separate buildings, or in sections of the same building cut off from each other in a standard manner?

9. Are bottleneck machines or production units speedily replaceable in the domestic market, or are they custom built or imported?

10. Is the merchandise sold by the Insured (if a Merchant), or are the raw materials from which the Insured (if a Manufacturer) produces a finished product, readily obtainable in domestic markets? If not, where is the source of

supply, and what is the probable time required to replace? Are substitutes feasible and available?

11. Does the Insured (if a manufacturer) have a considerable amount of materials in process of manufacture at any one time? What is the average time of processing from raw to finished product? Is aging or seasoning required, and for what period of time?

12. Which Business Interruption Insurance policy form is used to cover the risk being underwritten? What is the percentage of contribution? If the insurance is written subject to a period of indemnity, what is the period? If raw stock or stock in process is covered for more than 30 days, what is the period of such coverage?

The skill with which he selects or rejects risks, and weaves the answers to these questions into an accurate Business Interruption Insurance Loss Estimate determines the measure of the underwriter as a producer of a trading profit for the company he represents.

Underwriting Time Insurance—While the underwriter must know the physical divisions of the risk being underwritten, either by vertical or horizontal barriers to the spread of damage caused by the peril or perils insured against, he must always keep in mind that he is underwriting a form of insurance in which time is the principal element, and that physical divisions and distribution of property values by such divisions are not also indicative of the division of the productive capacity, the distribution of the earnings, or the loss expectancy in terms of the time required for rehabilitation.

The underwriter must not permit himself to use a low loss expectancy because the risk is divided into many sections by fire walls or open spaces between buildings, nor to use a high loss expectancy simply because the risk consists of a single building of one open area. A risk may have a loss estimate of 10% for property damage insurance but merit a 100% loss estimate for Business Interruption Insurance because of the loss expectancy of a bottleneck; or it may have a loss estimate of 100% for property damage insurance but merit a 50% or 75% loss estimate for Business Interruption Insurance.

Illustration of Time Bottleneck—To illustrate the extent to which the property damage and Business Interruption Insurance loss estimates of a risk might possibly differ, assume a factory consisting of many well detached buildings, one of which represents 10% of the total value of all buildings and contents, and contains the specially constructed machinery of an essential process involved in the manufacture of the finished product.

If the building (the bottleneck of the factory) is destroyed, the property damage insurance, which covers all buildings and contents blanket, will sustain a 10% loss, but the Business Interruption Insurance, which also blankets all buildings and contents, will sustain a loss equal to the earnings of the Insured prevented by a complete suspension of production of the entire factory for the period required to rebuild the bottleneck building and replace the special machinery it contains. This might be a matter of many months, resulting in a Business Interruption loss of a percentage many times the 10% loss sustained by the property damage insurance.

On the other hand, the destruction of a single building housing a factory or mercantile establishment causing a 100% loss to property damage insurance might cause only a 50% or 75% loss to Business Interruption Insurance, because the loss of net profit and necessarily continuing expenses sustained during the time required to rebuild the building and replace its contents do not exceed 50% or 75% of the amount of the Business Interruption Insurance.

Determining Acceptable Net Line—A few examples will illustrate the procedure followed by the underwriter in determining the net line he can accept on a risk upon which he is offered Business Interruption Insurance.

Assume the underwriter has determined upon a basic line of $10,000, and loss estimates of 50% for property damage insurance and 100% for Business Interruption Insurance.

1. If he were writing only property damage insurance on that risk, the underwriter would retain a net line of $20,000, 50% of which is the basic line of $10,000.

2. Were the underwriter to write only Business Interruption Insurance on that risk, he would retain a net line of only $10,000, which at a loss estimate of 100%, produces the basic line of $10,000.

Assuming the building insurance rate of the risk is 1.00 and the Business Interruption rate is .80 per $100 of insurance, the underwriter would in each case receive the following premium and sustain the loss indicated, provided his loss estimate proves to be accurate:

	Net Line		Rate	Premium	Loss Expectancy
(1)	$20,000	×	1.00 =	$200	$10,000
(2)	10,000	×	.80 =	80	10,000

But, as so frequently occurs, the underwriter is requested to participate in both the property damage and Business Interruption Insurance and therefore is confronted by the problem of apportioning most advantageously his participation between both forms of insurance so that his total net line on the basis of different loss estimates will not exceed the basic line of $10,000. This objective can be attained by any one of the following apportionments:

	Insurance	Net Line	Loss Estimate	Amount Subject	Rate	Premium
(A)	Property Damage	$10,000	50%	$ 5,000	1.00	$100
	Business Int.	5,000	100%	5,000	.80	40
		$15,000		$10,000		$140

230

(B) Property Damage	$15,000	50%	$ 7,500	1.00	$150
Business Int.	2,500	100%	2,500	.80	20
	$17,500		$10,000		$170
(C) Property Damage	$ 5,000	50%	$ 2,500	1.00	$ 50
Business Int.	7,500	100%	7,500	.80	60
	$12,500		$10,000		$110

Assuming the underwriter is committed for $15,000 property damage insurance, and is pressed to accept $15,000 Business Interruption Insurance in addition, giving him a total commitment of $30,000, which alternative will he take?

Probably he will try to arrange his participation in accordance with the apportionment (B), retaining all of the $15,-000 property damage insurance, and securing $12,500 Business Interruption reinsurance.

If he cannot secure that amount of reinsurance to apply wholly to Business Interruption coverage, which is very likely to be the case, he will try to secure reinsurance of $5,000 property damage and $10,000 Business Interruption, under Apportionment (A). If that fails, as it probably will, he is forced to apportionment (C), securing reinsurance of $10,000 property damage and $7,500 Business Interruption, and be satisfied with a premium income of $110 instead of $170 under Plan (B) or even $140 under Plan (A). The underwriter's predicament is caused by the unwillingness of reinsuring companies to accept a disproportionate participation in the low rated, high loss estimate Business Interruption Insurance, just as the underwriter is unwilling to do so for his own company.

What if the loss estimates were reversed, 100% for property damage and 50% for Business Interruption Insurance? On that basis, the apportionment would be as follows, corresponding to (A), (B) and (C) above:

231

Insurance	Net Line	Loss Estimate	Amount Subject	Rate	Premium
(D) Property Damage	$ 5,000	100%	$ 5,000	1.00	$ 50
Business Int.	10,000	50%	5,000	.80	80
	$15,000		$10,000		$130
(E) Property Damage	$ 7,500	100%	$ 7,500	1.00	$ 75
Business Int.	5,000	50%	2,500	.80	40
	$12,500		$10,000		$115
(F) Property Damage	$ 2,500	100%	$ 2,500	1.00	$ 25
Business Int.	15,000	50%	7,500	.80	120
	$17,500		$10,000		$145

If the underwriter was justified in assigning a loss estimate as low as 50% to the Business Interruption coverage, he would undoubtedly select Apportionment (F) as productive of the greatest premium income and, since it provides for the full amount of $15,000 Business Interruption Insurance to be written, it requires that the reinsurance would be entirely on property damage, which would probably be secured without difficulty.

However, realistically, the underwriter would probably not feel justified in assigning a loss estimate as low as 50% to the Business Interruption coverage, and would instead assign 75%, reasoning that the uncertainty as to the length of time required to rebuild and re-equip the risk does not justify a loss estimate less than 75%.

Therefore, the underwriter would probably select the following apportionment as offering the best prospects for securing the needed reinsurance from reinsuring companies desiring participation in both forms of insurance proportionately to the reinsured company's net lines.

Insurance	Net Line	Loss Estimate	Amount Subject	Rate	Premium
(G) Property Damage	$ 5,000	100%	$ 5,000	1.00	$50.00
Business Int.	6,666	75%	5,000	.80	53.33
	$11,666		$10,000		$103.33

From these examples, it will be seen that where the loss

estimates are 50% Property Damage and 100% Business Interruption, the premium income received for a basic line of $10,000 is as follows:

Insurance	Net Line	L/E	Basic Line	Rate	Premium
If only Property Dam.	$20,000	50%	$10,000	1.00	$200
If only Bus. Int.	10,000	100%	10,000	.80	80
If both by Plan (C)	12,500	——	10,000	——	110

Also, that where the loss estimates are 100% Property Damage and 75% Business Interruption, the premium income received for a Basic Line of $10,000 is as follows:—

Insurance	Net Line	L/E	Line	Rate	Premium
If only Property Dam.	$10,000	100%	$10,000	1.00	$100.00
If only Business Int.	13,333	75%	10,000	.80	106.66
If both by Plan (G)	11,666	——	10,000	——	103.33

These examples apply only when a single risk is the object. When two or more risks are the object by reason of property damage and Business Interruption Insurance, either or both, being written to blanket all risks involved, the process is not essentially different, as the following examples demonstrate:

Assume Plant A, to which the underwriter has assigned a basic line of $25,000 and loss estimates of 50% property damage insurance and 100% Business Interruption Insurance.

Assume Plant B, to which the underwriter has assigned a basic line of $50,000, and loss estimates of 100% property damage insurance and 75% Business Interruption Insurance.

Assume both forms of insurance are written blanket over both plants, with property values divided 50% at Plant A and 50% at Plant B, and that because of the interdependency of operation by reason of production bottlenecks, 100% of the Business Interruption Insurance must be regarded as applying to **either** plant.

Since Plant A has the lowest basic line, it is the key unit in the underwriting process.

In the following example

L/E=Loss Estimate
D   =Distribution of Value
B/L=Basic Line

Insurance	Net Line	At Plant "A" L/E × D = B/L	At Plant "B" L/E × D = B/L
Property Dam.	$40,000	50% of 50%=$10,000	100% of 50%=$20,000
Business Int.	15,000	100% of 100%= 15,000	75% of 100%= 11,250
	$55,000	$25,000	$31,250

By this apportionment, the underwriter has arranged his net lines so as to achieve two objectives: A total basic line of not exceeding $25,000 at Plant A and a preponderance of property damage insurance, which produces the greater premium income because of the higher rate.

If compelled to retain a greater Business Interruption Net Line in order to secure Business Interruption Reinsurance sufficient to permit him to write a large Business Interruption gross line, nevertheless holding his basic line at the key plant A to not exceeding $25,000, the underwriter might adopt the following apportionment.

Insurance	Net Line	At Plant "A" L/E × D = $25,000	At Plant "B" L/E × D = $50,000
Property Dam.	$20,000	50% of 50%=$ 5,000	100% of 50%=$10,000
Business Int.	20,000	100% of 100%= 20,000	75% of 100%= 15,000
	$40,000	$25,000	$25,000

The latter two examples also illustrate how Business Interruption Insurance, when written blanket over two or more risks because of interdependency of the Insured's business operations, acts to reduce the amount of the underwriter's net lines, as compared to the net lines he could retain if the Business Interruption Insurance were written to apply to each plant specifically, as in the following example:

234

Insurance	Specific at Plant "A"			Specific at Plant "B"		
	Net Line	L/E	B/L	Net Line	L/E	B/L
Property Dam.	$20,000	50%	$10,000	$20,000	100%	$20,000
Business Int.	15,000	100%	15,000	40,000	75%	30,000
	$35,000		$25,000	$60,000		$50,000

Even though the basic lines of $25,000 for Plant A and $50,000 for Plant B are not exceeded in this example, the total amount of insurance upon which he receives premium is the sum of the specific lines of $35,000 and $60,000, or $95,000 total, compared with $40,000 in the immediately preceding example, and with $55,000 in the second preceding example, in which both forms of insurance were written blanket.

Obviously, as many different results of the underwriting process can be obtained as there are different combinations of loss estimates and net lines. Just as underwriters differ in experience and temperament, ranging from the conservative to the rash, so loss estimates, particularly when they include appraisal of the uncertain time element involved in Business Interruption insurance, will differ and basic lines will vary.

CHAPTER 15

EXTRA EXPENSE INSURANCE

Any discussion of Business Interruption Insurance is incomplete if it omits consideration of Extra Expense Insurance as the alternative and sometimes supplementary coverage.

Historical Background—Although the first policy form and rating formula promulgated in any territory was published by the Board of Fire Underwriters of the Pacific on October 1, 1935, there is evidence that Extra Expense Insurance had been written in that and other territories during at least the preceding 15 years.

Who Needs Extra Expense?—Since the forms of Business Interruption Insurance available then and now require the maintenance of insurance in amounts large enough to cover loss of earnings for the major portion of the year, it is natural that businesses and service rendering enterprises, which can continue operations without loss of income with the assistance of other facilities, should desire a form of insurance designed to reimburse the Insured only for the expense of securing such assistance in excess of the expense that would be incurred had not property damage occurred. Extra Expense Insurance is designed to satisfy that desire.

The list of at least the principal businesses and service enterprises that may be attracted to Extra Expense Insurance, includes the newspapers, laundries, power plants, and milk and ice delivery businesses, for the exclusive use of which the original contract was promulgated on the Pacific Coast; also the following: Dry cleaners, garbage collection and incinerator companies, oil and gasoline distributing companies, bottling plants, bleacheries, magazine publishers, banks, educational institutions, churches, fraternal organi-

236

zations, hospitals, sanitariums, asylums, old people's homes, poor houses, orphanages, municipal buildings, court houses, funeral homes, offices (administrative, abstract, professional) and dwellings.

It is evident that if suitable temporary premises are available for immediate operation by the Insured, or if there are other organizations in the same line of business immediately available and willing to assist, for a consideration, in carrying on the business, Extra Expense Insurance will be enough, since it will reimburse the Insured for the expense, in excess of normal incurred to operate temporary premises, or purchase assistance from other organizations.

If there is any possibility that other organizations or suitable temporary premises will not be available when the emergency arises and, therefore, the income of the business, the premises of which have been damaged or destroyed, will be wholly or partially suspended, Business Interruption and not Extra Expense Insurance should be carried since it provides coverage only of the extra expense incurred to continue the Insured's operations.

Extra Expense Items—Among the many items of such extra expense are rent of temporary premises and equipment, cleaning and equipping temporary premises, moving equipment, extra production and clerical labor, advertising, printing, telephone, telegraph, messenger, traveling and legal charges, watchman, insurance, bonuses, cost of outside assistance, transportation.

Manufacturing Risks—Chief among the manufacturing businesses favorably situated and disposed toward Extra Expense Insurance are newspapers, because of the general understanding and frequently the specific agreement between newspapers in the same or nearby towns to go to each other's assistance in case of emergency.

However, conditions can be such that even a newspaper will prefer Business Interruption Insurance, as evidenced by the many that carry it in preference to Extra Expense Insurance. Some carry both forms for a reason explained later.

Since manufacturers or processors (such as laundries, creameries, ice, bottling and printing plants) must depend on others in their industry for assistance in carrying on their business, their ability to secure such assistance depends not only upon the willingness of competitors to furnish it by operating their machinery overtime, thereby risking breakdowns, but also upon the availability of the necessary labor.

The marked decrease in the amount of Extra Expense Insurance written during the recent war years was undoubtedly due to the extent to which industries were normally operating overtime, and were unable or unwilling to incur the risk of operating their plants overtime to assist a competitor.

Non-Manufacturing Businesses—Among the non-manufacturing and non-processing service enterprises for which Extra Expense Insurance may be an acceptable substitute for Business Interruption Insurance are educational institutions, hospitals, sanitariums, funeral homes, and offices such as abstract, professional, medical and others requiring special equipment. Enterprises for which only Extra Expense Insurance is suitable are banks, churches, fraternal organizations, public institutions (asylums, old people's homes, poor houses, orphanages, and court houses), and purely administrative offices. Dwellings constitute a third group requiring a form of Extra Expense Insurance known as "Additional Living Expense Insurance."

Offices—Chief among the non-manufacturing enterprises for which Extra Expense Insurance is being purchased are offices and banks. Due to the need for continuing their normal and very necessary operations with a minimum of lost time, offices must incur large amounts of expense to secure, prepare and equip temporary premises in which to carry on their operations.

Abstractors, architects, accountants, attorneys, consulting engineers, real estate and insurance agencies must incur substantial expenses to expedite the re-establishment of their offices, and the re-creation of their records.

Physicians, dentists and opticians are in the same situation, except that they must also incur extra expense to secure speedy replacement of their specialized equipment, and because of this should consider seriously whether Business Interruption Insurance is preferable to Extra Expense Insurance.

Administrative offices also should be covered by Extra Expense Insurance, to secure reimbursement for the extraordinary expense of securing and equipping temporary quarters and reproducing essential records.

The fact that a large number of Insurance Companies, Agents and Brokers are purchasing Extra Expense Insurance on their offices indicates that the sellers of this form of insurance thoroughly believe in what they sell.

Banks—Because of the essential public service they render, banks are in greatest need of Extra Expense Insurance, as was demonstrated by the largest Extra Expense Insurance loss of record which was paid to the Central National bank of Chicago (Deposits $65,000,000) because of the fire which destroyed the bank on March 31, 1947.

Fortunately, the cash, securities and vital records in the fire resistive vaults of the two story and basement brick building were saved, and the Extra Expense Insurance of $25,000, purchased several years previously, had been increased to $100,000 four days prior to the fire.

With the use of temporary quarters in a vacant building and some rented teller's cages of another bank, business was resumed at 10 A. M., eight hours after the start of the fire. Subsequently other and larger temporary quarters were secured.

BUSINESS INTERRUPTION INSURANCE

The extraordinary expenses incurred in the emergency measures, detailed in the following tabulations, exhausted the Extra Expense Insurance of $100,000 in less than half of the period of indemnity of 12 months, subject to which the insurance was written, and during which the Bank's Extra Expense loss was estimated to be at least $193,000.

TABULATION OF EXTRA EXPENSES—CENTRAL NATIONAL BANK

APRIL

Police protection.................................$	3,284.35
Watch service and A.D.T...............	9,675.39
Armored service to move money and records	3,579.41
Rent and heat—temporary quarters	6,321.19
Trucking and moving expense............	3,545.62
Special bonuses to employes............	8,871.50
Announcements, radio and newspaper advertising...............	11,384.02
Outside bank service. (Continental Illinois)	4,598.27
Engineering service	750.00
Meals and cabs for employes........	1,740.73
Special burglary insurance............	500.00
Installation of temporary telephones	245.00
Rental and use of cars...............	390.29
Rental of office equipment............	71.60
Misc. expense	1,049.55
Total, April	**56,006.92**

MAY

Police protection	170.00
Watch service and A.D.T...............	7,256.41
Rent and heat—temporary quarters	5,577.00
Trucking and moving expense............	147.70
Special bonuses to employes........	3,470.40
Engineering service	750.00
Installing telephones	719.86
Rental and use of cars...............	204.34
Rental of office equipment............	462.50
Misc. expense	499.58
Total, May	**19,257.80**

JUNE

Police protection, watch service and A.D.T.	3,217.14
Rent and heat—temporary quarters	5,799.02
Trucking and moving expense........	144.61
Special bonuses to employes............	275.00
Rental of air conditioning equipment	1,094.48
Misc. expense	127.52
Total, June	**10,657.77**

JULY

Police protection, watch service and A.D.T.	3,242.20
Rent of temporary quarters............	5,414.83
Rental of air conditioning equipment	1,094.48
Misc. expense	15.00
Total, July	**9,766.51**

AUGUST

Watch service and A.D.T...............	3,271.83
Rent of temporary quarters............	5,410.50
Rental of air conditioning equipment	1,094.48
Total, August	**9,776.81**

SEPTEMBER

Watch service and A.D.T...............	2,850.67
Rent of temporary quarters............	5,377.00
Rental of air conditioning equipment	1,094.48
Total, September	**9,322.15**

BALANCE OF YEAR

Extra watchman and watch service—estimate	6,000.00
Rental of temporary quarters........	26,852.19
Misc. expense—estimate	2,500.00
Total, Oct. 1, 1947 to March 31, 1948	**35,352.19**

Cost of miscellaneous fixtures and installations at temporary quarters

Signs and cards	1,607.89
Sanding floors and floor coverings	1,585.11
Partitions, tellers cages, counters and kindred temporary work............	32,075.52
Electric wiring and fixtures............	3,714.99
Window shades	232.55
Plumbing	477.96
Burglar alarm system............	1,811.35
Dictograph system from tellers cages to bookkeeping department	2,583.61
Bullet proof cage............	1,632.00
Painting of temporary quarters............	4,025.00
Purchase of safes for records (50% of actual cost)............	8,265.11
	58,011.49
Less salvage value of same—estimated	14,657.00
Total cost of misc. fixtures, etc.....	43,354.49
Total value and loss	**193,494.73**

That small as well as large banks need Extra Expense Insurance was demonstrated when the Zeeland (Michigan) State Bank burned and during the ten months in which temporary quarters were occupied, incurred the following extra expenses:

Watchman Services and extra help for drying and cleaning and refiling records	$1,500.00
Temporary scaffolding, wiring, plumbing, boarding up premises and extra vault and alarm expenses	905.00
Extra bank equipment expenses	450.00
Rental of temporary quarters	630.00
Temporary fixtures for banking quarters	400.00
Miscellaneous items	500.00

The foregoing and similar experiences of other banks doubtless influenced the American Bankers Association to include this statement in its publication—"Digest of Bank Insurance,"

"Banking is a business in which it is imperative that normal operations be continued after a fire regardless of the additional expenses incurred. For this purpose Extra Expense Insurance is particularly applicable. It furnishes indemnity for the excess cost of using other premises and equipment belonging to others and other necessary emergency expenses.—Decision as to buying Extra Expense Insurance for any banking quarters should rest upon the exposure hazards involved. Damage or destruction of bank premises may result from explosion, hurricane or flood, but the principal source of such loss would be fire or lightning. The exposure or potentiality of loss by fire, of course, must be measured by the quality of construction of the bank's premises and the contents thereof, whether a sprinkler system is maintained, etc. Equally important are the extraneous conditions, such as extra hazardous buildings or types of business therein which may adjoin or be located sufficiently close to the bank building to cause damage through the spread of or by "communicating" fire. Another outside factor is the degree of efficiency and prompt response to alarm which may be expected from the fire department and the quality of its fire fighting apparatus."

Newspapers—The importance of Extra Expense insurance to newspapers was demonstrated in December 1948 when the plant of the Daily News Tribune of LaSalle, Illinois was destroyed by fire. Following the procedure that has become established among newspaper publishers (because of which Extra Expense Insurance was originally devised) the publishers of the Republican Times of Ottawa, Illinois, 15 miles distant from LaSalle, came to the rescue of the Daily News Tribune by agreeing to print its editions until the destroyed plant was reconstructed. The extra expenses incurred by the Daily News Tribune, which aggregated $24,-778.53 during the two months and ten days required to resume operations in their rebuilt plant, included the following items: Operating expense charged by the Republican Times; contract job printing sublet; transporting employees between LaSalle and Ottawa; overtime wages; wages of temporary employees including additional janitor and watchman; express, freight and hauling; rent of temporary office and storage space and equipment; extra telephone charges; preparation expense at temporary premises. From the Extra Expense insurance carried in the amount of $10,000 divided $4,000 for the first month, $8,000 for the first two months, $10,000 if restoration exceeds two months, the Daily News Tribune recovered $10,000 but was short $14,778.53 of recovery of total of the Extra Expenses incurred. This 60% shortage and the 48% shortage experienced by the Central National Bank of Chicago because of inadequate amounts of Extra Expense Insurance, demonstrate that purchasers of this form of insurance will wisely double their original estimates to provide for unforeseen contingencies.

Policy Form—The function of Extra Expense Insurance is well expressed in the following definitions of the term "Extra Expense" which are included in the policy forms.

In Eastern and some Southern Forms—

"The term 'Extra Expense' wherever used in this form, is defined as the excess (if any) of the total cost during the period of restoration chargeable to the conduct of the Insured's business, over and above the total cost that would normally have been incurred to conduct the business during the same period had no fire occurred; the cost in each case to include expense of using other property or facilities of other concerns or other necessary emergency expenses. In no event, however, shall this Company be liable under this policy for loss of income, nor for Extra Expense in excess of that necessary to continue as nearly as practicable the normal conduct of the Insured's business, nor for the cost of repairing or replacing any of the described property that has been damaged or destroyed by fire, except cost in excess of the normal cost of such repairs or replacements necessarily incurred for the purpose of reducing the total amount of Extra Expense; liability for such excess cost, however, shall not exceed the amount by which the total Extra Expense otherwise payable under this policy is reduced. This Company shall also be liable for Extra Expense incurred in obtaining property for temporary use during the period of restoration necessarily required for the conduct of the Insured's business; any salvage value of such property remaining after resumption of normal operations shall be taken into consideration in the adjustment of any loss hereunder."

In the Midwestern State forms the term "Extra Expense" is defined as "the excess (if any) of the total cost during the period of restoration of the operation of the business, either at the insured location or on other premises, or both, over and above the cost of such operation that would normally have been incurred during the same period had no loss occurred; the cost in each case to include expense of using other property or facilities of other concerns or other necessary emergency expenses."

The early experimental Extra Expense policy forms with recovery limited to a specified sum per day (as in the Per Diem Use and Occupancy policy form then in current use) proving unsatisfactory to the Newspapers which were the chief applicants, and since a Contribution or Coinsurance Clause could not be required, the policy form adopted and now uniformly used bases recovery on a schedule of cumulative monthly limits designed to influence the maintenance of adequate amounts of insurance, as follows:

BUSINESS INTERRUPTION INSURANCE

"The limits of liability hereunder shall in no event exceed that percentage of the amount of this policy (at the time of loss) which is stated below for the determined "period of restoration":

............% when the "period of restoration" is not in excess of one month;

............% when the "period of restoration" is in excess of one month but not in excess of two months;

............% when the "period of restoration" is in excess of two months but not in excess of three months;

............% when the "period of restoration" is in excess of three months but not in excess of four months;

............% when the "period of restoration" is in excess of four months but not in excess of five months;

............% when the "period of restoration" is in excess of five months but not in excess of six month;

............% when the "period of restoration" is in excess of six months but not in excess of seven months;

............% when the "period of restoration" is in excess of seven months but not in excess of eight months.

In the event of the insurance hereunder being reduced by paying the longest period of restoration for which provision is above made does not exhaust the insurance hereby provided, then such unexhausted insurance shall apply for the remainder of the period of restoration.

In the event of the insurance hereunder being reduced by payment of claim, the percentage limits of liability for periods of restoration shall apply thereafter to the unexhausted insurance.

The word "month" however modified, wherever used in this contract shall be construed to mean thirty (30) consecutive days."

Requirements of Rating Bureaus—Coupled with this schedule of limits of liability are the following requirements promulgated by Rating Bureaus:

The period of indemnity to be not less than three months.

Not more than 40% of the amount of the policy to be allocated to any one month.

The monthly limits to be cumulative (see Note).

Fractional months not to be used.

Example—40% "when the period of restoration" is not in excess of one month.

80% when the "period of restoration' is in excess of one month but not in excess of two months.

100% when the "period of restoration" is in excess of two months but not in excess of three months.

Since the monthly limits are cumulative, it follows that, as the "period of restoration" increases, the limits named for the preceding months or shorter periods cease to apply, and the insurance applies blanket over the final actual period of restoration not exceeding the limit of liability named for the latter.

For example, if 30% of the amount of the policy in the foregoing example, is used to cover loss sustained during the first month, and 80% is needed to cover the loss sustained during the first two months, the insurance indemnifies up to the 80% specified when the "period of restoration" is in excess of one month but is not in excess of two months, notwithstanding the recovery is 50% for the second month of the "period of restoration."

Extension of Coverage—An important feature of the contract is the provision immediately following the schedule of limits providing that, if the extra expense incurred during the longest stated period of restoration does not exhaust the total amount of insurance, the unexhausted insurance applies for the remainder of the actual period of restoration. This extension of coverage was inserted when it was realized that the Insurer who had charged a high rate for a short period of restoration because of the total loss possibility, could not refuse to pay for the partial loss which might extend over a period longer than that specified in the schedule.

No Coinsurance Penalty—It should be noted that, although the schedule of limits does constrain Insured to maintain larger amounts of insurance than would be carried if no monthly limits applied, there is no penalty such as a contribution or coinsurance clause would inflict. The only penalty the underinsured Insured suffers is his failure to recover the full amount of loss sustained, as was the experience of the Central National Bank of Chicago. For the buyer of Extra Expense insurance who has not sustained a serious property damage loss and does not therefore know from experience the amount of Extra Expense Insurance to carry, the experience of the Central National Bank indicates that his best guess should be doubled.

Other Extra Expense Features—Other features of the Extra Expense policy worthy of comment are (1) the manifestly equitable provision that the salvage value of any property obtained at extra expense by the insured for temporary use during the period of restoration and remaining in use after resumption of normal operations, shall be taken into consideration in the adjustment of any loss, an example of which is contained in the exhibit of the adjustment of the Central National Bank's loss; (2) the provision that the Insurer is not liable "for the cost of compiling books of record or other documents," which is obviously unenforcible if contrued to apply to the extra cost (i.e., the cost in excess of normal) of such compilation. The normal cost is a property insurance loss, but the extra cost justifies a claim upon Extra Expense Insurance. For a discussion of the "excess insurance" clause in the Extra Expense form, see "Extra Expense and Business Interruption Expediting Expense," later in this chapter.

Multi-Location Blanket Coverage Prohibited—Since property damage and Business Interruption Insurance may be written to blanket properties situated at two or more locations, the question is sometimes asked, "Why may not Extra Expense Insurance be similarly written?" Extra Expense Insurance policies contain neither a contribution (coinsurance), average, or pro-rata distribution clause and, therefore, without such clauses Extra Expense Insurance in an amount sufficient for the requirements of an Insured's property at one location would be sufficient for each of his properties at other locations, no two of which would expose each other or be likely to be damaged or destroyed at the same time.

Rating Schedule—Since Extra Expense Insurance is a form of Time Element insurance in which recovery is apportioned to the number of months in the "period of restoration," the formula by which the premium cost is determined is arranged to coincide with the schedule of limits upon recovery by means of the following table of factors:

	Pacific Coast Factors	Elsewhere Factors
1st month period of restoration	1.69	2.60
2nd month period of restoration	1.20	1.85
3rd month period of restoration	.91	1.40
4th month period of restoration	.78	1.20
5th month period of restoration	.68	1.05
6th month period of restoration	.58	.90
7th month period of restoration	.52	.80
8th month period of restoration	.45	.70
9th month period of restoration	.39	.60
10th month period of restoration	.32	.50
11th month period of restoration	.29	.45
12th and succeeding months	.26	.40

To use this table, it is necessary to multiply the percentage of recovery for each respective month of the "period of restoration" named in the policy, by the 80% Coinsurance building rate, and then multiply the figure so obtained for each month by the factor for that month as shown in the foregoing table. The sum of the rates so determined is the full policy rate. When an 80% Coinsurance rate is not applicable, the No-Coinsurance rate is used.

EXAMPLE—Assume limits of liability or recovery in the policy as follows:

40% when the "period of restoration" is not in excess of one month.

80% when the "period of restoration" is in excess of one month but not in excess of two months.

100% when the "period of restoration" is in excess of two months but not in excess of three months.

BUSINESS INTERRUPTION INSURANCE

Assume 80% Coinsurance Building Rate $1.00
1st month = .40 × 1.00 = .40 × 2.60 ....$1.04
2nd month = .40 × 1.00 = .40 × 1.85 .... .74
3rd month = .20 × 1.00 = .20 × 1.40 .... .28

Extra Expense Policy Rate (except on Pacific Coast) $2.06

By the application of the Table of factors to various combinations of monthly Limits of Liability or Recovery, rates equal to the percentages of the building rate as shown in the tables in the immediately following paragraphs are determined for territories other than the Pacific Coast.

Suggestions on Choice of Most Advantageous Combinations of Limits of Recovery—Selection of the combination of limits depends upon the Insured's needs. If a large recovery is allocated to the early months of business suspension, the Insurer is subject to claim for a total loss during a short period of time, and therefore both the rate and premium cost are higher than for combinations of limits which spread liability over longer periods.

The amount selected for recovery during the first month determines the amount of insurance, while the amounts allocated to periods beyond the first month determine the rate and premium cost.

For example, assuming a building rate of 1.00 and the selection of $4,000 as the amount of recovery required for the first month, the amount of insurance is $10,000, regardless of how the balance of $6,000 is allocated to the subsequent periods, and the rates and premium costs for various combinations of limits (based on 40% allotted to the first month) are as in the first group below.

If larger amounts of recovery are required for the periods beyond the first month, but $4,000 recovery is required during the first month, any other combination of limits will result in total insurance exceeding $10,000 and higher premium costs. For instance the second group of figures shows the rates and premium costs for total insurance of $13,333, including recovery of 30% or $4,000 during the first month.

Months and Percentages in Schedule of Limits of Recovery in Policy Form (except Pacific Coast)							% of Building Rate of 1%	Premium on $10,000 Insurance
1	2	3	4	5	6	7		
40% $4,000	80% $8,000	100% $10,000					206%	$206.00
40% $4,000	70% $7,000	90% $9,000	100% $10,000				199.5%	199.50
40% $4,000	65% $6,500	80% $8,000	90% $9,000	100% $10,000			193.8%	193.80
40% $4,000	60% $6,000	70% $7,000	80% $8,000	90% $ 9,000	100% $10,000		186.5%	186.50
40% $4,000	50% $5,000	60% $6,000	70% $7,000	80% $ 8,000	90% $ 9,000	100% $10,000	176%	176.00

Second Group								Prem. on $13,333 Ins.
30% $4,000	60% $8,000	80% $10,666	100% $13,333				185.5%	$247.33
30% $4,000	55% $7,333	70% $9,333	85% $11,333	100% $13,333			179.1%	238.79
30% $4,000	50% $6,667	70% $9,333	80% $10,666	90% $12,000	100% $13,333		174.5%	232.66
30% $4,000	45% $6,000	60% $8,000	70% $9,333	80% $10,666	90% $12,000	100% $13,333	166.3%	221.73

By extending the schedule of limits beyond seven months, while assuring recovery of $4,000, i.e., 30%, during the first month it is possible to arrange a combination of limits that requires a rate of approximately 1.55, so that total insurance of $13,333 can be secured for approximately the same premium, i.e., $206.00, that is payable for total insurance of $10,000, based on limits of 40%, 80% and 100% recoverable in three months.

When there is doubt as to the amounts of recovery needed for periods extending beyond the first month of suspension of business, the combination of limits of 40%, 80%, 100% offers these advantages:

(a) the highest obtainable recovery (40%) for the first month when the extra expenses necessarily incurred are likely to be greater than for any other month,

(b) the highest obtainable recovery (80%) for the first

two months, when the loss is also likely to be greater than for succeeding months,

(c) recovery during the remaining months of the period of restoration of any portion of the insurance unused during the first three months,

(d) the lowest obtainable premium cost.

When the amount of insurance required by the combination of 40%, 80%, 100% limits is likely to provide an inadequate amount of insurance, unused by the Insured's claim for the account of the first three months, to apply to subsequent months, the combination of 30%, 60%, 80%, 100% at 20% more premium will provide the same amount of recovery during the important first and second months as is obtainable with limits of 40%, 80%, 100%, plus one third more insurance to apply to the subsequent months. Or for 36% more premium, limits of 25%, 50%, 70%, 100% will provide the same amount of recovery during the first two months plus 60% more insurance to apply to subsequent months.

No Monthly Limit of Liability—Where a policy is written without Monthly Limits of Liability or Recovery, the premium cost is computed at a rate five times the 80% coinsurance building rate, or five times the no-coinsurance building rate when an 80% coinsurance rate is not applicable. Since this provision was designed to discourage the writing of Extra Expense Insurance without monthly limits of liability, it is interesting to experiment with several examples to determine whether it achieves that purpose.

Assume the Insured anticipates that coverage in the amount of $1,000 will be sufficient to reimburse for any loss he may sustain and that his need for coverage will probably not extend beyond the first month following the date of fire damage. If the building rate is 1.00, the annual premium for $1,000 insurance at five times that rate is $50. However, were he to purchase a policy of $2,500 with monthly limits of 40% (the desired $1,000) for the important first month, 50% or $1,250 for the first two months, 60% or $1,500 for the first three months, 70% or $1,750 for the first four months, 80% or $2,000 for the first five months, 90% or $2,250 for the first six months and 100% or $2,500 for the first seven months of the period of restoration, the Insured, while securing the desired $1,000 insurance for the first month, would acquire $1,500 additional insurance to apply in the event of unforeseen contingencies, doing so for a premium of $44.00.

In short, he not only secures the desired $1,000 for 12% less premium, but also secures $1,500 additional insurance without cost to apply should his estimate of his need prove to have been inadequate. Obviously so long as five times the building rate is charged for a policy written without monthly limits upon recovery, it is to the Insured's advantage to accept any arrangement of limits other than 40%, 80%, 100% (for which the premium in this example would be $54.50) in preference to a policy written without limits.

Part Self-Insurance of Extra Expense—If to reduce premium cost where $5,000 coverage is needed for the first thirty days, the Insured carries $8,000 with limits of 40% (3,200) for the first thirty days, 70% ($5,600) for the first sixty days and 100% ($8,000) for the first ninety days and self insureds $1,800 of the first month's loss by means of a loan or otherwise, he will reduce premium cost from $201.50 for $10,000 insurance (with limits of 40%, 70%, 100%) to $161.20, a saving of $40.30 gross or $31.30 net after deducting one month's interest of $9.00 on $1,800 assuming annual interest of 6%. If there is a loss of $8,000 for 61 or more days period of restoration it will be recovered under either arrangement. However, the Insured will be short $1,800 of recovering a loss of $5,000 if it does not exceed the first critical thirty days, and $1,400 if there is a loss of $7,-000 which does not exceed the first critical 60 days. Moreover by his venture into the field of self-insurance he receives a rate of only $1.74 by earning a premium of $31.30, whereas for assuming the identical first month's risk the Insurance Company receives a rate of 2.015.

Contingent Extra Expense Insurance—Wherever a business A is dependent upon the premises of another business B for supplies of materials or services which will be interrupted if the premises of B sustain property damage, and A by incurring extra expense to secure the necessary supplies of materials or services from the premises of another business such as C, can continue business without loss of income, A can dispense with Contributing Properties Contingent Business Interruption Insurance (discussed in Chapter 9) and purchase Contingent Extra Expense Insurance. In such circumstances Contingent Expense Insurance will indemnify A for the extra expense incurred (such as the amount by which the price charged by C exceeds that charged by B, and transportation costs in excess of normal) to continue his business with the assistance of C substituting for B.

As this is written, neither manuals of rules nor Rating Bureau filings with state Insurance Departments specifically provide for Contingent Extra Expense Insurance. However, when it is written under a policy form employing the basic conditions of the standard Direct Extra Expense Insurance policy form, and limiting coverage to one contributing property, thereby observing the prohibition against blanket coverage which applies to direct Extra Expense Insurance, Contingent Extra Expense Insurance should be deemed permissible under existing filings and rules. Need for Contingent Extra Expense Insurance having risen, the promulgation of a policy form, rules and rates can be anticipated.

Work Sheet to Determine Amount of Extra Expense Insurance—The following work sheet is designed to expedite determination of the amount of Direct Extra Expense Insurance to be carried. The amounts tabulated should contemplate the greatest amount of expense which may reasonably be anticipated, including the possibility of entire dependence upon operations at temporary premises or by others under contract, plus the probable amount of expense necessarily continuing at the original location. It can also be used in the case of Contingent coverage, although only a few of the items will apply.

Because of limitations of space, provision is here made for only the first, second and third months following a loss. In practice, amounts, should be tabulated for as many additional months as the buyers' premises may be wholly prevented from operating.

Since the limits of recovery in the policy form are expressed as percentages of the amount of insurance carried, and are cumulative, when the tabulation is complete the total amount of insurance will be determined by adjusting the accumulated period totals as the buyer may desire, bearing in mind that 40% of the amount of insurance carried is the maximum which may be assigned to any one month, and three months is the minimum period of time for which coverage may be provided, except when the policy is written without monthly limits at five times the building rate.

EXAMPLE—Assume the total of the expenses tabulated are $4,000 the first month; $3,000 the second month; $2,000 third month; and $1,000 the fourth month. The amount of insurance would be $10,000, 40% of which is $4,000 needed for the first month. The limits of recovery would be entered in the table of limits in the Policy Form as 40% the first month; 70% ($4,000 plus $3,000 equals $7,000, i.e., 70% of $10,000) first and second months; 90% ($4,000 plus $3,000 plus $2,000) first, second and third months; and 100% for the total of four months or whatever longer period of time is required to completely exhaust the total amount of insurance carried.

Extra Expense and Business Interruption Expediting Expense—All standard Forms of Business Interruption Insurance in the United States provide that "This Policy also covers such expenses as are necessarily incurred for the purpose of reducing any loss under this policy, not exceeding, however, the amount by which the loss under this policy

BUSINESS INTERRUPTION INSURANCE

EXPENSES NECESSARY TO CONTINUE BUSINESS	FIRST MONTH		SECOND MONTH		THIRD MONTH	
Rent of Temporary Premises						
Cleaning Temporary Premises						
Labor equipping Temporary Premises						
Rent of Temporary Machinery, Equipment, etc.						
NET Cost (*) of Equipment, etc., purchased						
Expense of Moving Equipment, etc.						
Light, Power and Heat at Temporary Premises						
Labor at Temporary Premises						
Insurance Expense at Temporary Premises						
Janitor and Watchman at Temporary Premises						
Other Expenses at or because of Temporary Premises (Adv., Telep., Teleg., Legal etc)						
Total due to Temporary Premises						
Add Payments to others for manufacturing or processing						
Add necessarily continuing expenses at Original location AFTER a loss						
Add Bonuses for Quick Service etc.						
Total Expenses AFTER a loss						
Deduct Total of all Expenses which would have been incurred at the Original location for the corresponding period had no loss incurred.						
Extra Expense Ins. to be carried						

The word "loss" refers to fire, explosion, windstorm, or other peril causing a loss against which Extra Expense Insurance is carried.

(*) Item (5) applies to equipment, machinery, temporary buildings, etc., purchased for emergency use at original and/or temporary location. To determine Net Cost deduct salvage value of so much of such property as will be sold or utilized by the Insured upon resumption of operations at the original location.

254

is thereby reduced. Such expenses shall not be subject to the application of the Contribution Clause." In Canadian Business Interruption Forms such expenses are not exempted from the application of the Contribution Clause. Such expenses are known as "Expediting Expenses."

All standard Forms of Extra Expense Insurance provide that if, at the time of loss, there are other kinds of insurance which cover in any manner the loss insured against under the policy, then the Extra Expense Insurance shall apply only as excess insurance and in no event as contributing insurance, and then only to the amount of extra expense over and above the amount collectible by the Insured under such other forms of insurance.

Since the Expediting Expenses recoverable under policies of Business Interruption Insurance are extra expenses incurred by the Insured to continue business, Extra Expense Insurance indemnifies only for the amount of the Insured's loss of Extra Expenses which is in excess of the amount he recovers for Expediting Expenses when both Business Interruption and Extra Expense insurance cover a business at the time of a loss.

The following examples will serve to illustrate the procedure when only Business Interruption Insurance is carried; also when both forms of insurance are carried.

1. Assume that only Business Interruption Insurance is carried, and that the loss, if the Insured did not try to reduce it by incurring expediting expense, and a contribution penalty is not inflicted, would be $10,000. Then assume the Insured spends $5,000 resulting in reduction of the Business Interruption loss from $10,000 to $2,500. In accordance with the Extra Expense provision of the Business Interruption policy, the Insurance Company pays the net loss of $2,500 and, in addition, reimburses the Insured for the $5,000 spent to reduce the loss. Manifestly, the Insurance Company is glad to do so, since its total loss has been reduced from $10,000 to $7,500.

2. If, however, the Expediting Expenses of $5,000 incurred in Example (1) reduced the net loss by only $4,000 (from $10,000 to $6,000), the Insurance Company would be liable to reimburse the Insured for only $4,000 of the Expediting Expenses he incurred, and would pay the Insured $10,000, .ie., $6,000 on account of the net loss, plus $4,000 Expediting Expense. In this case, the Insured is short $1,000 of recovering his entire loss of $11,000 — $10,000 received from Business Interruption insurance and $1,000 Expediting Expense he failed to recover.

3. Assuming that both Business Interruption and Extra Expense Insurance have been carried, under the conditions of Example (2) the Insured would have recovered the excess Extra Expense of $1,000 from the Extra Expense Insurance. Although the amount of Excess Extra Expense involved in this example is comparatively small, the example illustrates operation of the Excess Clause in the Extra Expense policy, and demonstrates the value of the purchase of both Extra Expense and Business Interruption Insurance to cover a business such as a Newspaper, which to expedite resumption of business must incur expenditures greatly exceeding the amount by which they reduce the Business Interruption loss that would, but for such expenses, be recoverable from Business Interruption Insurance.

4. Reverting to Example (1). Assuming the same facts except that the Insured is a 20% coinsurer, he recovers $2,000, i.e., the net loss of $2,500 ($10,000 less $7,500 reduction resulting from payment of $5,000 to reduce the loss), less 20% coinsurance penalty. Since the Company's loss was reduced by $6,000 (from $8,000 to $2,000) the Company pays the entire extra expense of $5,000 and the Insured receives a total of $7,000. That the Insured is short $500 of recovering the total of $7,500 ($2,500 net loss plus $5,000 extra expense) is due solely to his coinsurance penalty of 20% on the net loss of $2,500.

Before the revision of Business Interruption forms, late in

1945, to provide that expediting expenses shall not be subject to the application of the Contribution Clause, the Insured in this example would have been coinsured 20% on the amount of Expediting Expenses also, so that his recovery would have been $2,000 ($2,500 net loss less 20% contribution) plus $4,000 ($5,000 Expediting Expense less 20% contribution), a total recovery of $6,000 instead of $7,000.

The revision was the culmination of a long controversy between Adjusters and between Underwriters, and reflected the belief of the majority that, in the long range interest of Business Interruption Insurance, and of the Insurance Companies that benefit by reduction in Business Interruption losses, the Insured should not be discouraged from cooperating to expedite resumption of business.

However "expediting expenses" as covered in the Canadian Gross Profits Form, in which they are referred to as "Increase in Cost of Working" are subject to the 100% Coinsurance Clause which is part of that form (See Chapter 11). While the Canadian editions of the Business Interruption Forms do not exempt expediting expenses from the application of the Contribution Clause, it is reported that in the adjustment of some losses coinsurance is not applied to such expenses.

Extra Expense Insurance and Rental Value Insurance. The rental value of a building is the sum of the cost of its maintenance and the owner's profit which is the difference between such cost and the rent payable for it or a similar building. Extra Expense Insurance indemnifies for the excess of the total cost during the period of restoration of maintaining the same building or renting and maintaining a temporary building, or doing both, above the normal cost had no loss occurred. When both Rental Value Insurance and Extra Expense Insurance are carried on an owner occupied building, the former indemnifies for the amount for which it is liable and Extra Expense Insurance indemnifies for the excess of the sum of the expense of maintnance of the original building and/or expense of renting, cleaning and outfitting and maintaining a temporary building, if any, above the normal cost of maintenance less any salvage value of property acquired for temporary use.

CHAPTER 16

MISCELLANEOUS

All standard form Business Interruption Insurance policies contain the following clauses:
1. Resumption of Operations
2. Special Exclusions (Consequential Losses)
3. Interruption by Civil Authorities
4. Special Conditions Applicable to Mining Risks (Underground Coverage)

These clauses, and the following items in their relation to Business Interruption Insurance, being more or less frequently the subject of misunderstanding and inquiry, are here discussed.
5. Coverage of only Fixed Charges and Expenses, or only Profits
6. Charges Insurance
7. Tutition and Camping Fees Insurance
8. Builders Risks and New Businesses
9. Income Taxes
10. Rent
11. Classification of Expenses
12. Allied Perils Coverages
13. Suggestions to Insurance Agents and Brokers
14. Suggestions to Prospective Buyers
15. Suggestions to Credit Men

1. Resumption of Operations Clause—This Clause requires the insured to resume complete or partial operation of the covered property, whether or not damaged, by making use of merchandise, stocks or other property, at the covered location or elsewhere, if thereby the loss can be reduced—the reduction to be taken into account in arriving at the amount of loss for which the insurance is liable.

The original edition of this clause ambiguously mentioned use of "other property, equipment or supplies" which be-

259

cause of loss experience was revised in 1955 to specifically mention "merchandise" in the forms for Mercantile and Non-manufacturing businesses, and in the forms for manufacturing businesses to specifically mention "stock (raw, in process or finished)" and to add the provision that "with respect to such use of finished stock, this policy covers any necessary extra expense that would be required to replace the finished stock used by the insured to reduce the loss resulting from interruption of business."

The loss experience referred to was obtained chiefly in connection with the large claim of a manufacturer covered by Gross Earnings Form No. 4 who, although admittedly able to maintain sales from an abnormal supply of finished stock in storage, pressed his claim for recovery on the basis of the sales value of prevented production. As the amount of the claim was large and suit was threatened, it was settled for a compromise amount—whereupon the "Resumption of Operations Clause" was revised to emphasize that recovery is for "actual loss sustained," by specifically requiring use of "finished stock" on hand at the described location or elsewhere, this was done to reduce the loss, but also, in fairness, to provide for recovery by the insured of any necssary extra expense incurred to replace the depletion in finished stock inventory occasioned by the sales which continued during the time production was interrupted. Since "sales value of production," which is stated to be the basis of recovery in Gross Earnings Form No. 4, is also used in the application of Two Item Form No. 2, and is involved in application of the "Resumption of Operations Clause," the reader is referred to the paragraph captioned "Earnings Produced at the Time Product is Manufactured" in Chapter 6.

2. Special Exclusions Clause—Standard policy forms in the United States include this clause which provides that the Insurer shall not be liable

(a) for any increase of loss which may be occasioned by any local or state ordinance or law regulating construction or repair of buildings;

The former reference to "any ordinance or law regulating construction or repair of buildings" (and the corresponding phraseology in the Canadian forms denying liability for increased loss due to additional time that would be required to replace or repair owing to ordinances or laws requiring the use of different construction, materials or equipment from the property destroyed) was the center of controversey during the early months of the recent World War with respect to whether it referred to Priority Regulations as discussed in Chapter 12.

In consideration of an additional premium, policies may be endorsed to assume liability for loss due to the enforcement of local ordinances, using clauses variously referred to as "Demolition Clause," and "Contingent Liability from Operation of Building Law Clause," which extend coverage to any increase in loss due to the demolition of undamaged portions of a building as required by the ordinance.

In some territories such clauses also extend coverage to include the time required to rebuild the demolished portions of the original type of construction; in other territories the coverage is extended to include the additional time required to rebuild of the superior type of construction required by the ordinance.

(b) by the suspension, lapse or cancellation of any lease or license, contract or order;

This portion of the Special Exclusions Clause (which in Canadian forms refers to loss due to the suspension, lapse or cancellation of any lease or license, contract or order, which may affect the Insured's earnings after the period following any fire during which indemnity is payable) is designed to deny recovery for the consequential loss of a tenant's leasehold profit due to the cancellation of his lease, a loss which may be insured against under "Leasehold Interest insurance" written to indemnify a lessee to the extent of the difference between the rent he is paying and the higher rent required for other suitable quarters.

261

In the case of cancellation or suspension of licenses, contracts, or orders, the denial of liability for the consequential loss of business earnings applies to so much of such loss as is sustained subsequent to the date of physical rehabilitation of the Insured's premises. Liability for the loss of business earnings sustained between the date of fire and the date of rehabilitation is not denied if cancellation or suspension of a license, contract, or order was due to the fire. The loss sustained subsequent to the date of rehabilitation, resulting from the cancellation of contract, is sometimes insurable under a special policy drawn in accordance with the contractual condition applying.

(c) for any increase of loss due to interference at the described premises by strikers or other persons with rebuilding, repairing or replacing the property damaged or destroyed, or with the resumption or continuation of business;

The denial of recovery for any increase of loss due to interference at the described premises by strikers or other persons with rebuilding, repairing or replacing the damaged or destroyed property, or with the resumption or continuation of business, is a provision in standard policy forms because of experience gained at the time of the rash of sitdown strikes that plagued industry in pre-war days.

This exclusion is designed to prevent misunderstanding by making it clear that Insurers are not liable for the consequential loss resulting from strikes which are not insured against.

Since the reference is to interference only "at the described premises," liability would not be denied for any increase of loss due to interference by strikers at the premises of contractors who are working on orders from the Insured to supply materials or equipment to be used to rehabilitate the Insured's premises.

(d) for any other consequential loss or remote loss.

Although Business Interruption Insurance is a form of

consequential loss insurance, in fact is so named in Great Britain, it is designed to indemnify only for the loss of business earnings resulting directly and immediately from physical damage to the Insured's premises. It is not intended to extend to indemnify for loss resulting from the indirect consequences of physical damage. Hence the dedenials of liability discussed in (a), (b), and (c), and the concluding statement in the Special Exclusions Clause that the Insurer is not liable "for any other consequential or remote loss."

Among the "consequential or remote" losses for which liability has been denied, are:

Loss of good will;

loss due to unpaid restaurant checks when patrons hastily departed because of fire in a nearby building;

loss of production of milk by discontented cows upset by strange quarters to which they were transferred following destruction of their accustomed quarters;

loss due to reduction in value of logs in forest caused by worms while sawmill was shut down by fire damage;

expense of recovering logs which sank in a mill pond during protracted idleness of sawmill due to fire damage;

loss due to spoilage of perishable stocks by changes in temperature.

The latter type of consequential loss may be covered by endorsing a Business Interruption Fire policy for an additional premium. If the Extended Coverage and Vandalism and Malicious Mischief Endorsements are attached to policy, it is necessary to also attach and pay additional premium for the standard "Consequential Riot and Vandalism Loss Assumption Clause" whereby liability is assumed for the change in temperature consequential losses to perishable stocks due to riot and malicious mischief, since liability for such losses caused by these perils is denied in the Extended Coverage and Vandalism and Malicious Mischief Endorsements. To eliminate claims for loss where such stocks are damaged by rioters or malicious persons without physical damage to the refrigerating, humidifying or heating apparatus, this Assumption Clause denies liability for loss caused by the "improper operation of, or the failure to operate, such apparatus or its control equipment."

Coverage against damage by strikers, in the absence of a legal riot, is unobtainable from tariff companies.

The consequential losses here discussed should not be confused with the consequential loss resulting from the normal *depreciation* in value of the undamaged property, if any, which remains following the destruction of a portion of a building or plant which has thereby been forced to suspend operations. Such depreciation, whether it be shown on the Insured's books as a fixed charge or be considered to be included in net profit, is covered by Business Interruption Insurance, since it is a charge that would have been met from the Insured's earnings had no fire occurred.

3. Interruption by Civil Authority Clause—By this clause, the Insurer assumes liability for loss sustained by the Insured during the period of time, not exceeding two weeks, while access to his premises is prohibited by civil authority, issued as a direct result of the perils insured against in the vicinity of such premises.

A demonstration of the operation of this clause occurred in a midwestern city several years ago when fire gutted a four story building. When one of the brick walls subsequently collapsed, the city authorities closed the entire block to the public until the remaining walls were removed or strengthened, thereby preventing all stores in the block from operating for periods of from three to six days.

Fortunately, five of the closed stores carried Business Interruption Insurance with the Interruption by Civil Authority Clause and, although their premises had not been physically damaged by the fire, recovered the aggregate Business Interruption loss of $6,000 sustained. In another city, claims were paid under this clause to 12 merchants who sustained loss of business because their street was completely closed for one day and only pedestrian access was permitted during the ensuing month.

This clause also assures recovery under a fire policy for loss of earnings sustained when the street on which the insured's business is situated is closed by the Fire Department during the progress of a fire on premises of others; or by the police when a large sign on adjoining building is in a dangerous condition due to wind damage, provided the Insured's policy covers against wind damage.

4. **Special Conditions Applicable to Mining Risks**—Business Interruption forms for manufacturing businesses, when applied to mining properties, deny liability for loss resulting from property damage or disturbances underground, unless: (1) By reason thereof any aboveground structure is damaged—in which event liability is assumed only for loss sustained during the time required to repair or replace such aboveground structure, or (2) unless coverage is extended to cover loss resulting from damage to underground property by means of standard form of Underground Coverage Endorsement in consideration of an extra charge for underground Fire coverage—plus charges for Underground Explosion or Riot coverage—by means of the Extended Coverage Endorsement, and for Underground Malicious Damage coverage by means of the Vandalism and Malicious Mischief Endorsement if these endorsements are also attached to the policy.

There are two forms of Underground Coverage Endorsements in the United States—the Limited Form and the Broad Form—which in the West Virginia and Mid-Western editions limits coverage to loss during the time required to repair, rebuild or replace specifically identified underground equipment which has been damaged, and denies liability for any loss sustained during the time that access to such equipment is prevented by any cause or peril, whether or not such peril is insured against by the policy.

The Virginia edition of the Limited Form omits reference to "access," although intended to be construed as though it were used.

The Broad Form, available only in West Virginia and Virginia at higher rates, extends coverage to include coverage of loss sustained during the time the identified underground equipment is prevented from being repaired, rebuilt, replaced or operated because of damage to underground property, including shafts, entrances and passages; excluding, however, loss for the period of time the described property is prevented from being repaired, replaced, rebuilt or operated as a result of interference by strikers or other persons, or by order of governmental authorities, such as orders of the Bureau of Mines prohibiting entrance to a mine until, for example, it has been purged of hazardous gas or until the Bureau has investigated the cause of the underground accident.

Prior to the adoption of the present editions of the Limited Form endorsement, an underground fire on December 17, 1946 in a Wisconsin Iron Ore Mine occurred under the then endorsement which denied liability for loss during the time that rehabilitation of damaged underground equipment was "delayed or prevented as a result of damage to or obstruction of underground workings, including shafts, entrances, passages and mine timbering by any cause." The electric hoist, which was damaged, could not be reached for approximately six weeks, due to sealing of mine passages in the affected area which were unsafe due to gas and smoke from burning timbers.

When the hoist was finally reached, it was repaired in four days, which the insurers contended was the maximum time for which they were liable. The insured claimed loss for total suspension of operations in the affected area until February 1, and for partial suspension until March 1, on the ground that the seals built to extinguish the fire and prevent unsafe access were not obstructions within the meaning of the exclusion, that the exclusion did not apply when the obstruction was a direct result of a peril insured against, and that therefore, the words "except from the hazards insured against" should be considered as added at the end of the endorsement after the words "by any cause," and that in any event, the exclusion did not apply until the fire was extinguished.

The insured's claim, which was litigated, was compromised, as was also the claim for a similar loss in a West Virginia coal mine occurring in April 1947 under the Limited Form of endorsement.

As a result of these losses, the present West Virginia and Mid-Western editions of the Limited Endorsement deny liability for "loss sustained during the time that access to such of the above described equipment as may have been damaged or destroyed is prevented by any cause or peril *whether or not such peril is insured against hereunder.*" The corresponding denial in the Virginia edition omits reference to "access," although intended to be construed as though it were used.

Another special form applicable to Mining Risks is the Business Interruption Policy Form No. 7A promulgated by the West Virginia Inspection Bureau in 1953 and by the Southeastern Rating Bureaus in 1955, to meet the peculiar needs of the Coal Mining Industry by providing (a) a Single Item Contract limiting coverage to be concurrent with Item 1 of the Two Item Form; (b) providing definition of deductible "Ordinary Payroll" and "Materials, Parts and Mine Supplies" in phraseology applicable to a Coal Mine; and (c) including provisions governing adjustment of premium coupled with a standard form of report of values.

Since coal mine operators refuse to insure "ordinary payroll"—consisting chiefly of miners' wages—either specifically as provided in Item II of the Two Item Form or blanket with other expenses as provided in the Gross Earnings Form, and since uncertain sales prospects in the coal industry indicated the need for coverage subject to adjustment of premium which is nowhere available in connection with the Two Item Form, the problem of providing necessary coverage for the coal mining industry was solved by devising a contract which combines in one form coverage identical with Item I of the Two Item Form, with the conditions of the Premium Adjustment Endorsement added. This form was unique in 1953 in that it dispensed with the term "Ordinary Payroll" by dividing all employees into two groups: Group I Employees being Officers, Executives, Superintendents, Foremen, Engineers, Chief Electricians, Office Employees, Employees required during an interruption of business for necessary maintenance, and other specified employees, if any, listed in the last report of values rendered prior to the date of damage or destruction of the described property. Group II Employees are "all other employees of the insured not covered under Group I."

By this new classification of employees and the detailed listing in the Standard Report of Values of the salaries and wages of the various categories of mine employees included in Group 1, the difficulties that would otherwise be encountered were avoided. The new form was also unique in providing a definition of "Business Interruption Value" which ties in with the standard "Report of Values" and the Contribution Clause.

5. Coverage of Charges & Expenses, or Profits, Only—
The idea that Business Interruption Insurance can be more economically written to cover only fixed charges and expenses by eliminating the coverage of net profit, or to cover only net profit by eliminating the coverage of fixed charges and expenses, is as misguided as it is persisting.

Business Interruption Insurance is designed to insure all earnings blanket—not merely that portion credited to net profit, or that portion charged to expenses and fixed charges. The interdependency between net profit and charges and expenses is so close as to require blanket coverage. Actually the rate charged for a Business Interruption policy may be considered an average rate, a blend of (1) the higher than average rate actuarily required for coverage of only net profit since net profit, being the last portion of income that is earned is the first part of earnings to be cut off when business is curtailed, and (2) the lower-than-average rate actuarily chargeable for coverage of only fixed charges and expenses which cannot be truly considered lost or reduced in the aggregate or individually, until net profit has suffered total extinction.

Therefore, the buyer of insurance against loss of only fixed charges and expenses is entitled to a premium rate lower than the full coverage Business Interruption rate, but such rate is nowhere obtainable, nor is a special rate obtainable for coverage of only net profit insured under a Time Element form of policy.

The fact that no net profit is currently being earned or is anticipated, is obviously not a valid reason for insuring only fixed charges and expenses since the Insured's prospects may improve with little advance notice.

For these reasons and because the coverage of only fixed charges and expenses, or only net profit, is to the Insured's disadvantage, as could be demonstrated by examples, space permitting, the approved method of accomplishing the underlying purpose of reducing premium cost is simple underinsurance under the full coverage policy, the result being a contribution (coinsurance) penalty in an amount approximating the net profit, or the fixed charges and expenses, as the case may be.

Except in territories where a non-standard policy form may be used at a substantial increase in rate, policies written to cover net profit only, or fixed charges and expenses only, are illegal in the absence of a filing approved by the State Insurance department.

6. **Charges Insurance**—in the above, the term "charges"

was used to refer to operating expenses of the Insured's business. In this discussion, the term is used to describe the income received by a warehouseman for storing property of others, or by a grain elevator operator for handling, storing, and delivering grain of others.

In either case, if the property of others is destroyed by the peril insured against in a Charges Insurance policy, the warehouseman or elevator operator—Insured is indemnified for his loss of the accrued storage and handling charges he would have earned, but which are forfeited because the property in storage was destroyed.

"Charges Insurance," or "Accrued Charges Insurance," or "Storage Charges Insurance," as this form is sometimes termed, being (like Profits and Commissions Insurance) coverage of past earnings accrued before the date of loss, does not conflict with Business Interruption Insurance carried by the same Insured, except in the case of Charges Insurance on grain in elevators, which is written under a special policy containing conditions which in some respects overlap the coverage provided by the Business Interruption policy.

There is, however, conflict between Business Interruption Insurance and "Non-Accrued Charges Insurance," a form of Charges Insurance covering future storage and handling charges which, but for the fire, would have been earned by the Warehouseman-Insured beginning with the date of the fire. Where both Business Interruption insurance and any form of Charges Insurance are written to cover the same premises so as to provide overlapping coverage, any loss for which both are liable will be apportioned between them.

7. **Tuition Fees Insurance**—This is a form of Business Interruption Insurance designed to meet the needs of Educational Institutions which receive income from students for tuition and other services. It differs from Business Interruption Insurance in that the policy form is phrased in terms applying specifically to schools and colleges, and indemnifies for loss sustained beyond the period of time required to

rebuild, repair, or replace the destroyed or damaged property.

Following are the distinctive conditions of the form standard in most territories:

(2) It is a condition of this insurance that if the above described building(s), structure(s), or their contents, be damaged or destroyed by the peril(s) insured against during the term of this policy, this Company shall be liable for the actual loss of tuition fees sustained less such operating expenses as do not necessarily continue during the period (not limited by the date of expiration of this policy) commencing with the date of such damage or destruction and ending, except as provided in paragraph 3, on the day preceding the beginning of the first school year following the date that the damaged or destroyed building(s), structure(s), and their contents could, with the exercise of due diligence and dispatch, be rebuilt, repaired or replaced.

(3) If the period of time, as provided under paragraph 2, for rebuilding, repairing or replacing the damaged or destroyed building(s), structure(s), and their contents shall end on a date within 30 days immediately preceding the beginning of the first school year specified above, the period of liability for loss under this policy is hereby extended to end on the day preceding the beginning of the second school year.

The words "beginning of school year," however modified, wherever used in this policy, shall mean the opening date of school in the Fall as prescribed, or as would be prescribed, in the school catalogue.

Definition of Tuition Fees: The term "tuition fees" wherever used in this contract, shall mean tuition, fees and other income from students, less the cost of merchandise sold and materials and supplies consumed in services sold to such students. In determining "tuition fees," due consideration shall be given to the experience of the Insured before the date of damage or destruction and the probable experience thereafter had no loss occurred.

Contribution Clause: In consideration of the rate and form under which this policy is written, this Company shall be liable, in the event of loss, for no greater proportion thereof than the amount hereby covered bears to (insert 80 or 100) % of the tuition fees that would have been earned (had no loss occurred) during the 12 months immediately following the date of damage to or destruction of the described property.

Expense to Reduce Loss: This policy also covers such expenses as are necessarily incurred for the purpose of reducing any loss under this policy (except expense incurred to extinguish a fire), not exceeding, however, the amount by which the loss under this policy is thereby reduced. Such expenses shall not be subject to the application of the Contribution Clause.

Interruption by Civil Authority: This policy is extended to include the actual loss as covered hereunder during the period of time, not exceeding 2 consecutive weeks, when as a direct result of the peril(s) insured against, access to the property described is prohibited by order of civil authority.

Resumption of Operations: If the Insured, by resumption of complete or partial operation of the property herein described or by making use of other property, equipment or supplies, could reduce the loss under this policy, such reduction shall be taken into account in arriving at the amount of loss hereunder.

Special Exclusions: This Company shall not be liable for any increase of loss which may be occasioned by any local or state ordinance or law regulating construction or repair of buildings or structures, nor by the suspension, lapse or cancellation of any lease or license, contract or order, nor for increase of loss due to interference at the described premises by strikers or other persons with rebuilding, repairing or replacing the property or with the resumption or continuation of operations; nor shall this Company be liable for any other consequential loss or remote loss.

The definition of the term "tuition fees" in this form is the latest of three definitions prescribed during the time since the original form was promulgated in 1934. The definition in that original form authorized the deduction from tuition and other income, of "operating expenses as do not necessarily continue." Any other construction being impracticable, and 100% Coinsurance being mandatory, this definition was construed to permit the deduction of operating expenses as would not necessarily continue in the event operations were totally suspended for an entire fiscal year. This applies whether the actual suspension following a loss be partial, total, short or long.

Beginning in 1948, a revised form was promulgated in which the term "tuition fees" was defined as the gross tuition and other income from student sources without deduction of any discontinuable expenses whatever, and the insured was given the choice of a 60%, 70%, or 80% Coinsurance clause at rates, 100%, 90%, and 82% respectively of the building rate. This revised form proved to be disadvantageous, costwise, to many educational institutions, because the scale of rates was designed to produce the same premium as was charged for the original 100% Coinsurance form where the discontinuable expenses of an instiution are 40% of gross income.

Since Tuition Fees insurance is of greatest value to boarding schools, the discontinuable expenses (including food, dormitory supplies, and laundry) which range from 44% to 67%, the present form which permits the deduction from income of cost of merchandise sold and the cost of material and supplies consumed in services sold to students, was adopted.

Tuition Fees Insurance is available in recognition of two conditions peculiar to educational institutions supported by fees paid by students:

1. That their executives and professional employees have limited opportunities for new employment during the school year, and therefore their contractual salaries in many instances are a necessarily continuing expense for the entire school year, and

2. That most students have a planned educational schedule which does not allow for interruption, and therefore, if, due to fire damage, the institution of their first choice is prevented from receiving them or from continuing their education, they will transfer to another institution, resulting in the former's loss of their tuition and other fees for the entire current school year, and even beyond.

Therefore, even though rehabilitation of damaged or destroyed school property has occurred, and operations can be resumed on a date considerably in advance of the close of the school year, Tuition Fees insurance indemnifies for loss sustained until the beginning of the first school year following the date of completion of rehabilitation, unless that date falls within the 30 days immediately preceding the beginning of a school year, in which event the period of recovery is extended until the beginning of the second school year following the date of completion of rehabilitation of the damaged or destroyed property.

Such extension of the period of recovery provides for the cases where students, fearful that the school will not be able to open, enroll at other schools.

EXAMPLE. Assume a school's year begins September 15 of this year and closes the following June 15. Fire destroys the building on November 1, and all students transfer to other schools. If the school is rebuilt and ready to operate May 1, Tuition Fees insurance indemnifies for loss of gross income less discontinuable expenses sustained during the period ending September 14, of next year.

If rebuilding operations are not completed until September 1 of next year (i.e., less than 30 days prior to September 15), Tuition Fees insurance indemnifies for loss sustained during the period ending September 14 of the year after next.

If the school in this example were covered by Business Interruption Insurance, indemnity would be limited to loss sustained up to May 1, or September 1 of next year, depending upon which of these dates rebuilding operations are completed.

Comparison of Extra Expense and Tuition Fees Insurance —Extra Expense Insurance is an alternative, and sometimes a supplementary coverage for Tuition Fees Insurance, as well as for Business Interruption Insurance as discussed in Chapter 15.

Where an institution consists of several or more buildings, all of which are not subject to destruction by a single fire or windstorm and, therefore, by incurring extra expense, undamaged buildings can be used to carry on the functions of the destroyed buildings; or where, in the case of the destruction of a school's only building and suitable premises situated outside the campus can be expeditiously secured and adapted for school purposes without loss of income from student sources, Extra Expense Insurance is a satisfactory substitute for Tuition Fees Insurance.

Extra Expense Insurance is manifestly a necessary coverage for **public schools.** Even where such schools receive some tuition fees from students residing outside the school district, Tuition Fees Insurance is not suitable because of (1) the difficulty of apportioning necessarily continuing expenses between the tuition paying non-residents and the non-tuition paying resident students, and (2) the difficulty also of proving any loss of tuition fees where school work can be continued in temporary quarters at extra expense.

Since a considerable portion of the income received by many educational institutions is derived from gifts and endowment funds sometimes qualified as to permissible use, the standard Tuition Fees Insurance policy form confines coverage to income received from student sources to prevent misunderstanding.

Tuition Fees Insurance Rates—Although all rating bureaus use the building rate as the rate for Tuition Fees Insurance, all bureaus are not uniform in their methods of determining an average rate for blanket coverage over two or more differently rated school buildings.

Some bureaus have computed average rates on the basis of building values. Some quote the numerical average of the building rates and some follow the floor area method used in computing average Business Interruption rates. Evidently the trend is toward uniformity in using the floor area method. Tuition Fees Insurance rates generally exceed Business Interruption rates because the period of recovery does not end on the date rebuilding, repairing and replacement operations are completed and, therefore, the loss payable is greater than the loss recoverable from Business Interruption Insurance.

Camping Fees Insurance—Camping Fees Insurance is merely Tuition Fees Insurance adapted to seasonal camps by using the Tuition Fees Insurance form, changing the term "Tuition Fees" to read "Camping Fees"; the phrase

"Tuition Fees and other Income from Students" to read "Camping Charges and other income from guests" and changing all references to the "school year" to read "camp year."

Seasonal camps, like private schools, were covered by some Business Interruption Insurance prior to 1934 (when the Standard Tuition Fees policy was promulgated). Like the schools, they found it unsatisfactory because the period of recovery in case of loss ended upon the date rebuilding, repairs, and replacement of damaged property was completed, whereas considerable amounts of expense continue for the balance of the camping season although earnings are reduced or totally suspended because campers transfer to other camps. Many seasonal camps have therefore purchased Camping Fees Insurance under the adapted Tuition Fees form.

The fact that such insurance against the perils of fire and windstorm was being written was doubtless to some extent responsible for the creation of "Camp Epidemic and Quarantine Insurance," designed to indemnify camp operators for loss of camping fees refunded because a camp is compelled to close, due to epidemic diseases, or an individual camper withdraws for more than a specified number of days because of injury, or profit is lost because a camp is quarantined beyond its normal closing date.

Viewed by underwriters as a hazardous form of insurance, it is being written by only a few Fire and Casualty companies as an accommodation to purchasers of policies covering the preferred forms of insurance.

Seasonal Hotel "Camps"—Although Camping Fees Insurance is intended to be restricted to legitimate "camps" operated commercially for children, with educational objectives, or by schools, churches, Y.M.C.A.'s or similar organizations, the possibility exists of misusing it to cover seasonal hotels and boarding houses masquerading as "camps," thereby securing for such business enterprises a contract with all the benefits of Business Interruption Insurance, plus coverage of loss sustained beyond the time required to rebuild, repair or replace destroyed property.

This is not to say that such use of Camping Fees Insurance is reprehensible for reasons other than absence of authorized filings with State Insunrance Departments. In fact, a good case can be constructed in behalf of permitting Business Interruption Insurance to be written on seasonal hotels and boarding houses, canneries, and other seasonal businesses, extended to cover loss of earnings sustained beyond the time required to rehabilitate physical damage, or until business returns to normal.

Such extended period of recovery applies under the English Consequential Loss policies, the Canadian Profits policies, the Louisiana Warehouse Endorsement and the Seasonal Stock Endorsement promulgated in Pacific Coast States. An extended period of recovery will doubtless be available some day under Business Interruption policies written to cover any business desiring extended recovery similar to that provided by Tuition Fees Insurance, and willing to pay a correspondingly increased rate of premium.

8. Builders' Risks and New Businesses—Since buildings in process of construction (termed "Builders' Risks") to be occupied for business purposes are potentially sources of earnings the production of which will be delayed during the time completion of construction is delayed by property damage, they should be covered by Business Interruption Insurance.

The inception date of such insurance is preferably the date of commencement of construction operations or any date during the process of such operations may be selected, but the period of time during which indemnity is payable is the period beginning with the date as of which the building would have been completed and able to function as a source of business earnings, had not property damage prevented.

Provision for such coverage (formerly endorseable only) is now contained in the "Alterations and New Buildings Clause" in revised forms.

If an operating plant covered by Business Interruption Insurance is being altered or enlarged, the Alterations and Repairs Permit in the policy form, if it does not contain the following provisions, should be revised as follows to avoid misconstruction of the contract in the event of loss:

"Alterations and New Buildings: Permission is granted to make alterations in or to construct additions to any building described herein and to construct new buildings on the described premises. This policy is extended to cover, subject to all its provisions and stipulations, loss resulting from damage to or destruction of such alterations, additions or new buildings while in course of construction and when completed or occupied, provided that, in the event of damage to or destruction of such property (including building materials, supplies, machinery or equipment incident to such construction or occupancy while on the described premises or within 100 feet thereof) so as to delay commencement of business operations of the Insured, the length of time for which this company shall be liable shall be determined as otherwise provided herein—but such determined length of time shall be applied from the date that business operations would have begun had no loss occurred. This clause does not waive or modify any of the conditions of the Automatic Sprinkler Clause, if any, attached to this policy."

Underwriters are disinclined to write Business Interruption Insurance on buildings in course of construction for persons inexperienced in a new business until they have demonstrated their ability to operate profitably.

Similarly a new business enterprise which occupies or is about to occupy an existing building, may purchase Business Interruption Insurance to cover such building either from the date of the lease or contract to purchase, or the date of commencement of occupancy or operations, or as of any subsequent date desired. As in the case of "Builders Risks," if the applicant for Business Interruption Insurance has had previous experience in the same business at another location, it will predispose underwriters to furnish insurance.

When such experience is lacking and even where it exists, underwriters may be expected to be reluctant to furnish Business Interruption Insurance anticipating difficulty in adjusting claim for a loss that may occur before the new business has become sufficiently established to provide a basis for determining what the Insured's earnings would have been but for the property damage. Accordingly the longer the period of time a new business has been in operation the less difficulty will be experienced in locating underwriters willing to furnish Business Interruption Insurance.

The Premium Adjustment Endorsement, for obvious reasons, should be useful on Builders' Risks and new businesses. "Valued" policies have been issued to pay fixed sums per day or week regardless of actual loss but underwriters are reluctant to issue them. They are discussed in Chapter 2.

9. Income and Profits Taxes—Since there are two kinds of net profit—before and after income taxes, the proposal is occasionally advanced that Business Interruption Insurance be so written as to eliminate coverage of such taxes, thereby relieving the Insured of the burden of paying premium on insurance for the benefit of the Government.

Although, on first consideration, the proposal appears practicable, it does not stand up against mature consideration. Since the amount of an Insured's income tax as of the indefinite future date of a claim for a Business Interruption loss is unpredictable, to specifically exclude coverage of such tax and also maintain insurance to the amount required by the contribution clause would be difficult if not impossible.

Any amount recovered for the account of net profit in the event of a loss claim would be taxable thereby defeating the Insured's objective of not paying for insurance for the Government's benefit. And if underinsurance in the amount of the estimated tax, without specific exclusion of the tax, be undertaken, the result will be a contribution penalty which will reduce the Insured's recovery for the account of his own loss of net profit and necessarily continuing expenses.

Any such attempt to interfere with the normal functioning of Business Interruption Insurance, as insurance designed to do for the Insured's business what it would have done for itself in the production of earnings "before taxes," is unwise. Moreover such attempts disregard the fact that, since premiums paid for business insurance are a business expense deductible from income when computing tax, the major portion of the cost of full coverage falls upon the government indirectly.

Although sums received by Insured in settlement of Business Interruption losses are substitutes for the sums that his business would have earned had not property damage prevented, attempts have been made to evade the payment of income tax on the proceeds of Business Interruption Insurance loss recoveries.

Where such insurance is written to indemnify for loss of net profit, the Federal Board of Tax Appeals has invariably ruled that the sum recovered by the Insured is fully taxable income just as the income and profit would have been normally taxed. Even where Business Interruption Insurance was written under a "valued form" policy paying a fixed sum per day without reference to coverage of profit, the Board has held that whatever sum was recovered must be treated the same as sums recovered under property insurance policies, i.e., not taxable if entirely used for replacing the damaged or destroyed property of the same size and quality, but taxable at the Capital Gains Tax maximum rate of 25% in respect of so much of the amount recovered as is not so used and therefore is gain. (See Board of Tax Appeals Case No. 5 BTA Decision No. 1955, Flaxinum Insulating Company, November 30, 1926.) Some accountants have expressed belief that the Board of Tax Appeals might apply the regular income tax to the amount of gain if there were evidence that the amount of flat insurance per day was predicated upon past and anticipated profits.

Not only are "valued form" Business Interruption policies prohibited in most states but, where written with the purpose of evading payment of income tax and succeeding in that objective, cease to be insurance against loss of earnings. To purchase "valued form" Business Interruption Insurance as a substitute for Property Damage Insurance is to purchase a form of insurance wholly unsuited for the purpose since recoveries in case of loss are on the basis of time to replace and not on the basis of value of physical property damaged or destroyed. For additional discussion of Valued Policies, the reader is referred to Chapter 2.

10. **Rent**—Both as a source of income and as an item of expense, Rent, and insurance against loss of it, are frequently subjects of queries with respect to their relation to Business Interruption Insurance and Extra Expense Insurance. Where, because of lease requirements, rent is a necessarily continuing expense, it is covered by the Business Interruption Insurance carried by the Lessee. When rent is abated it is not covered by the Lessee's Business Interruption Insurance and the Lessor needs Rent Insurance. Where the Lessor occupies part of a building for his business and leases part to a tenant, several alternatives are presented as follows:

(1) If the Lessee operates a department of the Lessor's business (such as a restaurant in a department store), the Lessor's rental income should be covered by Business Interruption insurance.

(2) If the Lessee's occupancy is separate from the Lessor's, the Lessor can

(a) carry separate Rent Insurance and exclude coverage

of rent income from his Business Interruption insurance, doing so by endorsement to avoid misunderstanding, or

(b) include coverage of rent income under his Business Interruption Insurance and dispense with separate Rent Insurance.

Frequently Lessor's elect the (a) alternative when the rate for Rent Insurance is lower than the rate for Business Interruption Insurance, and/or where the following advantages of Rent Insurance over Business Interruption Insurance are important to the Insured,

(1) Coinsurance based on time to rebuild instead of annual value,

(2) Absence of limitation on recovery to "actual loss sustained" which is provided in rent forms in some states

(3) Gratis coverage against untenantability resulting from damage to outside sources of electricity or heat which is provided under rent forms in some states.

The practice of carrying Rent Insurance on guest rooms of hotels or rooming houses supplemented by Business Interruption Insurance applying to other portions of the Insured's premises with the Rental Value Exclusion Clause attached to the latter, is prohibited in some territories.

The (b) alternative is likely to be adopted where the foregoing are not important and/or the Lessor is financially interested in the Lessee's business, and insurance is written in the joined names of Lessor and Lessee. In this event, however, both interests may suffer a coinsurance penalty, because of the uncertain Business Interruption value, which would not be suffered under a Rent Insurance Policy because the rent income is fixed. The (b) alternative can be construed to be in violation of filed rules in some states because the rates and the bases and permissible percentages of contribution under Rent and Business Interruption policy forms differ, raising the question of discrimination. The safe and clear cut method is to insure separately each insurable interest.

For a discussion of the relation between Extra Expense and Rental Value Insurance see end of Chapter 15.

11. Business Interruption Classification of Expenses Paid by Insured—

(1) Deductible from income when determining application of Contribution Clause.

(2) Not deductible from income when determining application of Contribution Clause.

(3) Recoverable as necessarily continuing expense in the event of loss.

(4) Not recoverable because discontinuable in the event of loss.

The above classifications of expenses apply to various expense items as indicated by their key numbers following the names of expense items in the listing below.

Advertising (2). When contract not cancellable (3) otherwise (4). Recoverable when incurred as expediting expense to establish temporary quarters.

Bad Debts (1) (4)

Collection Expense (1) (4)

Commissions to Salesmen (1) and (4) (unless guaranteed) or (2) and (3) depending upon circumstances such as the essentiality of salesmen. See also Selling Agents Commissions and Personal Income coverages at end of Chapter 9.

Depreciation (2) ; (3) in respect of undamaged property. (See Subdivision (2) of Chapter 16)

Discounts (1) (4)

Donations (2) (3)

Dues (2) ; (3) or (4) depending upon circumstances.

Heat, Light & Power (1) under Item I, Two Item Policy Form. (2) under Gross Earnings Policy Form, but refer to discussion of service businesses in Chapter 6. (3) if supplied under non-cancellable contract, otherwise (4).

Insurance Premiums (2) and (3). Premiums or assessments for Workmen's Compensation, Unemployment, Hospitalization and Group Life Insurance, Social Security, and Pensions, to the extent applicable to Payroll of Group II Employees are treated as part of Item II under the Two Item Policy Form. Premiums for Life insurance on executives and essential employees class as (2) and (3).

Interest on Indebtedness (2) (3)

Payroll (2) and (3) as respects executives and essential employees. As respects payroll of Group II Employees "Ordinary Payroll" (1) if policy covers only under Item I of Two Item Policy Form; (2) and (3) if insured under Item II of Two Item Policy Form; (2) and (3) if policy written with Gross Earnings Form.

Professional Services (2); (3) or (4) depending upon necessities.

Rent—(See Sub-division (10) of Chapter 16)

Repairs and Maintenance (2); (3) or (4) depending upon necessities.

Royalties (2) when based on actual production. (3) if contract non-cancellable. (4) in direct proportion to reduced production.

Subscriptions (2); (3) or (4) depending upon circumstances.

Supplies (1) and (4) as respects wrapping and packing materials; expendable machine and tool accessories; explosives, water; gasoline, lubricants and tires unless deducted under Transportation. (See Work Sheets Chapters 4, 5 and 6, and discussion respecting non-manufacturing businesses in Chapter 6)

Taxes if on property (2); (3) on whole, or on undamaged property depending upon negotiations with taxing authority. If on income (2); (3) or as profit item depending upon bookkeeping. (See subdivision (9) of Chapter 16)

Transportation and Vehicles When supplied by outside parties entire expense is (1) and any guaranty is (3). When supplied by the Insured's vehicles (4) and only that portion chargeable to feed, gasoline, lubricants and maintenance is

(1) and drivers are treated as essential or Payroll of Group II Employees according to necessities. (See Formulas "X" and "Y" in Work Sheets—Chapters 4 and 5)

Traveling (2) ; (3) or as expediting expense incurred to reduce loss.

12. **Allied Perils Coverages**—Business Interruption insurance can and should be purchased against any peril a property insurance company is chartered and authorized by law to insure against. The "allied perils" (allied more or less with fire and lightning) most frequently the object of coverage are windstorm, tornado and hurricane, hail, explosion, riot and civil commotion, damage by aircraft and vehicles and smoke from defective heating or cooking apparatus, all of which are included in the "Extended Coverage Endorsement" which, to a steadily increasing extent, is attached to Fire insurance policies, but may also be insured against individually under separate policies.

Next in importance and frequency of coverage are Vandalism and Malicious Mischief, Sprinkler Leakage, General Water Damage, Flood and Earthquake, and building collapse. To these in time of war is added War Risk coverage.

The peril of explosion of steam boilers and certain other steam containers, explosion of flywheels and breakdowns of electrical machinery, as written by Casualty insurance companies, is beyond the purview of this book.

Wherever loss of earnings may result from property damage or destruction by any peril, Business Interruption Insurance can and should be carried, but for recovery to be secured the loss must be the result of direct and not consequential damage, unless the Insurer assumes liability for loss resulting from such damage. (See Section (2) of this chapter.)

Usually Business Interruption Insurance is written under Fire insurance policies to cover only against loss of earnings sustained as a result of property damage by fire and extended coverage perils to the Insured's fixed business premises, or to the fixed premises of others upon the operation of which the Insured's earnings are dependent.

Little use has been made of Business Interruption Insurance written under Inland Marine or Multiple Peril forms of policy. Comparatively few salesmen of Inland Marine forms of Property insurance on mobile apparatus or materials or equipment in transit or on instrumentalities of transportation and communication, have realized that when such property is essential to the production of the insured's earnings, such earnings should also be protected by Inland Marine Business Interruption insurance. Examples of property essential to production of earnings are mobile contractors equipment—such as tractors, pile drivers, shovels and cranes, materials, equipment or machinery in process of shipment to the fixed premises of the insured by land, inland waterways or air; toll bridges and tunnels, piers, wharves, docks, marine railways, and radio and TV broadcasting equipment. This latter group constitutes the largest volume of Business Interruption writings—doubtless because manuals of rules specifically direct attention to their eligibility for Business Interruption Insurance.

Moreover, few insurance buyers and salesmen seem to realize that earnings dependent upon materials or equipment in transit to the insured's plant by ocean conveyances may be protected by Ocean Marine Business Interruption Insurance. Even less attention has been devoted to Multiple Peril or Line forms of Business Interruption Insurance— doubtless because the perils for which Multiple Peril Property insurance is of value (other than the catastrophic perils of fire, windstorm, explosion and riot—which are coverable under Fire policies, and earthquake for which separate policies are available) are not catastrophic, and therefore are unlikely to produce time element losses of much consequence to earnings. However, in view of the trend toward "package policies," Multiple Peril Business Interruption Insurance will doubtless be developed when experience with Multiple Peril Property Insurance forms indicates practicable ways and means of also insuring against loss of earnings involving the time element.

Although this book is designed to deal with Business Interruption Insurance as written to protect against loss of earnings resulting from damage to or destruction of physical property, it seems appropriate at this point to briefly call attention to available corresponding forms of Life and Personal Accident and Health insurance—designed to indemnify a business for the loss of a key man by death, or an individual for the loss of earnings or necessarily continuing business expenses resulting from incapacitation by accident or illness. Whether the bottleneck of a business is a machine, process, or an executive, the principle is the same. Therefore, complete insurance protection for a business— whether a large corporation, partnership, or a one-man affair—should include some form of Business Interruption Insurance—not only against damage to business premises and property, but also against death, personal accident, or illness of the key executive.

13. SUGGESTIONS TO INSURANCE AGENTS AND BROKERS

1. Be certain of your prospect's insurable interest (see Chapter 2).

2. Secure the Fire and Extended Coverage Endorsement rates chargeable for each of the policy forms applicable to your prospect's premises.

3. Inspect your prospect's premises, noting the "bottlenecks" (see Chapter 2). Begin interview with your prospect by outlining in simple language the purpose and operation of Business Interruption insurance, referring to the "bottlenecks" of his operations and premises which may be closed by property damage resulting in loss of earnings. Read the "Suggestions to Prospective Buyers" presented

287

in paragraph (14); also use the Dollar Bill Demonstration in Chapter 1 and the testimonies of satisfied loss claimants in Appendix 9.

4. If your prospect is a merchant, tactfully develop information as to his annual sales and cost of merchandise. If he is reluctant to disclose the amount of his sales, develop the annual cost of merchandise sold and the average "mark up," i.e., the percentage by which the cost of merchandise is marked up (increased) to determine selling price. (If the mark up is 30%, sales are 130% of cost of merchandise.) Subtract cost of merchandise from sales to secure "Gross Earnings."

Assuming the Gross Earnings Form with 50% Contribution Clause is to be used, develop whether insurance amounting to 50% of Gross Earnings will be sufficient to indemnify for the prospect's loss of net profit (gross earnings less all expenses), plus the loss in expenses which will necessarily continue during suspension of business, all for the longest period of time that the Insured's business can be shut down because of property damage or destruction.

If 50% of Gross Earnings is sufficient, after allowing for a possible increase in the prospect's business and earnings, quote the premium cost of the determined amount. If 50% is insufficient, quote premium cost for the 60%, 70% or 80% Contribution Clause.

In basing your proposal on the Gross Earnings form, you will be offering your prospect the contract that four out of five merchants are buying because of its simplicity (see Chapter 6.)

If, however, your prospect inquires about any other available contract, or discloses that he is adverse to insuring ordinary payroll, subtract the sum of annual "ordinary payroll," and of heat, light and power, from Gross Earnings; take 80% of the remainder as the amount of insurance to be carried under Item I of the Two Item form (see Chapter 5), and quote premium cost at the rate prescribed for that form. Determine whether more than the 30 days gratis coverage of stock is required. (See Chapter 10) If a merchant objects to the Contribution (Coinsurance) Clauses in both the Gross Earnings and Two Item policy forms, offer him the "Earnings Insurance Form," which does not contain such a clause and is described in Chapter 7.

5. If your prospect is a manufacturer, you cannot assume that the Gross Earnings form is the better purchase. Because many manufacturers are opposed to carrying any insurance on "ordinary payroll," your prospect's attitude toward it should be ascertained, and the annual amount of "ordinary payroll" and the expense of heat, light and power determined.

If the sum of these items of expense is in excess of the critical percentages of gross earnings shown in Chapter 6, the premium cost of the Two Item form will be less than the cost of the Gross Earnings form. However, your prospect should be made to realize that the advantages of the Gross Earnings over the Two Item form may offset its greater premium cost. If the prospect is disinclined to insure ordinary payroll even for the minimum of 50%, the fact that recovery for the ordinary payroll which is necessarily continuing during a suspension of business is possible under the Gross Earnings form, plus the simplicity of that form, may make it worth the difference in cost.

When the choice of policy form has been determined proceed as previously suggested for merchants. Determine whether more than 30 days gratis coverages of "raw stock" or "stock in process" are required (see Chapter 10.)

6. If your prospect operates a service type business (hotel, restaurant, garage, theatre, or other amusement enterprise) read "Service Type Businesses" in Chapter 6 before determining the amount of insurance required by the Contribution Clause. If he objects to the Contribution Clause, offer the Earnings Insurance Form described in Chapter 7.

7. Having secured your prospect's order for direct Business Interruption Insurance, his possible need for Contingent Business Interruption Insurance should be determined. If his business is dependent upon electric light or power, heat, gas, or water, furnished by a public service plant show him how his policy can be extended to cover loss of earnings caused by the interruption of the supply of such utilities. Also find out whether he needs any other forms of Contingent Business Interruption Insurance described in Chapter 9.

8. In any case, avoid the use of a formal printed Work Sheet when determining the amount of insurance, except when the amount cannot be determined during your interview, and it is necessary to leave a Work Sheet with the prospect to be filled out at his convenience.

An informal work sheet, outlined on any available sheet of paper, will emphasize the simplicity of the process of determining the required amount of insurance.

9. If the prospective buyer objects to the quoted premium cost, suggest that it can be reduced (for example) by 50% if he will stand 50% of any loss of earnings that may occur. (by being a coinsurer). Usually, the great difference between the premium saved, and the substantial shortage in the prospect's recovery of loss sustained because of a prolonged suspension of business, will convince him that he cannot afford to be "penny wise and pound foolish."

Also compare the loss that may be recovered for suspension of business for, say, one day with the pro-rata premium paid for one day's coverage.

For example, if the annual premium for insurance of $12,000 is $60, the daily premium cost of a daily recovery of $40 loss sustained, in case of suspension of business, is only 20¢ and for only 20¢ per day, $240 may be recovered for an average week's suspension of business.

Moreover, the entire premium of $60 paid for a full year's

protection may be recovered for a complete suspension of business for only $1\frac{1}{2}$ days when earnings are average, or for only one day when earnings may be high because of seasonal business conditions.

10. Be prepared to answer objections raised by the prospect such as the following:

(a) *"My business cannot be interrupted for more than a short time and any property damage can be so quickly repaired that I don't need Business Interruption Insurance."*

Answer: "Even a slight damage can result in some loss of earnings which can exceed the premium paid. Conditions beyond your control, such as bad weather and strikes, can delay repairs and transportation of essential materials and equipment. Bear in mind that insurance is designed to indemnify against loss caused by unforeseen events."

(b) *"We don't need Business Interruption insurance because our customers will wait until we resume operations."*

Answer: "Maybe they will and maybe they won't. The temptation will be strong to patronize your competitors to secure what they need when they need it, particularly in the case of seasonal merchandise. If you satisfy your customers with goods bought from a competitor, paying his emergency price and reducing your profit, Business Interruption Insurance will pay for the loss."

(c) *"We have several stores (or factories) from which we can supply customers."*

Answer: "Granted, but suppose they are operating full time to satisfy their trade. If they operate overtime, there will be extra expense to reduce your profit, and loss of time in making deliveries will antagonize customers and curtail sales."

(d) *"By working my factory overtime after operations are resumed, lost production will be made up."*

Answer: "Lost time and what it represents can never be regained, particularly in case of prolonged suspensions of operations because of serious property damage. Overtime labor is expensive, and increased expenses mean reduced profits. Besides, lost orders from customers who cannot wait are lost forever."

(e) "Our company is so strong financially that we are able to self-insure its earnings."

Answer: "Will your stockholders be satisfied to forego their dividends while expenses that necessarily continue during suspension of business are paid from surplus or reserve funds? If they discover that you refused to buy Business Interruption Insurance, by which their dividends would have been paid and reserve funds protected against depletion, what will your job be worth?"

(f) "We cannot afford to buy Business Interruption Insurance because business is poor."

Answer: "While Business Interruption Insurance is important to a profitable business when business is good, it is indispensable to a struggling business when business is poor, because it can save it from complete failure and bankruptcy, by paying the inescapable expenses during the time of business suspension. It will do for a business what it would have done for itself, had it not been interrupted by property damage. Temporary poor business of a well established business is a reason for carrying Business Interruption Insurance, not for rejecting it."

11. Be consistent. Buy Extra Expense Insurance on your own office thereby protecting your business against loss of earnings resulting from extra expense incurred to continue necessary office operations, and demonstrating your own belief in the value of Time Element forms of insurance.

14. SUGGESTIONS TO PROSPECTIVE BUYERS

1. Review Chapters 1 and 2.

2. Inspect your business premises, studying every situation to decide whether it is a "bottleneck" of your operations. Having identified the bottlenecks (which may be essential equipment, machines, materials, features of building construction, records, etc.), estimate conservatively the length of time your business may be totally or partially shut down in case one or more of such bottlenecks, or your buildings and all contents, are damaged or destroyed by fire, explosion, windstorm, hurricane, hail, rioters, malicious persons, sprinkler leakage, falling aircraft, vehicles, or smoke from defective heating units.

3. Then consider whether your business can afford to be shut down for the length of time required to repair, rebuild or replace the damaged or destroyed property, meanwhile losing the net profit plus the expenses that will necessarily continue and that would have been earned had the disaster not occurred.

If you are an employee, consider whether you and your associates can afford to lose your salaries and wages while the damaged or destroyed premises or contents of your business are being rehabilitated. Then realize that, if Business Interruption insurance is carried, the insurance companies will indemnify the business for the loss of net profit and necessarily continuing expenses, including dividends for stockholders, salaries and wages, taxes, interest on indebtedness, etc., until rehabilitation is completed and the premises are ready for resumption of business.

4. Assuming that you will conclude, as every foresighted and prudent businessman must, that your business should be protected by Business Interruption Insurance call, in a capable insurance agent or broker, and authorize him to provide the coverage you require based upon the following information which you will furnish:

(a) Amount of your annual net sales.

(b) Annual cost of the merchandise you sell if you operate a retailing or wholesaling business; or annual cost of the raw stock and supplies used to produce your finished product if you operate a factory. If you operate a hotel, restaurant, garage, or amusement enterprise, read "Service Type Businesses" in Chapter 6 and furnish the annual cost of materials and supplies consumed in the service you render.

(c) Provide information as to the annual expense of heat, light and power; the annual expense of payroll of Group II Employees (see discussion of Payroll in Chapter 5.); and your attitude toward insuring such payroll.

(d) Give your agent or broker your conservative estimate of the longest period of time your business can be completely shut down by property damage to or destruction of your buildings and their contents or the essential materials, such as lumber, stored outside of your buildings; also, your estimate of the loss of net profit and necessarily continuing expenses that may be sustained during that period of time.

(e) Read Chapter 9 and inform your agent or broker whether you operate more than one store or factory, and whether each such store or factory is operated independently of others; also whether your business can be interrupted by lack of electricity, gas, heat, water, or materials, or parts of your products furnished to your business by other businesses, and identify the sources of such essential services.

(f) Read Chapter 8 and, if you operate a mercantile or non-manufacturing business, consider substituting the Agreed Amount Contribution Clause for the percentage type Contribution Clause. In any event, whether you operate a store, factory, or service type business, consider the Premium Adjustment Form of Policy.

(g) Having purchased Business Interruption Insurance watch the trend of your business earnings, and periodically adjust the amount of insurance carried, bearing in mind the requirement of the Contribution Clause in your policies and that Business Interruption Insurance covers prospective and not past earnings.

Having followed these suggestions, you will have acquired the peace of mind enjoyed only by managers of businesses protected against loss to the only objective for which they exist—EARNINGS—resulting from damage to or destruction of business premises.

15. SUGGESTIONS TO CREDIT MEN

1. Read Chapter 1 and the immediately preceding "Suggestions to Prospective Buyers."

2. Realize that among your objectives when you grant credit to a business, are the following:

(a) The safety of your loan.

(b) The preservation of a profitable customer.

Consider how Business Interruption Insurance carried by a customer achieves these objectives, by providing funds during the time his business is shut down by property damage resulting in the following benefits to him and to you.

Preservation of the efficiency of your customer's organization by paying salaries and wages of necessary employees so that business can be promptly and efficiently resumed when repairs and replacements are completed.

Payment of your customer's bills for necessarily continuing fixed charges and expenses including taxes and interest on indebtedness, without drawing upon his surplus funds or upon the funds received from Property Insurance which are needed for repairs and replacements.

Assurance of the resumption of your customer's business by sustaining his credit, providing indirect collateral security for your loans, preventing good loans from becoming bad debts and thereby preserving a profitable customer.

3. Influence all your customers to maintain adequate amounts of Business Interruption Insurance, thereby assuring their solvency and continuation in business in case of

destruction of their business premises by fire or other catastrophe.

4. Be consistent. Be certain that your own business premises are covered by Business Interruption Insurance. If you represent a bank, or maintain an office not part of a mercantile or factory premises covered by Business Interruption insurance, be certain that your bank or office is covered by Extra Expense Insurance (see Chapter 15).

APPENDIX 1

(By permission of Western Adjustment & Inspection Co.)

Loss Adjustment Under Per Diem Policy Form On Manufacturing Plant

Use and Occupancy Claim for Fire Nov. 14, 1929

U and O Value and Loss based on insured's books showing an accurate division of departments—Loss to "Department No. 1"

	Department No. 1		Other Departments	
Net Sales 11/1/28 to 11/1/29	$273,745.25		$146,248.28	
Manufacturing Costs				
Inventory 11/1/28	$ 49,969.25		$ 84,407.76	
Purchases 11/1/28 to 11/1/29	163,026.37		57,434.60	
Labor 11/1/28 to 11/1/29	36,642.52		33,989.95	
Fuel 11/1/28 to 11/1/29	2,540.37		1,839.58	
	$252,178.51		$177,671.89	
Less Inventory 11/1/29	52,995.93	199,182.58	67,466.86	110,205.03
Gross Profit		$ 74,562.67		$ 36,043.25

EXPENSE

Executives' Salaries	$ 12,541.67		$ 4,125.00	
Office	2,673.61		1,936.07	
Repairs	2,667.02		2,901.49	
Miscellaneous Expense	602.67		296.85	
Taxes	1,387.57		1,004.80	
Insurance	772.99		559.76	
Salesmen's Expense	2,369.14		789.64	
Supplies and Miscellaneous	9,299.75		5,071.21	
Association Dues and Legal	600.69	32,915.41	435.20	17,066.02
Net Profit		$ 41,647.26		$ 18,977.23

	Use and Occupancy Value		
	Dept. No. 1	Other Depts.	Total
Executive Salaries	$ 12,541.65	$ 4,125.00	$ 16,666.65
Skilled Labor and Office Salaries	6,916.65	3,900.00	10,816.65
Taxes	1,387.57	1,004.80	2,392.37
Insurance	515.42	378.99	894.41
Dues and Legal Retainer	600.99	435.20	1,036.19
Net Profit	41,647.26	18,977.23	60,624.49
	$ 63,609.54	$ 28,821.22	$ 92,430.76

Agreed Loss Dept No. 1
5 days 100%
10 days 50%
Insurance $75,000.00
Daily Insurance Liability 1/300 of $75,000.00=$250.00
Daily U and O Value 1/300 of 92,430.76= 308.10

LOSS & DAMAGE

		Loss	Claim
Insured's books indicate Dept. 1 would have produced 68.2% of the total production in November			
68.2% of the daily U and O Value=	$ 210.12 Value		
Total U and O Value for Year	$ 92,430.76		
5 days loss at 210.12		$ 1,050.60	
Under Operation of Partial Suspension Clause Companies' Liability Is			
210.12/308.10 of $250.00=170.50 x 5			$ 852.50
10 days loss @ $105.06		1,050.60	
Under Operation of Partial Suspension Clause Companies' Liability Is			
105.06/308.10 of $250.00=85.25 x 10			852.50
	$ 92,430.76	$ 2,101.20	$ 1,705.00

297

APPENDIX 2

(By permission of Western Adjustment & Inspection Co.)

Loss Adjustment Under Weekly Policy Form
Mercantile Business

Use and Occupancy Claim—Fire Jan. 11, 1930

U and O Value and Loss based on books and
records of insured—verified and corrected
by adjuster

Sales 1/1/29 to 1/1/30		$136,643.23
Cost of Merchandise Sold		
Inventory 1/1/29	$ 22,742.68	
Net Purchase 1/1/29 to 1/1/30	83,371.08	
	$106,113.76	
Less Inventory 1/1/30	26,880.40	79,233.36
Gross Profit		$ 57,409.87

EXPENSE		U and O Value
Salaries Officers	$ 12,525.00	$ 12,525.00
Salaries Employers	17,725.58	475.50
Rent	7,875.00	1,394.69
Repairs and Maintenance	720.67	
Insurance	696.42	15,240.00
Heat, Light and Water	1,394.69	7,875.00
Advertising	2,764.56	
Auditing	490.81	490.81
General Expense	214.71	
Supplies	541.39	
Telephone and Telegraph	254.60	
Towel Service	19.90	19.90
Traveling Expense	162.49	
Depreciation	459.44	459.44
Charity	44.00	
Taxes	443.96	443.96
Association Dues	205.40	205.40
Interest	150.83	150.83
	$ 46,689.45	
Net Profit	$ 10,720.42	10,720.42
		$ 50,000.95

Loss As Agreed
January 11—Total.
January 13-14-15—Total; 16-17-18—Partial

NOTE

Loss being for so short a time most of the insurable expense continues.

INSURANCE

December 29 to April 26, inclusive	17 weeks @	$1,000.00	$17,000.00
April 27 to September 27, inclusive	22 weeks @	600.00	13,200.00
September 29 to December 27, inclusive	13 weeks @	2,000.00	26,000.00
			$56,200.00

	Sales	Net Profit	Continuing Expense	U & O Value	Insurance	Loss	Claim
Dec. 29-Jan. 4	$ 2,642.40	$ 207.31	$ 755.40	$ 962.71	$ 1,000.00	None	None
Jan. 5-Jan. 11	2,550.82	200.14	755.40	955.54	1,000.00	$168.57	$168.57
Jan. 12-Jan. 18	2,574.80	202.02	755.40	957.42	1,000.00	677.39	677.39
Jan. 19-Jan. 25	2,720.60	213.46	755.40	968.86	1,000.00	None	None
Jan. 26-Feb. 1	2,960.74	232.30	755.40	987.70	1,000.00	None	None
47 other weeks	123,193.87	9,665.19	35,503.53	45,168.72	51,200.00	None	None
	$136,643.23	$10,720.42	$39,280.53	$50,000.95	$56,200.00	$845.96	$845.96

Profit ratio of Sales, 7.846.

Anticipated Sales January 11	$ 450.00 Loss 450.00/2550.82 of 955.54=168.57
Anticipated Sales January 13-14-15	1,200.00
Reduction of Sales January 16-17-18	621.70
	$1,821.70 Loss 1821.70/2574.80 of 957.42=677.39

298

(By permission Western Adjustment & Inspection Co.)

Loss Adjustment Under Two Item Policy Form On Manufacturing Plant Without Ordinary Payroll Coverage. With Allowance for Expediting Expense

	Value	Loss
Use and Occupancy Value based on the calendar year 1-1-44 to 12-31-44. Sales and production in 1945 indicate the experience for the year immediately following the loss would have been the same as the calendar year of 1944:		
Net Sales _____	$2,008,739.54	
Less:		
Cost of Materials Used_____$974,226.66		
Ordinary Payroll and Payroll Taxes 477,555.31		
Heat, Light and Power_____ 18,973.45		
	1,470,755.42	
Use and Occupancy Value_____		$537,984.12

Loss Computation:

This loss seriously damaged the buildings, machinery, raw stock and stock in process. A severe damage by water occurred to cutting dies located in a basement vault. The loss to buildings and countents amounted to $200,-974.61. This figure is after depreciation was deducted and before the application of con-contribution clauses.

The damages described suspended operations completely in the Punch Press Dept. through the loss of use of the dies destroyed in the basement areas. In addition the destruction of raw stock and stock in process caused a loss of production.

Immediately after the loss occurred it was agreed that insured should remove all possible machinery equipment and stock that was usable from the damaged buildings and re-install these items in another building the insured owned so as to resume operations at the earliest possible time. The involved buildings could not be restored for several months, necessitating use of other property. Arrangements were also completed to obtain replacement of dies destroyed through overtime work and at extra costs from outside manufacturers. In about one month the insured had re-established all machine operations but the lack of necessary dies caused a partial suspension of operations for another four months.

This loss was therefore adjusted on the basis of the loss of U & O earnings on that production actually prevented plus the extraordinar expense incurred to obtain replacement of dies and setting up machinery at a temporary location. All the insureds' normal expenses continued in their entirety without any abatement throughout the interruption of production:

Sales value of production prevented as determined from examination of orders on hand and production records for period 3-29-45 to 9-1-45:

Punch Press Department_____$ 48,333.40		
Die Press Department_____ 70,833.40		
Production Prevented _____	$ 119,166.80	

Less:

Cost of Materials Used	$ 49,677.46		
Ordinary Payroll and Payroll Taxes	29,838.74		
Heat, Light and Power	904.20	90,420.40	
Loss of Earnings			$28,746.40

Extraordinary Expense Incurred to Reduce Loss:

Labor and miscellaneous expense removing machinery, equipment and stock from involved buildings and installing in temporary locations	$ 3,669.90
Trucking and machinery movers expense	1,234.74
Temporary power and light wiring at new location	1,399.31
Labor and miscellaneous expense moving offices, records and supplies	1,199.47
Labor and cartage handling raw stock to and from temporary warehouses to serve manufacturing operations in temporary buildings	1,547.50
Rental of temporary warehouse space for raw materials to facilitate temporary operations	2,640.00
Overtime labor and above normal costs of outside manufacturers in the replacement of dies destroyed so as to avoid further loss of production for period 3-29-45 to 9-1-45	6,533.33
Estimated extra cost of obtaining substitute raw materials for those destroyed so as not to delay production	1,500.00
Labor, truckers, machinery movers and miscellaneous expense returning machinery, equipment, office fixture and stock from temporary locations to original building when restored	4,775.62
Overtime expense incurred in replacing shop and office materials so as to resume operations promptly	297.82

*Total Extra-Ordinary Expense	$24,797.69
Total Use and Occupancy	$53,544.09

Recovery is:
Under the application of 80% Contribution Clause liability for loss of earnings is limited to:

300,000.00/430,387.30 of 28,746.40 or	$20,037.58
Extra-Ordinary Expense	24,797.69
Total Recovery	$44,835.27

*Adjusters' computation of test of what loss would have been if the insured had not used temporary measures to carry on operations;
Sales value of production that would have been prevented;

Die Press Department—5 months	$177,150.00
Punch Press Department—5 months	241,650.00
Total Production that would have been lost	$418,800.00
U & O Earnings on such prevented production would have been (Est.)	83,760.00
U & O Recovery after application of contribution clause (300,000.00/430,387.30 of $83,760.00)	58,384.62
Less: Amount of this adjustment	44,835.27
Savings of U & O Loss by use of temporary building	$13,549.35

APPENDIX 4

(By permission Western Adjustment & Inspection Co.)

Loss Adjustment Under Two Item Policy Form
On Manufacturing Plant
With Coverage of Ordinary Payroll

ITEM I

Value as agreed, viz:

Anticipated Sales—12 months____		$735,018.32
Cost of Sales		
Materials _____	$284,186.40	
Direct Labor & P.R. Tax_____	166,168.52	
Heat, Light & Power_____	8,090.12	458,445.04
Use and Occupancy Value_____		$276,573.28

Loss as agreed, based on analysis of partial suspension period— December 16, 1945 to March 17, 1946)

	Anticipated Operation		Actual Operation	
Net Sales _____		$183,754.58		$139,481.35
Materials _____	$ 71,046.60		$ 61,962.20	
Direct Labor & Taxes_____	41,542.13		35,762.70	
Heat, Light & Power_____	2,022.54	114,611.26	1,763.88	99,488.78
		$ 69,143.32		$ 39,992.57
Departmental Expense _____	2,677.53		2,677.53	
Foundry Expense _____	6,177.77		2,143.71	
Building Repairs _____	15.16		15.16	
Machinery Repairs _____	262.92		262.92	
Job Freight & Express_____	615.98		615.98	
Insurance _____	2,052.03		2,052.03	
Depreciation _____	1,783.41		1,585.59	
Taxes _____	1,134.75		1,134.75	
Rent _____	15.00		15.00	
Exec. Salary & Bonus_____	4,938.64		2,940.75	
Office _____	3,169.46		3,169.46	
Watchmen _____	1,652.90		1,652.90	
Engineering _____	638.40		638.40	
Other Adm. Expense_____	2,921.68	27,995.63	2,921.68	21,825.86
Net Profit _____		$ 41,147.69		$ 18,166.71

SUMMARY

	Anticipated	Actual	Loss
Production _____	$183,754.58	$139,481.35	$ 44,273.23
Cost & Expense_____	142,606.89	121,314.64	21,292.25
Net Profit _____	$ 41,147.69	$ 18,166.71	$ 22,980.98
Value—as Developed_____	$276,573.28		
Insurance Required—80% _____	$221,252.62		
Insurance carried _____	$245,000.00		

80% Contribution Clause complied with

ITEM II—ORDINARY PAYROLL EXPENSE

Value 90 days_____$ 41,542.13

Loss as agreed, based on expense incurred during suspension period, checked and approved by adjusters—

Week Ended

January	6	10 men	$ 287.75
January	13	10 men	291.00
January	20	10 men	291.00
January	27	10 men	291.00
February	3	10 men	291.00
February	10	10 men	291.00
February	17	10 men	291.00
February	24	10 men	291.00
March	3	10 men	291.00

| March | 10 | 10 men | | 280.92 |
| March | 17 | 8 men | | 221.00 |

		$ 3,117.67
Payroll Taxes _____		65.47
Loss _____		$ 3,183.14
Value—as developed_____		$ 41,542.13
Insurance required—80%_____		$ 33,233.70
Insurance carried _____		$ 45,000.00
80%Contribution Clause complied with.		

		Value	Loss
UNEARNED PREMIUMS		$986.68	$86.08

RECAPITULATION

Item	Value	Loss	Insurance	Claim
I—Use and Occupancy_____	$276,573.28	$ 22,980.98	$245,000.00	$ 22,980.98
II—Ordinary Payroll _____	41,542.13	3,183.14	45,000.00	3,183.14
Unearned Premium _____	986.68	86.08	986.68	86.08
TOTALS _____	$319,102.09	$ 26,250.20	$290,986.68	$ 26,250.20

APPENDIX 5

(By permission Western Adjustment & Inspection Co.)

Loss Adjustment Under Gross Earnings Policy Form Non-Manufacturing Business

Business conducted by insured is a theatre lounge bar selling wines and liquors. No food is sold and their records indicate a successful business operated on a very profitable basis, and strictly legal.

The lack of sufficient insurance caused the operation of the 50% Coinsurance Clause which was explained to the insured and accepted in a fair-minded manner. The main discussion during the adjustment centered around the length of time required to get ready to do business and the final outcome is entirely in accord with the facts.

FIRE: DECEMBER 14, 1943

"Gross Earnings" anticipated for 12 months following date of fire as agreed, based on actual operations for 12 months' period from 12-1-45 to 11-30-43, viz.:

Sales showing trend of business:
December, 1942 _____	$11,994.72
January, 1943 _____	11,839.13
February, 1943 _____	12,103.50
March, 1943 _____	13,568.77
April, 1943 _____	13,178.11
May, 1943 _____	13,667.01
Total Sales, 6 months_____	$76,351.24

"Gross Earnings" based on actual operations for six months just prior to fire: Sales—Net
June, 1943 _____	$13,115.17
July, 1943 _____	14,576.66
August, 1943 _____	14,172.65
September, 1943 _____	14,427.97
October, 1943 _____	14,431.11

```
November, 1943 _____  14,159.35
        Total Sales 6-1-43—11-30-43_____$84,882.91

Merchandise Inventory 6-1-43_____  31,880.47
Purchases 6-1-43—11-30-43 _____  19,143.18
                                      $51,023.65
    Less Inventory 11-30-43_____  26,855.26
        Cost of Sales—28.47%_____          $24,168.39

            "Gross Earnings," 6 months_____  $60,714.52
            Estimated Gross Earnings, 6 months_____  60,714.52

"Gross Earnings" as agreed for 12 months immediately fol-
    lowing loss _____  $121,429.04
Average anticipated monthly "Gross
    Earnings" _____$10,119.08
Period of suspension is agreed as 2
    months total and loss of "Gross Earn-
    nings" as agreed, 2 x 10,119.08 or____                         $20,238.16
```

	Actual 6 mos 6-1-43 to 11-30-43	Anticipated for 2 mos. Operation	Expenses not Continuing for period of Suspension	
Operating Expenses				
Salaries _____	$24,924.18	$ 8,308.06	$ 4,890.51	
Rent _____	1,825.00	650.00	162.50	
Licenses _____	900.00	300.00	_____	
Insurance _____	550.00	200.00	20.00	
Advertising _____	2,130.55	710.18	594.36	
Miscellaneous Expense _____	392.73	130.90	130.90	
Ice _____	508.09	169.36	169.36	
Heat, Light and Water_____	804.21	454.06	248.06	
Linen _____	458.00	152.66	152.66	
Donations _____	12.50	4.16	4.16	
Interest _____	271.82	123.94	78.00	
Dues _____	113.00	34.34	_____	
Music (A.S.C.A.P.) _____	245.35	81.78	81.78	
Bank Charges _____	60.39	20.12	20.12	
Audit and Legal_____	451.35	150.44	_____	
Repairs _____	912.98	304.32	304.32	
Supplies _____	619.98	206.66	206.66	
Travel _____	358.24	119.42	119.42	
Cabaret Tax _____	4,045.24	1,348.42	1,348.42	
Burglar Alarm Service_____	50.40	16.80	_____	
Social Security Tax_____	1,002.83	334.28	197.58	
Depreciation—Fix. and Imp._____	1,785.26	598.42	518.88	
	$42,422.10	$14,418.32	$ 9,247.69	$ 9,247.69
Loss _____				$10,990.47

```
Claim:
    Insurance required under 50% Coinsurance
    Clause is 50% of $121,429.04 or_____  $60,714.52
    Insurance _____  $40,000.00
    Company's limit of Liability is 40,000.00/
        60.714.52 of $10,990.47 or_____          $ 7,240.75
    Unearned Premium Computation Policies Ex-
        piring 3-30-46 _____
    Unearned Premium for unexpired term 837/
        1096 of $426.61 or $325.80_____
    Proportion of unearned premium due insured
        on account of loss 7240.75/40,000.00 of
        $325.80 or _____                 58.98
            Total Claim _____       $ 7,299.73
```

APPENDIX 6

(By permission Western Adjustment & Inspection Co.)

Loss Adjustment Under Gross Earnings Policy Form
On Manufacturing Plant

BUSINESS INTERRUPTION VALUE

for the period of 2-17-48 to 2-17-49 based
on anticipated net sales for 12 months
subsequent to loss, with due consideration to experience before the loss, verified from insured's records, viz; _____ $54,877.71
Raw materials _____   20,030.36

Gross Earnings & Business Interruption
tion Value _____ $34,847.35
Insurance thereon _____$52,000.00
Insurance required _____ 27,877.88

COMPUTATION OF LOSS

Fire destroyed acid room used in finish-
ishing cut glass and period of full suspension agreed upon at 4 months accounting for seasonal operations estd.
Sales for period 2-17-48 to 6-17-48_____ 16,935.65
Less Raw Materials_____ 6,181.51

Gross Earning Loss _____   10,754.14
Other expenses for period of suspension
2-17-48 to 6-17-48

	Anti-cipated	Non-Con-tinuing
Direct labor _____	$ 6,326.80	$ 1,464.00
Heat, light and power_____	309.76	68.77
Rent _____	500.00	
Depreciation _____	202.74	202.74
Commissions _____	2,116.96	2,116.96
Discount _____	85.37	85.37
Officers salaries _____	2,975.00	
Office salaries _____	499.00	
Adv. & sales expense_____	197.00	
Auto expense _____	82.07	
Donations _____	187.00	
General expense _____	411.98	211.98
Insurance _____	666.83	227.54
Interest _____	62.81	
Legal and auditing_____	200.00	
Repairs _____	135.00	135.00
Taxes and licenses_____	406.82	45.38
Telephone & telegraph_____	156.85	
Traveling expense _____	386.00	200.00
	$15,907.99	$ 4,757.74

Gross earnings loss less Non-Continuing
expense _____   4,757.74
LOSS _____ $ 5,996.40

80% COINSURANCE CLAUSE COMPLIED WITH

APPENDIX 7

Loss Adjustment Under Canadian Gross Profits Policy Form Mercantile Business

Fire December 23, 1951

Because of damage to Building and Contents of approximately $140,000 the Insured's store remained closed until May 12, 1952 and all repairs were not completed for several additional months.

1951 "Turnover"		$245,329.27
20% added for anticipated increase		49,065.85
Estimated turnover year after fire		294,395.12
Less estimated cost of merchandise sold		196,263.42
		98,131.70
All other expenses		89,550.00
	"Net Profit"	$ 8,581.70

"Insured Standing Charges" estimated

Taxes	$ 1900.00	
Interest	5000.00	
Director's Fees	375.00	
Auditor's Fees	2500.00	
Salaries (permanent staff)	30800.00	
Travelling	1200.00	
Advertising	4750.00	
Insurance	2500.00	
Depreciation	5200.00	
Auto upkeep	1100.00	
Light, heat, etc.	1000.00	
Postage, etc.	500.00	
	56,825.00	
Miscellaneous —5%	2,841.00	
	$ 59,666.00	59.666.00
	Gross Profit	$ 68,247.70

"Rate of Gross Profit" is therefore

$$\frac{\text{Gross Profit}}{\text{Turnover}} = \frac{68,247.70}{294,395.12} = 23.2\%$$

Taking into consideration the loss of Christmas sales and the estimated loss of sales in the Toy Department which loss continued subsequent to May 12, 1952 the Reduction in Turnover was estimated to be ... 89,280.00

"Rate of Gross Profit" ... 23.2%

Loss of Gross Profit on Reduction in Turnover	$ 20,712.96

Less discontinuing expenses

Salaries & wages	816.05	
Heat, light etc.	350.00	
Depreciation—equipment	447.44	
Depreciation—building	263.74	
	$ 1.877.23	1.877.23

Loss sustained under Item 1(a) "Reduction in Turnover"	$ 18,835.73

Loss sustained under Item 1(b) "Increase in Cost of Working"
Advertising expense incurred to reclaim customers $5606.00 actual reduced by compromise to ... $ 4,500.00

Application of Coinsurance Clause

Insurance carried $\frac{60,000.00 \times \$ 4500.00}{68,247.70} = \$ 3.956.17$ Item 1 (b)

Insurance required $\frac{60,000.00 \times \$18,835.73}{68,247.70} = \$16,559.43$ Item 1 (a)

Insured's total Recovery	$ 20,515.60

(By Permission Underwriters Adjustment Bureau, Ltd., Toronto)

APPENDIX 8

Loss adjustment under Earnings Insurance policy

COVERAGE—$32,000 under Earnings Insurance, insuring the operation of a large delicatessen and food store. As per the form, liability of the insuring Companies is limited to 25% of the face amount of the insurance in any 30-day consecutive calendar period.

Demonstration of Bus. Int. Value:
(Based upon Profit and Loss Statement for fiscal year ended 1/31/54, prepared by C.P.A., reflecting operations at the market conducted at 7250 ———— Ave., Sales and Gross Earnings obtained at new location from date of opening (5/27/54) through Aug 15, 1954 proved to be virtually identical with those for the same period of fiscal 1954 at the ———— Ave. location; and, accordingly, operating details at that point are used here as being representative of operations at the insured location)—

SALES:

Delicatessen	$186,183.02			
Groceries	262,925.56			
Produce	90,655.72			
		3,478.85		
Deduct Sales returns & refunds		$539,764.30		
			$536,285.45	(100%)

Cost of Sales—

Inventory 2/1/53	$ 11,008.59			
Net Purchases	439,886.23			
Store Supplies	3,018.28			
		$453,913.10		
Deduct Inventory 1/31/54		12,585.62		
Cost of goods			$441,327.48	
			$ 94,957.97	(17.7%)
Add concession rental			4,212.94	(00.78%)
GROSS EARNINGS			$ 99,170.91	

LOSS COMPUTATION:
(Based upon operations for fiscal 1954 at 7250 ———— Ave., those for April, 1954, being adjusted to give effect to increase normally experienced during Passover holiday period. (starting 4/9/54). In view of limit of liability imposed by contract provisions (25% of total amount of coverage within any 30 consecutive days), suspension period is broken down into two 30-day periods, covering the agreed 60-day period of suspension from date of original anticipated opening (3/27/54) to actual opening date, 5/25/54)—

Period #1—(3/27-4/25/54)—

Net Sales anticipated	$39,440.39			
Add for Passover holiday increase	5,112.09			
	$44,552.48			
Gross Profit lost (17.7%)	$ 7,885.79			
Add concession rental loss (00.78%)				
	347.51			
GROSS EARNINGS LOST—PERIOD #1			$8,233.30	

Discontinued Expense—

Heat & Light	$ 90.54		
Store expenses	317.69		
Telephone & Telegraph	26.50		
Truck expenses	58.55		
		$ 493.28	
Anticipated payroll expense	$ 3,927.35		

Actual payments (from records)—

2 wks.—S. Shemsky	$ 90.00		
3 wks.—E. Roth	345.00		
3 wks.—J. Karafin	380.25		
3 wks.—D. Rosenthal	249.00		
4-3/7 wks.—R. Williams	297.99		
4-3/7 wks.—S. Solnick	522.75		
4-3/7 wks.—H. Dichter	454.06		
4-3/7 wks.—A. Lightman	395.91		
3 wks.—H. Earps	165.00		
		$ 2,899.96	
Discontinued payroll expense		$ 1,027.39	
Social Security and Union Welfare Fund (6.5%)		66.78	
			$1,587.45
EARNINGS LOSS—PERIOD #1			$6,645.85

306

```
PERIOD  #2—(4/26-5/25/54)—
  Net Sales anticipated _____        $48,779.21
  Gross Profit Lost (17.7%) _____       $ 8,633.92
  Add concession rental lost (00.78%)_____          380.48
  Gross Earnings Lost—Period #2_____                          $9,014.40
Discontinued Expenses:
  Heat & Light, Store Expenses, Telephone
  & Telegraph and Truck Expenses (identical
  with Period #1, above) _____                 $   493.28
  Anticipated payroll expense—_____       $ 3,800.65
  Actual payments (from records)—
  4-2/7 wks.—S. Solnick _____$505.89
  4-2/7 wks.—R. Williams _____ 288.39
  2-4/7 wks.—H. Dichter _____ 263.65
  1-2/7 wks.—A. Lightman _____ 114.94
                                              $ 1,172.87
  Discontinued payroll expenses _____                  $ 2,627.78
  Social Security & Union Welfare Fund (65%)                    170.81    $3,291.87
  EARNINGS  LOSS—PERIOD  #2_____                                   $5,722.53
RECAPITULATION OF EARNINGS LOSS
  Period  #1—(3/27-4/25/54)  _____—$ 6,645.85
  Period  #2—(4/26-5/25/54)  _____    5,722.53
                                                                    $12,368.38
```

APPENDIX 9

Following are testimonial letters actually written to insurance agents by satisfied Business Interruption Insurance and Extra Expense Insurance policyholders who recovered losses sustained; also by regretful business proprietors who had considered the purchase of Business Interruption Insurance but did not have it when their businesses were shut down by fire damage.

"The Insurance Was a Gift"—Retail Store

"On September 2nd of last year, we were unfortunate enough to suffer a severe loss by fire, completely destroying the stock and partially destroying the fixtures. Because of this, we were forced to stay closed until the 30th of October, or approximately two complete months.

"Fortunately, among the insurance policies carried by our store, we had one covering business interruption. This type of policy is one that every businessman should consider, as it completely covered the fixed expenses of the store as well as covering the net earnings of the business for the period the store was closed.

"We felt that the insurance was a gift, as the premium was ridiculously low for the settlement made."

Bar Closed for 28 Days

"On July 5th, 1948, we suffered a serious fire loss due to defective wiring of one of our electric glass washers. Because considerable fire damage was done to the bar and equipment, and the entire premises were damaged by smoke, we were forced to close our doors for 28 days.

"We wish to express our gratitude to you for seeing to it that our fixed expenses and net earnings were adequately protected by Business Interruption Insurance.

"We realize that we were particularly hard to convince that this coverage was necessary because we were tenants in a fireproof building but, after receiving a check covering our entire loss of profits for this 28 day period—normally our busiest month—we are thoroughly convinced that every businessman should protect his earnings with this type of insurance. We were surprised to learn how much of this protection we were able to buy for so little premium."

Highly Recommended "U. & O."—Retail Store

"On June 9th of last year, we were unfortunate to suffer loss by fire, due to a total loss to the store adjoining our property. Because of this fire we were forced to close our store, with complete loss of profits, for a few weeks, with partial business loss for July, August and September.

"Among insurance policies in our possession we had a Use and Occupancy insurance policy issued by your agency, which completely covered our fixed expenses of the store as well as covering the net earnings of the business for the period of the loss. We highly recommend Use and Occupancy insurance to all merchants as it is as important as the Fire Insurance on stock, furthermore the cost is surprisingly low."

"A Manufacturer Praises U. & O."

"The importance of Use & Occupancy Insurance should not be underestimated. The president of one milling firm which had suffered two fires called us immediately after the fire to offer us his plant facilities to aid in servicing our customers. In our conversation, he mentioned that it was fine that we had some U. & O. Insurance but it was going to be a difficult job to get it adjusted because of its indefinite clauses, etc.

"We are happy to report that, by bringing in our regular accounting firm to aid us, we were successful in arriving at a satisfactory agreement, as to what the loss was under the Use & Occupancy policy and we are very pleased with the manner in which the adjusters handled the settlement of this claim. Everything that was done was fair and reasonable. This company could not have considered rebuilding had we not had the Use & Occupancy coverage. Our employees were very happy to get the announcement that we would rebuild and that they would have work close to their homes."

Extra Expense Insurance Loss On An Office

"Thank you for the check in the amount of $2,000 which reimburses me for practically the entire expense to which I was put to continue my insurance agency business following the total destruction of the building on North Mitchell Street containing my office during the night of December 22, 1954 by a fire which originated in the basement of the adjoining building. Because of this experience, I am very thankful you persuaded me to purchase Extra Expense Insurance two years ago.

"With some records recovered from my safe which dropped to the basement, and others duplicated by my companies, I was able to resume business with little delay in the Viking Building on West Harris Street but only at considerable extra expense. This extra expense consisted of salvaging costs, extra rent for temporary quarters and office equipment, expense of moving safe, etc., and cleaning temporary office, installation of necessary temporary lights and telephone service, cost of newspaper, radio and television advertising, also wages for necessary overtime and extra help and meals for mployees working overtime.

"Now that I am again located in permanent quarters following four months in a temporary office, I will continue to carry Extra Expense Insurance since my experience has demonstrated that only Property insurance on the contents of an office is not sufficient protection."

Extra Expense Insurance Loss On A Bank

"Having received payment of $5,000 which reimburses us for part of the extra expense we incurred as the result of the conflagration which originated in an adjoining building spreading to and destroying our banking premises on the night of Saturday, April 3, 1954, we are writing to express our appreciation to you for having persuaded us to purchase Extra Expense Insurance. Our only regret is that we did not purchase a larger amount, since our loss is nearly double the amount of our policy.

"As you know, we were fortunate to secure temporary quarters in a nearby vacant building and be open for business Monday morning, April 5, entailing considerable extra expense for rent, overtime, employees' meals, wages of police guards, advertising, signs, moving safe deposit vaults, cost of temporary equipment, insurance carpentry, painting, wiring, heating, plumbing and telephone service at temporary premises.

"Having had this experience, we consider Extra Expense Insurance to be a form of insurance essential to every bank."

Regrets Indecision

"In April we had a bad fire loss and following were shut down completely for two months and normal operations were not resumed until nine months after the fire.

"We had adequate Fire Insurance to cover our property loss but we had no Business Interruption Insurance. We were considering this subject two weeks prior to the fire, but had not done anything definite. This was very unfortunate for us because our loss, net profit and our continuing fixed expenses, amounted to approximately $45,000. This occurred at a time when we were, after some years of effort, clear of all liability to the bank of roughly $45,000.

"In the face of this we naturally carry Business Interruption Insurance now and we recommend it highly to other manufacturers."

"Loss Would Pay the Premium 40 Years"—Store

"Last September you called on us for the purpose of selling us a Business Interruption Insurance policy. Unfortunately for us, the purchase of this protection was postponed. On December the 23rd last we suffered a severe fire loss and it is estimated we will be out of business for about two months.

"With the lack of other suitable premises, we cannot even partially carry on our business. Our sales will be reduced as a result of the shutdown by $20,000 or more and, as we are continuing to pay the salaries of our nine employees and losing the profit on sales, our Gross Earnings will be substantially reduced.

"We can now definitely appreciate the advantage of insuring the operations of a business apart entirely from ordinary Fire Insurance, and regret we did not buy Business Interruption, particularly when we could have purchased the coverage to insure our loss of earnings for as much as twelve months following a fire, for the very reasonable premium of only approximately $85 per annum. The loss which we have suffered would alone pay the premium for over 40 years.

"Merchants would do well to give careful consideration to this subject. We certainly will when our store is reopened."

Dropped Policy to Save Money for Expansion

"In October you sold us Business Interruption Insurance covering the operations of both our Tire Vulcanizing and Auto Accessories Sales Departments.

"This policy was kept in force till October, 1947, at which time it was dropped, the reason being that we felt we needed to save the cost of the premium, as we were under heavy expense in connection with the expansion of our business.

"On February 14th this year, a bad fire occurred in our premises which completely shut down our Vulcanizing department, and reduced our sales in the Accessories division.

"While we were well reimbursed by your company and the others carying our Fire Insurance, we have suffered a very substantial loss of earnings to date, and it seems this condition may continue for some time yet.

"We now have a practical knowledge of the advantages of Business Interruption Insurance and the saving of the small premium involved was actually a very costly experience. Instead of our business expanding, it was very nearly completely destroyed.

"As you are aware, we have now repurchased a new contract from your company insuring the earnings of our business. We will always consider this policy as one of the most important items of our insurance program."

LEGAL DECISIONS

The following decisions (with the exception of the concluding decision in the case of National Union vs. Anderson Prichard Oil Co.) are reproduced with the permission of K. W. Withers, Executive General Adjuster of the General Adjustment Bureau of San Francisco, from his booklet "Use & Occupancy Insurance" (1943).

Litigation under Use and Occupancy coverage has not been frequent probably because adjustments, involving so many elements of practical judgment, have in most cases been worked out through satisfactory negotiations and compromises. Then, too, the very nature of this type of insurance makes it attractive only for profitable business operations.

Such cases as have come to our attention are in the following list together with the opinions expressed in connection with the judgments rendered. We have included the case of Miner-Edgar Company vs. North River Insurance Company which was tried in the Supreme Court of New York. This is a trial court and although the court's opinion would probably not be considered the final rule of law, the case was not appealed and the insurance companies have evidently placed some confidence in the findings with the exception of the incomplete analysis involved in the opinion that "Profits cannot be made on production but can be made only on sales." Profits may not be "realized" until production is sold but may be "earned" with production of some products —at least those products whose "cash value" is based on selling price. The Miner-Edgar case is of value in that it contains the court's complete analysis of the "Per Diem Form."   K. W. WITHERS

These and other decisions are indexed in Mr. Withers book—"Business Interruption Insurance Coverage and Adjustment" published in 1953 and now in its 2nd Edition.

Ascertainment of Loss

STANDARD PRINTING AND PUBLISHING CO. vs. BROTHWELL
(Md. 1923) 122 Atl. 195
61 Insurance Law Journal 366

Under strike insurance policy provision that, in case of total prevention of production liability shall cease when the average daily production equals 80% of the "average daily normal production," such average daily normal production is to be ascertained by the method employed in estimating the average daily net profits. The court states that, at best, these are estimates, but takes the period of one year prior as a fair basis, and arrives at an average for that period.

GOETS vs. HARTFORD FIRE INSURANCE CO.
(Wisconsin 1927) 215 N.W. 40
70 Ins. Law Journal 108

Held that where business was not earning any net profits and not earning fixed charges and expenses no claim for loss could be sustained.

Fire insurance provision providing for payment of actual loss sustained from total or partial suspension of business, consisting of net profits and fixed charges necessarily continuing, held inapplicable where had no fire occurred, business would have operated at a loss, since the provision was intended to indemnify only for "actual loss" caused by fire, and the insured was to be reimbursed for fixed charges only if the fire prevented the business from meeting this obligation.[1]

HARTFORD FIRE INS. CO vs. WILSON & TOOMER
FERTILIZER CO. 4F (2) 835

"Loss hereunder" means the loss of any profits; of course it includes fixed charges and expenses, because until they are earned there cannot be any net profits.

---

[1]Same held in Puget Sound Lumber Co. vs. Mechanics (Washington) 79 Ins. Law Journal 350.

ATLANTIC STEEL CO. vs. HARTFORD FIRE INSURANCE CO.
(Georgia 1929) 148 S. E. 286
73 Ins. Law Journal 484

Insured has burden of showing temporary closing of mill caused actual monetary loss under contract covering Use and Occupancy. Insurance contract is one of indemnity.

HUTCHINGS vs. CALEDONIAN INSURANCE CO.
(So. Carolina 1931) 52 F (2) 744
78 Ins. Law Journal 88

Provision in Fire policy requiring that due consideration be given to experience of business before fire and probably experience thereafter should be applied in determining probable profits of warehouse during suspension of business. [2]Here took auditors figures together with experience of similar business and probabilities as to insured.

PUGET SOUND LUMBER CO. vs.
MECHANICS & TRADERS INS. CO.
(Washington 1932) 10 P (2) 568; 79 Ins. Law Journal 350
(Use and Occupancy)

In action on policies covering loss from suspension of business caused by fire, the question is not, in what account did insured place various items for the purpose of computing income tax or making a statement for its banker, but rather to what account should the respective items be allocated for the purpose of determining liability, if any, on the policies sued on, and the question to be decided is, where do the different items of account, as the same affects the issues, properly belong, not where were they placed by insured pursuant to the system of accounting which it followed before the fire.

SAME CASE
(Ascertainment of loss)

Insured could not recover on policies covering loss from suspension of business caused by fire for loss of opportunity to earn fixed charges during suspension, save in so far as insured would have earned some portion thereof by operation of its business.

NUSBAUM vs. HARTFORD FIRE INS. CO.
(Pa.) 120 Atl. 481

"Fixed charges" were those due to the disablement of the power plant, causing cessation of operation of the plant, and could not include loss of interest, wages, etc.

BENEDICT COAL CORP. vs. FIDELITY PHENIX FIRE INS. CO.
4 F (2) 347; 81 Ins. Law Journal 277

Item of anticipated loss to mining company which would result from intended closing of one of its mines held not deductible from profits from the sum lost as result of fire in determining recovery under use and occupancy policy, although it might be charged on the books as the profits would have been those earned over cost of production and fixed charges.

---

²Also held in: Puget Sound Lumber Co. vs. Mechanics & Traders, Washington Supreme Court, 79 Ins. Law Journal 350, adding: "In action on policies covering loss from suspension of business caused by fire, insured could introduce evidence tending to show that insured would have increased earnings in suspension period. And Benedict Coal Corp. vs. Fidelity Phenix Fire Ins. Co., Circuit Court of Appeals, Fourth District 1933, 81 Ins. Law Journal 277: Losses arising from interruption of business under Use and Occupancy policy are determined in a practical way, having regard to experience of business before fire and probable experience thereafter, without being confined to basis on which books are kept for income tax purposes or for dealings with stockholders. Citing Hutchings vs. Caledonian; Puget Sound Lumber Co. vs. Mechanics & Traders.

Appointment of Auditor
NEWARK FIRE INS. CO vs. BISBEE LINSEED CO.
33 F (2) 809

Court may appoint auditor (or special master) whose report will be prima facia—subject to being disproved by parties in accordance with

313

decisions in Heirs, etc. vs. U. S. 8 L. ed. 807 C. M. & S. & P. vs. Tompkins 176 U. S. 167; 44 L. ed. 417; Ex Parte 253 U. S. 300; 64 L. ed. 919.

Coverage — General

MINER-EDGAR CO. vs. NORTH RIVER INS. CO.

(N. Y. S. 1928) 70 I .L. J. 1084

"Use and Occupancy policy covering building situated at designated location covers only those buildings in which business as defined in policy is conducted. Where such business is defined as the production of goods, policy does not cover storage warehouse in which no manufacturing is conducted."

See Insurance Dec. Dig. Sec. 507

"Use and Occupancy, sometimes called Business Interruption insurance, is intended to secure to insured who is engaged in a profitable business all net profits lost because of fire and to indemnify him for all 'fixed charges' which necessarily continue during periods of total or partial suspension resulting from fire. It covers all profits lost as result of fire including profits on products which might have been manufactured if fire had not occurred. In determining insured's liability for loss, insured must prove that he restored his premises to normal operating conditions as quickly as possible, and he must prove extent of periods of total or partial suspension, amount of net profits which he would have earned if there had been no suspension and amount of 'fixed charges' which necessarily continue during periods of suspension."

SAME CASE

In construing contract of insurance court should lean toward such construction as will make contract definite and certain and not to one which will leave question for determination in every case submitted thereafter. Every part of contract should be considered in arriving at an interpretation consistent with design and object of whole instrument.

See Insurance Dec. Dig. Sec 146 (2)

The older New York cases held that losses and profits were not covered and that the policy was a valued policy covering only the business use of the building. It was even held that the company was entitled to reduce the loss by actual income still received.

Michael vs. Prussian National_____171 N.Y. 25, 63 N.E. 810
Tanenbaum vs. Freundlich_____81 N.Y.S. 292
Tanenbaum vs. Simon_____81 N.Y.S. 655
Chatfield vs. Aetna_____75 N.Y.S. 620

They did permit recovery for partial loss, however.
Lite vs. Firemen's Ins. Co._____193 N.Y. 639; 86 N.E. 112
See also:
O'Brien vs. North River_____212 Fed. 102

Coverage — Value

WHITNEY ESTATE CO. vs. NORTHERN ASSUR. CO.
155 Cal. 521; 101 Pac. 911; 38 Ins. Law Journal 1909

Rents—Values for coinsurance includes gross rentals. Recovery was based on Gross Rentals, not less saved expense, as policy provided company should be liable for actual loss of rent for time to put building in tenantable condition. Required insured to carry insurance in full amount of rents, hence, if expense deducted, paying for insurance on which there could be no recovery.

Coverage — Construction

FIREMEN'S vs. LASKER
18F (2) 375; 69 I. L. J. 65

Rule requiring liberal construction in favor of insured applies only when ambiguity renders contract susceptible of two interpretations.

In national courts insurance contracts are construed according to meaning of terms used when given their ordinary and popular sense.

Coverage—Description of Property Covered

STUDLEY BOX & LUMBER CO. vs. NATIONAL F. INS. CO.
(New Hampshire 1931) 154 Atl. 337; 75 A-R 248; 77 Ins. Law Journal 1942

Description of insured's principal buildings, in business interruption policies held not exclusive of other structures used in business. The court states that in fire insurance different items are separately valued; whereas under Business Interruption (or U & O) it is impossible to assign to each unit the amount of business loss its destruction or damage would occasion. It is clearly the object to insure loss to the business as a whole, whatever part may be conducted in or with the part which is damaged.

NUSBAUM vs. HARTFORD F. INS. CO.
(Pa.) 132 Atl. 177

The court held there may be insurance for loss of profits and expense arising out of disablement of power plant and machinery, and that loss occasioned by cessation of operation of plant covers loss resulting from destruction of ice storage building containing no machinery and is not limited to loss due directly to disablement of machinery.

Coverage — Operation Insured

BENEDICT COAL CORP. vs. FIDELITY PHENIX
64 F (2) 347; 81 Ins. Law Journal 277

Corporation operating coal mine opening new mining seam held no such change in corporation's business as defeated recovery under use and occupancy policies indemnifying against losses from business interruption. Court also infers that mill operating different tract of lumber, or factory using new machinery would not change business—but that changing to entirely new business would void policy.

SAME CASE

Loss of profits of mining company from its commissary, from smithing and sales of powder to miners, and from rental of miners' houses, should be included in determining losses arising from interruption of company's business by fire under Use and Occupancy policy. These enterprises were an integral and necessary part of the mining business.

Coverage — Expediting

MINER-EDGAR Co. vs. NORTH RIVER INS. CO.
(New York 1928) 70 Ins. Law Journal 1084
"Where policy provides that insured shall use outside facilities during suspension, insured should be compensated for their proved cost and product made therein should be included in determining total business done during suspension."

Coverage — Partial Suspension Clause

FIREMEN'S INS. CO. vs. LASKER
18 F (2) 375; 69 Ins. Law Journal 65
Partial Suspension Clause not ambiguous and upheld.
BENEDICT COAL CORP. vs. FIDELITY PHENIX
Use and Occupancy policy covering "actual loss sustained not exceeding 1/300 of the amount of this policy for each business day of suspension" held referable to business days included in period of suspension of mining operations, not to probable days that mine would have operated if fire had not occurred.

Coverage — Per Diem Limits of Liability

HUDSON MFG. CO. vs. N. Y. UND. INS. CO.
33 F (2) 460; 73 Ins. Law Journal 890
Upholding Per Diem limits of liability in Wisconsin, and limiting recovery to actual time to repair, not for delay by reason of law.

Coverage — Partial Suspension Clause — Expediting Costs

HARTFORD vs. WILSON LOOMER FERTILIZER CO.
4 Fed (2) 835
Expediting arrangements which provided partial operation where fire caused total suspension would not bring partial suspension clause into operation where there was no actual reduction in the loss by expediting 2/5ths of production was salvaged but actual loss was as great as it would have been during total suspension.

STUDLEY BOX & LUMBER CO. vs. NATIONAL FIRE INS. CO.
154 Atl. 337; 75 ALR 248
77 Ins. Law Journal 1942
Policy provisions, limiting insurers' per diem liability during partial

suspension of business because of fire, held inapplicable to expenses incurred in reducing loss. Here horses were burned and the expense consisted of hiring horses, labor in clearing the roadway and barn, expense of sawing lumber by other parties, as sawmill was shut down so employees could do this other work.

OCEAN ACC. & GUAR. CORP. vs. PENICK & FORD
101 F (2) 493

Expediting costs, in this case purchase of electric power, are not recoverable unless permitted by the policy.

Fixed Charges and Expenses
STANDARD PRINTING & PUBLISHING CO vs. BROTHWELL ET AL
122 Atlantic 195 (Maryland) 61 Ins. Law Journal 366
Strike Insurance U. & O.

Fixed charges within a policy covering loss from strike of average daily net profits and fixed charges are the salaries of officers and men, whose services could not have been dispensed with by insured without loss to insured, and, without rendering insured unable either to resume promptly normal production when the strike ended, to continue the business during the period of partial production, and also comprise other necessary expenses, incurred in maintaining the efficiency of insured organization, including those charges which spread over the entire establishment, such as rent, insurance, taxes, mortgage interest, depreciation, and the like, according to whether the plant is leased or owned, and which continue whether or not the business is operated; but depreciation in the value of manufactured articles or goods on hand are not fixed charges. [3]This case includes an analysis of "fixed charges" as the term is used in Strike U & O policy.

Same case quoted Bassett on Accountancy, page 244, as follows: "Charges which spread over the entire establishment, such as rent, insurance, taxes, mortgage interest, depreciation, and the like, according to whether the plant is leased or owned . . . "Fixed Charges" arise out of the very being of the plant, and continue whether or not the business is operated."

_____

[3]See "Words and Prases," First and Second Series, "Fixed Charges."

BUFFALO FORGE CO. vs. MUTUAL SECURITY CO.
83 Conn. 393; 76 Atlantic 995
STRIKE INSURANCE

By fixed charges is meant "those expenses necessarily incurred in maintaining the organization in such a state of efficiency as would enable it to resume normal production without substantial delay after the strike was ended, or as the strike might be broken by a gradual return of employees."

MINER-EDGAR CO. vs. NORTH RIVER INSURANCE CO.

70 Ins. Law Journal 1084

Decided in the Supreme Court of New York 1928, Not appealed, which is a lower court; fixed charges were defined as follows:

"Fixed charges are those expenses necessarily incurred in maintaining the organization in such state of efficiency as would enable it to resume normal production without substantial delay after fire or to continue business as efficiently as practical during periods of partial suspension.

"Fixed charges should include all continuing charges, such as rent, insurance, taxes, mortgage interest, depreciation, general maintenance expense, salaries of employees who could not be discharged during suspension without detriment to business. Classification of any item as 'fixed charges' depends upon its nature; the fact that it was deducted from sales in determining net profits is immaterial."

In this same case the following was said of Advertising: "Normal advertising expenditures during suspension are 'Fixed Charges.' Advertising is of continuing nature, results not being immediately secured."

As to salesmen's salaries: "Normal expenditures for salesmen's salaries during suspension are 'fixed charges.' Orders secured to be filled after manufacturing has been resumed do not compensate insured for salesmen's salaries. In the absence of evidence that reduction in sales was due to failure of market, he is presumed to have lost sales which could have been made had he been able to produce. Compensation under policy merely indemnifies insured and does not constitute double compensation."

As to salesmen's commissions: "Salesmen's Commissions are not 'fixed charges' because they are not paid unless sales are made. Commissions are direct charges against profits on sales to which they apply."

As to salesmen's traveling expenses: "Salesmen's traveling expenses unless incurred for a specific sale are not fixed charges. Where it is customary for salesmen to travel, traveling expenses are 'fixed charges,' because continuing in nature and not related to specific sales. Insured would lose good will if it discontinued having salesmen travel."

The above opinions are worth only their value as basis for analysis, as this lower court's findings do not constitute recorded law.

Fixed Charges & Expense — Depreciation — Depletion

STANDARD PRINTING AND PUBLISHING CO. vs. BROTHWELL

(Maryland) 122 Atl. 95; 61 Ins. Law Journal 366

"Depreciation in the value of manufactured articles or goods on hand are not fixed charges."

BENEDICT COAL CORP. vs. FIDELITY PHENIX FIRE INS. CO.

64 F (2) 347; 81 Ins. Law Journal 277

Items of depletion and of depreciation on property destroyed held properly disallowed as fixed charges, in computing loss resulting from interruption of business by fire, under use and occupancy policies, for manifestly depreciation and depletion stops when property is destroyed.

___

*Note: By the same reasoning, appreciation of manufactured articles would not be an item increasing net profits.

Fixed Charges & Expense — Payroll
HUTCHINGS vs. CALEDONIAN INS. CO.
52 F (2) 744; 78 Ins. Law Journal 88

Auctioneer and Bookkeeper of tobacco warehouse employed for two months period. Held their salaries recoverable under item covering "Fixed charges and expense" as insured liable for them due to short period of employment.

In final order Court directed insured to pay amount of judgment for these salaries to employees for their protection as some elements of judgment compromised.

Fixed Charges Are Expenses — Recoverable Expenses Under Per Diem Form
PUGET SOUND LUMBER CO. vs. MECHANICS & TRADERS
(Washington) 10 P (2) 568; 79 Ins. Law Journal 350

Club and association membership dues of offices held properly included in computing insurer's liability as it would be contrary to sound business policy to drop them and it could not be maintained that, immediately on the occurrence of the fire, these club and association memberships should have been dropped, possibly to be later resumed at greater expense and at the cost of time, money and annoyance.

SAME
Insurers not liable for expense incurred in making proofs of loss.

SAME
Fixed expense of New York Office, if maintained for some time prior to fire proper item of recoverable expense for period fire prevented office from performing its functions.

Expense
BENEDICT COAL CORP. vs. FIDELITY PHENIX
64 F (2) 347; 81 Ins. Law Journal 277

During development stage of mine many expenditures, which later would be charged to expense, should be charged to capital, as regards computation of loss under use and occupancy policy, and need not be charged to expense.

Period of Suspension

GRAND PACIFIC HOTEL vs. MICHIGAN COMMERCIAL INS. CO.
(Illinois); 90 N.E. 244; 39 Ins. Law Journal 268

Where fire cancelled lease having 64 days to run and period necessary to replace 84 days, held that tenant could only collect on basis of 84 days, within which time the property could have been repaired. Could only recover for period during which repairs, with due diligence, could have been completed, not for termination of lease.

HARTFORD FIRE INS. CO. vs. PIRES
Texas Civ. App. 165 S.W. 565

RENTS

Delay not unavoidably occurring in the course of repair or one not caused by insurer is not a part of the time for which the insured is entitled to indemnity from the insurer. (Also Palatine Ins. Co. vs. O'Brien, 107 MD 341.)

But time to restore included time to place contract therefor.

AMUSEMENT SYNDICATE CO. vs. PRUSSIAN NATIONAL INS. CO.
116 Pac. 620 (Re-hearing denied 118 Pac. 76)

Rents—Only time to rebuild same building. Not one required by ordinance.

Same 136 Pac 941

Rents—Time to rebuild same building as though there was no reconstruction. Where not reconstructed, the season of the year, weather or other fact or circumstance which might have interfered is not considered.

SAPERSTON vs. AMERICAN & FOREIGN INSURANCE CO.
Supreme Court, Niagara Co., N. Y., 1932
255 N.Y.S. 405

Company not liable for delay occasioned by adjustment of loss under fire policy which delayed repairs until adjustment completed. But if same company insurer under fire policy, their acts in delaying repairs would stop them from claiming insured did not proceed with reasonable diligence and dispatch.

Net Profits

MINER-EDGAR CO. vs. NORTH RIVER INSURANCE CO.
N. Y. (Lower Court) (No appeal) 1928
70 Ins. Law Journal 1085

"Profits cannot be made on production but can be made only on sales. Where any reliable method of ascertaining net profits is available, they should not be estimated by regarding goods produced as worth selling price."

SAME CASE

"It covers all profits lost as result of fire, including profits on products which might have been manufactured if fire had not occurred."

SAME CASE

"Transfer of raw material, goods in process, or finished goods from one department to another are not sales and do not result in the earning of a profit. No profit can be made except on sale for which consideration is received. Such transfers must be eliminated in determining insured's net profit to be used in computing his loss."

Other References

WILSON & TOOMER FERTILIZER CO. vs. AUTOMOBILE INS. CO.
(D. C.) 283 Fed 501

Question of pleading, but distinguishes early N. Y. case—method to be used is that set forth in policy.

OCEAN ACCIDENT & GUAR. CORP. vs. PENICK & FORD
MACHINERY BREAKDOWN
101 F (2) 493

Company is liable only in accordance with terms of its policy, but the question as to whether there was a breakdown is a question of fact for the jury.

MICHAEL vs. PRUSSIAN NATIONAL INS. CO.
171 N. Y. 25-63 N.E. 810
NUSBAUM vs. HARTFORD
132 Atl. 177

CAMERON LUMBER CO. vs. MT. ROYAL ASSCE.
47 B. C. R. 52 (Canada)
2 W. W. R. 129 (Canada)
Insurance, Dec. Digest

NATIONAL UNION FIRE INS. CO. vs. ANDERSON PRICHARD
OIL CO.
U. S. Circuit Court of Appeals Tenth Circuit (1944) No. 2699,
141 Fed. Rep. 2d 443

In this case involving Business Interruption Insurance on an Oklahoma oil refinery damaged by fire in 1941 the court held a manufacturer's profit in his manufactured products is realized as, if, and when they are manufactured and not when they are sold and such profit is ascertained on the basis of the prevailing market prices when the products are manufactured. (Patapsco Insurance Company vs. Coulter, 28 U. S. 222; Standard Marine Insurance Company vs. Assurance Company 283 U. S. 284.) This decision also upholds "sales value of production" as the logical basis of determining the actual loss sustained by manufacturers under Business Interruption Insurance policies, as the U. S. Circuit Court of Appeals, Ninth Circuit (1944) also held in General Insurance Company of America vs. Pathfinder Petroleum Company No. 10,494, 145 Fed. Rep. 2d, 368.

INDEX

Abstractors, 239
Accident & Health Cover, 287
Additional Living Expense, 238
Adjustable Premium Endorsement, 111, 130
Advertising Expense, 283
Agents Aids, 287
Agreed Amount Endorsement, 111, 130
Alterations & Repairs Clause, 278
Amusement Enterprises, 91
Analytic Rating Schedule, 207
Animal Bottlenecks, 23
Answers to Objections, 291
Associated Factory Mutuals, 121
Associated Reciprocal Exchanges, 116
Automobile Expense, 284
Average Blanket Rates, 136, 214
Bad Debts, 283
Banks, 239, 295
Blanket Policies, 133
Boiler Casualty Cover, 18
Bottlenecks, 19, 227
Bottlers, 236
Bowling Alleys, 93
Bridges, 28, 286
Brokers Aids, 287
Builders Risks, 277
Buyers Aids, 292
Camping Fees, 275
Canadian Methods, 203
Charges, 269
Chomage Insurance, 9
Churches, 236
Civil Authority Clause, 264
Climate, 26
Coal Mines, 218
Coinsurance, 31, 58, 111
Collection Expense, 283
Combined Manufacturing and Mercantile Coverage, 160
Commissions Coverage, 162
Consequential Losses, 262
Construction Bottlenecks, 20
Contingent Coverages, 140, 221, 259

Contracts Cancellation, 261
Contributing Property, 141
Contribution Clause, 31, 58, 112
Cotton Seed Oil Mills, 165
Counter Signature End't., 139
Credit Men, 5, 295
Dairies, 236
Debts, 283
Demolition Clause, 261
Depreciation, 283
Discounts, 283
Dollar Bill Demonstration, 288
Donations, 283
Dues, 283
Dwellings, 27, 238
Earnings Insurance Form, 103
Educational Institutions, 236, 270
Electricity Supply Coverage, 147
Erion's Form, 73
Exclusions Clause, 260
Expediting Expenses, 253
Expenses, 268, 283
Extended Coverage, 285
Extra Expense Insurance, 236, 274
Factory Insurance Association, 123
Finished Stock, 97, 159, 163, 172
Fire Limits, 26
Fixed Charges, 268
Floor Area Method, 136, 214
Foreign Machinery, 23
Function, 1
Funeral Homes, 237
Gas Supply Coverage, 147, 222
Government Contracts, 132
Government Directives, 28, 198
Gross Earnings Form, 72, 302, 304
Gross Profits Canadian Form, 175
Heat Expense, 283
Heat Supply Coverage, 147, 222
History, 8
Hospitals, 238
Hotels, 91, 294
Housing, 27
Inland Marine Coverage, 286
Insurable Interest, 14

Insurance Premiums, 283
Interest, 284
Interstate Coverage, 137
Kimball, Warren F., 73
Laundries, 236
Laws, 28, 260
Leasehold Interest, 261
Leases, 261
Legal Decisions, 11, 12, 311
Lessees, 14, 281
Lessors, 281
Licenses, 261
Life Insurance, 287
Light Expenses, 283
Local Ordinances, 28, 261
Loss Adjustments, Appendixes 1-8
Machinery Casualty Cover, 18
Machinery Bottlenecks, 21, 22
Maintenance Expenses, 284
Manufacturing, Definition, 161
Marine Cover, 286
Market Price Clause, 161
Mercantiles, 43, 53, 73, 90, 103
Merchandise Profits, 161
Mining Properties, 218, 265
Molten Glass and Metal Clauses, 158
Monthly Form, 46
Motor Vehicles, 28
Multi-Locations Coverage, 132
Multiple Perils Cover, 286
Municipal Buildings, 237
Municipal Ordinances, 26, 260
Mutuals, 120
Names, 11
New Businesses, 277
Newspapers, 236, 241
Objections, 291
Ocean Marine Cover, 286
Offices, 28, 237
Off Premises Power, etc., 147, 222
Oil Mills, Cotton, 165
Ordinances, 28, 260
Ordinary Payroll, 65, 83, 284, 301
Origin, 8
Partial Suspension Clause, 32
Payroll—see Ordinary Payroll
Per Diem Form, 30, 297
Period of Indemnity, 173, 197, 201

Personal Services Income, 150, 222
Per Week Form, 36
Plans and Patterns, 27
Power Bottlenecks, 23
Power Expenses, 283
Power, Off Premises, 146, 222
Power Plants, 236
Premium Adjustment Form, 110, 130, 175
Priorities and Clauses, 28, 199
Process Bottlenecks, 21
Professional Services, 284
Profits Earned, 96, 321
Profits Form, Canadian, 175
Profits on Merchandise, 162
Profits Only Coverage, 268
Publishers, 236
Rates, Average, 136, 214
Rating Methods, 205
Recipient Property, 144
Reciprocal Exchanges, 116
Remote Losses, 262
Re-negotiated Contracts, 132
Rent, 231
Repairs, 284
Reporting Form, 123
Restaurants, 91
Resumption of Operations Clause, 97, 259
Royalties, 151, 284
Sales, 96, 98
Sales Value of Production, 96
Salesmen's Commissions, 283
Schedule Rating, 207
Schools, Private, 236, 270
Schools, Public, 275
Selling Agents Coverage, 149, 222
Selling Price Clause, 162
Selling Suggestions, 287
Service Businesses, 91
Specified Time Forms, 180, 188
Sprinklered Properties, 223
Stock Bottlenecks, 25
Stockholders, 1, 2
Stock Coverage Rates, 212
Stock Finished, 97, 159, 162, 172
Stock in Process, 25, 156
Stock Profits, 165

Stock Raw, 25, 153, 194
Strikers Interference, 262
Subscriptions, 284
Superior Risks, 123, 223
Supplies, 284
Taxes, 279, 284
Testimonial Letters, 307
Texas, 187
Theatres, 93
Time Element Endorsements, 199
Transportation Expense, 284
Traveling Expense, 284
Tuition Fees Insurance, 270
Two Item Contribution Form, 52, 299, 201
Underlying Policies, 137, 145
Underground Coverage, 219, 265
Underwriting Methods, 223

Unemployment Compensation Funds, 66, 87, 122
Use and Occupancy Insurance, 9
Valued Policies, 17
Vehicles Expense, 284
Warehouses, 173
Wartime Methods, 195, 203
Water Supply Coverage, 147, 222
Weekly Form, 36
White, Frederic C., Foreword, 11
Windstorm Losses, 24, 149
Work Sheet, Weekly Form, 47
Work Sheet, Two Item Form, 61
Work Sheet, Gross Earnings, 76
Work Sheet, Extra Expense Insurance, 252

324

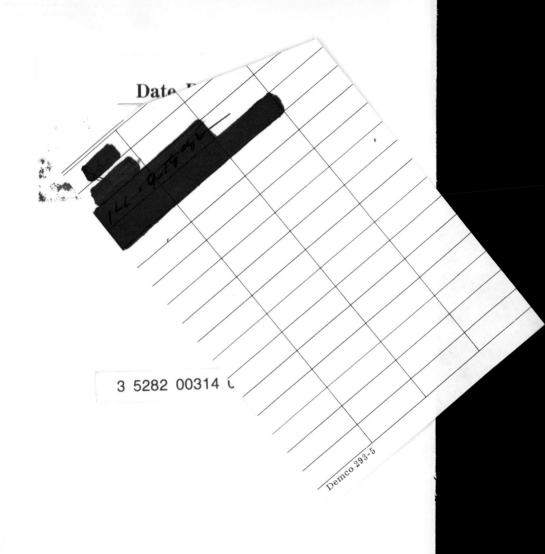

Date

3 5282 00314 0

Demco 293-5